LOSS PREVENTION

A Management Guide To Improving Retail Security

Edited by Len Daykin

Progressive Grocer Co., New York

This edition of LOSS PREVENTION: A Management Guide to Improving Retail Security is based on the book entitled THE CRIME THAT NO ONE TALKS ABOUT by Harold Cohen and compiled and edited by Len Daykin.

Design — Magdalena Malachowski

Printed in the United States of America

ISBN 0-911790-51-9

CONTENTS

PREFACE

The sad litany of crime in the United States continues unabated. The Federal Bureau of Investigation reported crime up 9.1% in 1979, the sharpest rise since 1975; even worse, all seven types of crime in the FBI's Uniform Crime Index were up for the second straight year.

Property crime, including the vast majority of crimes against retail businesses, itself accounts for 90% of all of the crimes reported in the FBI annual figures, thoroughly dwarfing the more sensational media-covered crimes of violence. Clearly, crimes against retail businesses that do receive widespread publicity only represent the tip of the iceberg.

Retailers themselves—particularly medium and smaller-sized operations—often have little conception of the severity of their problem. A U.S. Department of Commerce news release referring to the Department's 1977 annual survey of the cost of crimes against business notes, "Only slightly more than half the companies surveyed indicated that inventory shrinkage was recorded in sufficient detail to determine whether it was due to employee theft, breakage or shoplifting."

Loss prevention. It has a nice, modern, technical sound to it. It also happens to be a critical need. We live in an age of specialization by job function. The diversity of the free enterprise system and the increasing complexity of life have helped make this so. Few security specialists are equally at home in the world of merchandising strategies, buying policies and retail business cash flows. Likewise, store managers and management trainees by and large dislike the idea of "playing cop" in a system that depends on access, self-service, volume and traffic to succeed.

But, since the self-service retail system that dominates our marketplace requires the "umbrella" of security, as I refer to it in Chapter 1, there must be an interface between the loss prevention or security responsibilities and duties borne by each employee, and those that require the attention and control of professional loss prevention personnel.

The focus of this text is on the retail employee who will come in contact with security operations, have some responsibilities for loss prevention, perhaps manage or have loss prevention personnel reporting to him or her in a corporate setting. The focus is also on private entrepreneurs who have recognized the potential severity of security problems affecting them, and now must select resources, services and suppliers to deal with their particular situations.

While many of the examples cited and illustrated dwell heavily on the retail grocery industry for convenience sake, the basics set forth here apply to virtually all self-service retail formats, with many suggestions and recommendations pertinent for serviced operations as well.

Although the scope of the loss prevention function goes beyond that of retail crime, this text confines itself to involuntary loss due to internal and external forms of theft. Such subjects as safety, fire prevention and sanitation are each too large to examine in one book in the context of retail crime.

This text draws to some extent on *The Crime That No One Talks About,* a book I compiled and edited in 1974 from the accumulated experiences and know-how of Harold Cohen, now, as then, Director of Loss Prevention for Wakefern Food Corporation, Elizabeth, N.J., the distribution arm of Shop-Rite Supermarkets, one of the most dynamic operations in the retail grocery industry. The changes in systems, attitudes, equipment available, not to mention the size of the problem itself, have been so great in the intervening six years that a totally new security overview from the perspective of the retail management candidate is thoroughly needed.

The present volume also takes its cues from the "Plugging the Profit Drain" series, a sequence of in-depth articles on aspects of security I wrote during my years as Associate Editor of *Progressive Grocer.* Many of the statistical references cited to *Progressive Grocer* studies in this text originated in the research conducted for "Plugging the Profit Drain."

I would like to acknowledge the advice and assistance of Norman Bussel, Shirley Palmer, Micaela Rosenzweig, Lucy Tarzian, Lenore Stanoch and Ron Tanner at *Progressive Grocer.* Lillian E. (Betty) Edds and George S. (Bud) Hayward of the Cornell University Food Industry Management Program have both been instrumental in determining the direction and scope of coverage of this text.

Len Daykin
New York, N.Y.

1 UNDERSTANDING THE SECURITY UMBRELLA

This chapter will describe:

- **The role of security in the modern retail operation**
- **Organization and operation of the security or loss prevention division**
- **Bringing employees into the security picture**

One of the last things an employee wants to hear in the retail business structure is a lecture on the need for and operation of a security or loss prevention department. The vast majority of employees entering a business organization are like shiny new pennies; confronting the need for a loss prevention department is like an abrasive that can dull the finish of those bright coins.

Yet an awareness of the staggering growth in all forms of crime is more than just a gut feeling. We read the stories in newspapers and see them on television every day. "Normally law-abiding citizens," reports *U.S. News & World Report*, "aware of the lenient treatment usually accorded to white-collar criminals, are engaging in a wide range of larceny and fraud that includes passing bad checks, embezzling funds and stealing goods from employers, shoplifting, cheating on taxes, luring friends and neighbors into illegal pyramid schemes, defrauding insurance companies."[1]

Security departments that look upon themselves merely as cops searching for as many rotten apples as they can find in the barrel can help contribute to an attitude of cynicism and distrust on the part of employees. The attitude rapidly becomes one of "us against them," which is nothing more or less than a self-fulfilling prophecy. At the same time, as explored in the next chapter on internal theft, companies with little or no visible security function can end up with a security problem equally as severe as the "police-state" organization. In both operations, morale of the employees can be negatively affected as a result.

It is a guiding principle of this text that a more efficient security operation results from telling employees more, not less, about the functions of security and exactly how it operates. Further, this process should start with an employee's initial orientation to the company, and continue via updating seminars at headquarters, in stores, at distribution centers, even "off-campus" for a relaxed yet structured change of scene. In the spirit of "full disclosure," such an approach can demonstrate to employees that the security department is knowledgeable and well-organized. Taking employees into the confidence of the security department in revealing elements of the security operation can prove to be a strong deterrent to an employee tempted by dishonesty. At the same time, it can make each employee feel a part of the security process, enhancing each individual's feeling of self-importance and self-respect.

One major chain, for example, considers security training for cashiers to be extremely important, since the front end is often the greatest source of loss due to internal theft in high-volume stores. The chain calls this training "Cash Control," which entails a full explanation of the company's strict procedures for handling cash.

New cashiers are often asked if they would like to be trained as security cashiers, first learning security procedures directly from the security department, then going on to cashier training. Their role would be to assist security in spotting or apprehending dishonest employees. The chain also trains all front-end supervisors responsible for the scheduling of cashiers and the smooth operation of checkout area security. Procedures to eliminate so-called "community drawers," where cashiers may pass cash drawers from one to the other without totalling out the drawer are stressed.

In other areas, the security department teaches each employee, assigned to a specific department, the violations the security department is aware of regarding the handling of cash or merchandise in that department. Every employee is fully briefed as to what constitutes a dishonest act by either employees or customers.

The attempt, therefore, is to eliminate personnel indifference to security and to pursue efforts that tend to enforce discipline. Telling employees that they are really part of the management team is beneficial. Reassuring all employees that the company's security rules pertain to everyone, regardless of rank or length of service, is even more important. Positive rules and procedures presented by security to all personnel from the moment they are employed, and then carried through on a constant basis, set an example that employees respect and appreciate.

It is also important, as the title of this chapter implies, to make all employees aware of the scope of coverage of the security "umbrella." Its use as a symbol for one of the largest multiform insurance companies in the country is very much akin to the spirit of security embodied in this text.

Just what is, or should be, the security or loss prevention function of a retail organization? One major supermarket chain isolates these critical functions:

1. Maintenance of maximum security for the company.
2. Protection of personnel, merchandise, monies, properties, reputations and all other assets owned by the company.
3. Operation of a complete security organization with clear loss prevention standards.
4. Authority to interview, hire and direct personnel in key specialties: this includes floor detectives, honesty shoppers (security operatives posing as customers) and guards, as well as people involved in investigation, fire and safety.
5. Responsibility for instituting proper methods for detection and apprehension of all persons committing a crime within the confines of the company, and of all persons committing a crime against the company.
6. Creation of programs required for alarm systems, employee identification, key controls, lock controls, security hardware such as closed circuit television cameras, mirrors and any other mechanical systems or devices that can curtail shrinkage loss.
7. Responsibility for conducting investigations when apprehensions are made, gathering of legal evidence, preparation of cases which satisfy the letter of the law in regard to the actions and methods of security personnel.
8. Elimination or minimization of false arrest or damages suits against the company.
9. Coordination of a liaison between law enforcement agencies, fire departments, first aid stations, ambulance services and all other emergency organizations that can be of service to the company, its employees and customers.
10. Development of first aid and fire brigade training classes.

It should be clear from this listing that *security* in the retail organization goes beyond the narrow constraints of police-style apprehensions; security in the retail sense also means *safety.* Vesting this responsibility in the security or loss prevention department makes eminent good sense because, properly managed, security is on the job 24 hours a day, seven days a week, under the jurisdiction of a director of loss

SECURITY DEPARTMENT

FIRE, EXPLOSION, ELECTRICAL MALFUNCTION REPORT

INCIDENT REPORT ______________ FIRE [ ]

DATE OF REPORT ______________ EXPLOSION [ ]

TIME OF REPORT ______________ ELECTRICAL MALFUNCTION [ ]

EXACT LOCATION ______________

____

INCIDENT REPORTED BY : PHONE [ ] ALARM [ ] ______________ [ ]

REPORTING PARTY IF KNOWN ______________

____

DATE OF INCIDENT ______________ TIME ______________

EMERGENCY SERVICES NOTIFIED: L.A.P.D. [ ] FIRE [ ] RESCUE [ ]

AMBULANCE ______________ FIRST AID [ ] TEL–CO [ ] DEPT. OF WATER & POWER [ ]

OTHER ______________ DATE ______________ TIME ______________

NO. INJURED [ ] FATALITIES [ ] WITNESSES [ ]

(SUBMIT DETAILS OR EACH ... ABOVE ON ATTACHED FIRST AID ... PORT, VICTIM OR WIT... ORM.)

...CIOUS ... BO...

SECURITY DEPARTMENT

EMERGENCY FIRST AID REPORT

INCIDENT REPORT ______________ EMPLOYEE [ ]

DATE OF REPORT ______________ EMPLOYEE NUMBER ______________

TIME OF REPORT ______________ VISITOR [ ]

VICTIM'S NAME ______________ PHONE ______________

ADDRESS ______________

ADULT [ ] JUVENILE [ ] SEX [ ] AGE [ ] PHOTO TAKEN [ ]

(If juvenile, parent or guardian's name and address)

____

______________ PHONE ______________

WITNESS' NAME ______________ PHONE ______________

WITNESS' ADDRESS ______________

WITNESS' NAME ______________ PHONE ______________

WIT... ______________ ______________

The "security umbrella" for a retail company includes more than the prevention and detection of internal theft, shoplifting and other types of crime. Forms on these pages, from one firm's security department, show the range of security activities.

SECURITY DEPARTMENT

PROPERTY LOSS REPORT

INCIDENT REPORT ____________ ☐ AUTO ☐ THEFT

DATE OF REPORT ____________ ☐ BURGLARY ☐ THEFT FROM PERSON

TIME OF REPORT ____________ ☐ ROBBERY ☐ ____________

REPORTING PARTY____________ ☐ VISITOR ☐ EMPLOYEE BADGE ____________

ADDRESS ____________

TELEPHONE (RES.) ( ) ____________ (WORK OR EXT.) ( ) ____________

DESCRIPTION OF PROPERTY ____________

____

____________. VALUE $ ____________

IF VEHICLE (OR FROM VEHICLE) LICENSE ____________ AND DESCRIPTION OF VEHICLE:

____

VEHICLE PARKED ____________

WHEN WAS LOSS DISCOVERED DATE ____________ TIME ____________

PROPERTY LAST SEEN (LOC.) ____________ DATE ____________ TIME ____________

...ME AND ADDRE...

BOMB THREAT REPORT

Name of operator, or person receiving call ____________

Date of call ____________ Time ____________ a.m. p.m.

ORIGIN OF CALL:

Local ____________ Long Distance ____________ Phone Booth ____________ Internal ____________

IDENTITY OF CALLER:

VOICE

____ Loud ____ Soft
____ High Pitch ____ Deep
____ Raspy ____ Pleasant
____ Intoxicated ____ ____ (other)

SPEECH

____ Fast ____ Slow
____ Distinct ____ Distorted
____ Stutter ____ Nasal

LANGUAGE

____ Good
____ Foul
____ Poor
____ (other)

ACCENT

____ Local ____ Foreign
____ Racial ____ Regional
____ (type)

MANNER

____ Calm ____ Angry
____ Rational ____ Irrational
____ Coherent ____ Incoherent
____ Deliberate ____ Emotional
____ Righteous ____ Nervous Laugh

BACKGROUND NOISE

...nes

Security department activities include responsibility for investigating any fires, explosions or electrical malfunctions, first aid crises, property loss of individual employees and, reflecting our troubled times, bomb threat reports.

prevention whose job it is to see that those rules are enforced around the clock. As with the detection of crime, safety requirements don't exist only from nine to five; they are constant, and as such, require constant vigilance.

The safety function can encompass an injuries policy, vehicular safety, fire safety, even the overall direction of sanitation operations and responsibilities within the company. While many retail companies vest sanitation responsibilities with a store operations or maintenance department, placing it under the control of security may eliminate the danger of partiality. For example, if an operations manager responsible for sanitation is a former merchandising specialist, it may be felt that the removal of an unsanitary condition might have a negative impact on sales in terms of stricter rules on displays or fixtures. As a result, the problem might not be pursued with total sincerity and dedication.

One firm's security department with sanitation responsibility has developed a system of periodic rotation of sanitation inspectors so that none of its inspectors are covering the same stores for any great length of time, and thus are not growing too close to any one store manager. Such a system also ensures that the inspection procedures and standards will be applied evenly throughout the company.

Security As A Profit Center

With the broad perspective of security functions going beyond those of stopping crime, the idea of a symbolic umbrella takes on sharper focus. And with that, the view of security as part of management. From this, it is an easy jump to the fact that, properly organized, directed and operated, the security department is a recognizable profit center of the company. It is a profit center in the sense that any prevention of crimes or safety losses before they occur can improve the net profit of a retail store; in fact, this is probably the easiest way to improve profits at the retail level. Crime or shrinkage losses work not on gross receipts, but directly on the bottom line. Merchandise stolen from a store or warehouse must still be paid for by the retailer; cash theft represents an identical loss. By investing in a good, sound security operation, a retail organization is undoubtedly forestalling the loss of more pure profit dollars from the firm.

THE OUTSIDE VENDOR ALTERNATIVE

Many smaller retail companies, and even some larger operations, utilize the convenience of outside security vendors in preference to the creation of an in-house loss prevention department. Such vendors must be chosen with great care, since outside firms may have strength in numbers, but be absolutely wrong for a given company's set of security problems or needs. Security vendors chosen should be selected on the basis of plans tailor-made to the prospective retail organization. Agencies which have specialized in stemming security losses incurred in shipments and deliveries may have insufficient expertise in handling front end or checkout security problems. A security firm with strong credentials in the guarding of buildings or property may be totally unqualified to create a program for a small independent drugstore plagued by shoplifting or narcotics-motivated robbers.

The qualifications of any security agency under consideration must therefore match as closely as possible the needs of the client. Particulars on the professional service should include the following:

1. That the company is knowledgeable and has had experience in security areas covering not only similar problems but also similar types of operations.
2. That the company is willing to fully discuss its plan, including costs and a time frame deemed necessary.
3. That the vendor's plan breaks out costs according to short-term goals, while establishing standards for long-term maintenance programs that lead to an ongoing service.
4. That the company's program covers all of the security problems a retailer is aware of, plus possibilities that had not been considered—another indicator of the prospective vendor's experience in dealing with specific businesses or classes of trade.

This outline for a review is normally conducted with several candidate security agencies. A decision should be reached only after each agency has surveyed the particular retail operation, submitted its proposals and discussed them in detail with the firm.

Most retail organizations are somewhat surprised to discover the large number of companies in the security field, and the fact that many have outstanding qualifications for dealing with a retail organization's particular problems. However, client involvement should not stop with the choice of a vendor. The same type of internal audits and inventories that may have brought a particular security problem to light may now indicate the success or failure of the security vendor's efforts on the retailer's behalf. In any event, an outside vendor's program should be reviewed and discussed in detail periodically, to verify that the program is constantly being fine-tuned or refined and customized to solve the client's specific, often changing needs.

THE CASE FOR "IN-HOUSE" SECURITY

The establishment of a totally dedicated security division, in the sense that it serves no other master, is the kind of decision taken by a retail organization as it contemplates immediate and long-term growth possibilities. The criteria thus are not only problems at hand but also an appraisal of the company's long-term needs and the collateral benefits that an outside security vendor cannot provide. These may include good employee/customer safety programs, improvement in the nature and quality of employee recruitment programs, development of an energy and cost-saving internal "watchdog" agency, a sanitation or Occupational Safety and Health Act (OSHA)-enforcement unit, a liaison with labor unions in vital areas of concern, and so on.

Most often, the decision to establish an internal security department is one that should be made and implemented by the senior officer of the company. The integration of security into corporate management can create closer ties between the company and law enforcement agencies, a greater awareness of applicable security, safety and sanitation regulations, and a more thorough screening of vendors doing business with the company. Thus, when emergencies arise, each employee is aware that there is a department capable of handling emergencies with professionalism.

The natural inclination toward growth in retail businesses, coupled with the severity and extent of security breaches and violations in these high-volume operations, has led most retail companies to develop internal security departments with varying degrees of sophistication, size and capability. Special vendors, such as uniformed guard services, armored car pickup and delivery service, or undercover-type services, are generally handled on a long-term contractual basis, with these vendors reporting directly to the retailer's loss prevention department manager or director.

USE OF UNDERCOVER WORKERS

Undercover personnel represent a complex situation. While not involved with the life-and-death danger of covert espionage agents, undercover personnel in business security roles provide the same important type of first-hand investigative information. Because of the often complex, technical nature of the work, and the clear value of obtaining undercover personnel with good experience, most loss prevention directors find that vendor agencies provide a higher caliber of such personnel than would be obtained by direct recruitment.

In retail firms, undercover personnel have been used as truck drivers, accountants, maintenance engineers, stock clerks, cashiers—even buyers. Obviously, secrecy is the most important factor in instituting and supervising undercover work. Knowledge of an undercover agent and his or her location in the company should be limited to a minimum number of people: the security director, the security supervisor in charge of undercover operations, where applicable, and the top management executive to whom the entire loss prevention function reports. Most retail security professionals advise that all other security operatives, all other management executives of the firm—in short all other rank-and-file employees—should never be aware of the existence of a particular undercover agent. In many instances, the fact that such an operation even exists under the security umbrella should be masked.

Thus, security departmental budgets may be programmed so that when bills for undercover services are forwarded by the vendor agency, they may be simply captioned, "For services rendered," and paid through a built-in reservoir of funds for such services, requiring no further explanation. With the consent of top management, this shields the accounting and payroll departments from any knowledge of these activities. In general, the security department's top management supervisor should be fully briefed as to the need for and ramifications of undercover work within the company. With all the facts in hand, the final decision for using undercover agents should be made by top management only.

Uniformed Guard Services

The protection of the perimeter of any company's headquarters and warehouse operations is vital as a first line of defense. This involves patrolling physical premises of key areas such as warehouses, controlling and screening traffic in and out of offices, distribution centers, transportation depots, company parking lots, and, at times, even retail locations. Most security departments will draw upon vendor services to obtain uniformed guard services rather than create their own force.

While the operation of such guard services is dealt with more incisively in Chapter 7, important prerogatives should be retained by the security department in the employment of guard forces through vendor companies. For example, the security department should have the right to conduct its own interviews of guards, both prior to employment, as well as ongoing or exit interviews.

With bids from several vendors in hand, the evaluation of guard services should include the services rendered as well as the cost. Vendor guard services can be like small private armies, complete with their own supervision. For the company with its own security or loss prevention department, at no time should a uniformed guard service become a separate, individual security operation. One way to ensure this is to have the supervision of the guards fall directly under the company's own security director, rather than supervisory personnel employed directly by the guard company.

SECURITY DEPARTMENT AS A MODEL

Within the security department, pursuit of a high standard of morale is not only important for efficient operations, but also helps set an example for the entire company. Aware, alert, caring security operations should follow guiding principles in dealing with their own employees and other employees in the company that represent the "state of the art" in human relations. Some of the principles would include:

- Developing a communications network within the department.
- Instilling self-esteem in workers.
- Giving workers deserved recognition.
- Encouraging creative expression on the part of workers.
- Encouraging new experiences, via assignment rotations, new responsibilities, etc.
- Taking personal interest in workers.
- Holding special departmental meetings and training sessions.
- Developing a written manual for each function in the department.
- Discussing problems, ideas and suggestions with management.
- Practicing prevention rather than self-aggrandizement.
- Satisfying each worker's need for security and reward via merit increases.
- Discussing company policies and benefits prior to hiring.
- Setting good examples.
- Opening up a pipeline with peer groups from other departments.

Such operating policies take their cues from the basic needs we all have, needs many psychologists agree include:

1. The need for love.
2. The need for security.
3. The need for recognition.

4. The need for creative expression.
5. The need for new experiences.
6. The need for self-esteem.

SECURITY DEPARTMENT AS AN EDUCATOR

It is the security department that will normally educate the entire company in the need for and practice of retail security preventive maintenance. The security department must believe in its own value and importance, as well as its need to exist, before it can communicate its attitudes and operating rules to the company at large.

One security consultant notes that security education is not an isolated concept which can be put into the same category as fringe benefits, wherein such benefits are not seen until needed. Security education is a real and vital need in any organization, as a front-runner in supporting company objectives as well as reducing the opportunity for crime. Security information must reach every level of the company, and to work effectively, must be supported from the very top.

Security education must make clear what is expected of each employee and what action is being taken to ensure that the working environment is a safe place. Cooperation must be sought from each and every employee for this program to be effective. The attitude of the first-day employee will be much different from that of the ten-year veteran, and conditions will change during the career of each employee, but this does not lessen the need to instill a positive attitude.

The Security Manual

The bible of loss prevention within any one company is the security manual compiled for store and warehouse locations. Prepared by the security department, the manual should answer almost every question an employee might have relating to security, safety or sanitation—or any other areas under the jurisdiction of the loss prevention department. It should cover the protection offered by alarm systems and what to do if alarms occur. It spells out all actions to be taken should emergencies arise, including burglaries, robberies, injuries, or fires.

The manual provides emergency telephone numbers, singling out exactly whom to contact depending on the situation involved. It identifies the color-coding system warehouses or distribution centers

MODEL TOPIC OUTLINE FOR A SECURITY MANUAL

SUBJECT

ALARM SYSTEMS
AUTOS PERMITTED ON COMPOUND—RED "W"
BAKERY DIVISION:
  PARKING
BARRED FROM THE COMPOUND
BREAK TIMES—DIVISIONS'
CONTACTS:
  AFTER HOURS
  LOSS PREVENTION
DRIVERS—NO ID CARDS
EMERGENCY CALL
EMERGENCY PLAN
EMERGENCY TELEPHONE LIST
ENGINEERING—EMERGENCY PROCEDURES
ENGINEERING—PERSONNEL, CORPORATE
FIRST AID—POISON AND DRUG ANTIDOTES
GUARD ROSTER
HELPERS, TEMPORARY
ID—COLOR CODES
LAYOUT OF COMPOUND
LOSS PREVENTION ORGANIZATIONAL CHART
LOSS PREVENTION PERSONNEL
MAINTENANCE, AFTER HOURS
MEMOS
PARKING—RESERVED
PASS HOLDERS—TEMPORARY
PRIVATE LABELS
STATEMENT—TAKING OF
STORES
TELEPHONE LINES—DIRECT
TRACTOR/TRAILER—MISSING, STOLEN
WALKIE-TALKIES

A good working "security manual" should be in the hands of every retail manager or "decision-maker." The manual does not pre-empt the functions and duties of a security department, but provides store and warehouse-level personnel with the information they need relevant to security/safety/sanitation procedures, what forms, documents and credentials are needed, emergency call numbers, etc. This manual index indicates information provided on situations as diverse as poison and drug antidotes and proper taking of a statement.

may use for passes and identification. It presents a complete layout of all premises, including locations of security-related equipment and property. The manual includes a list of all security and maintenance personnel business extensions and personal telephone numbers. It enumerates the order in which specific people or institutions should be called, depending on what type of situation occurs.

Full details as to what to do and what not to do when crimes are uncovered are listed. Procedures for opening and closing stores, for cash control, and for fire-fighting should be fully and completely spelled out. Finally, dates and times of regularly scheduled security sessions at stores and distribution centers are listed so that all locations are prepared in advance for training meetings and seminars, and all appropriate personnel are on hand.

Every company is different, but in retail businesses, there are more similarities than differences. Thus, while no two security programs will be exactly the same, basic concepts are universal. The security and crime prevention program offers knowledge of the correct way to accomplish a job as an alternative to being held accountable for incorrect job performance. In translating this to a single most important principle in the understanding and appreciation of the security umbrella, the old adage "an ounce of prevention is worth a pound of cure" will do nicely.

It is almost always far less expensive to prevent internal theft, shoplifting, bad check loss, etc., than it is to investigate it. Prevention dollars are an instrument which is controllable in both time and amount. Since prevention is planned, and not based upon emotional response, it is likely to be more accurate and much more cost-effective than a response to a committed crime. Business profitability is dependent upon uninterrupted and efficient operations. Very few businesses incorporate plans to have extended down-time due to loss which could have been prevented in the first place.

To reduce crime, one must first predict crime. Temptation, especially in retail businesses which sell finished goods directly to consumers, can affect anyone. If prevention is the primary goal of the security operation, it should be tempered by the fact that no one is above suspicion.

THE EMPLOYEE FOLDER

A key item in dealing with employees is the documented folder. Such documentation is often the most important tool in determining a person's growth potential, merit for promotion, or, at times, cause for termination. Small accumulated documentations in a folder will collectively reveal an amazingly accurate and complete story, including the good and the bad. If an employee shows initiative in the field of sales vs. stock, this should be documented. If an employee is an outstanding salesman, but has been reprimanded several times for poor security—keeping a door open when it should be locked, not placing the jewelry immediately back in the showcase, etc.—this should also be documented.

Naturally, any accusation of a dishonest act or criminal violation of rules and regulations must be backed up by hard evidence. But documented evidence can reveal several occasions in which an employee was called to task because of a disregard for company regulations. In the real world, an accumulation of small offenses, not each in themselves a cause for immediate dismissal, can provide sufficient documentation to terminate an employee at a point when that employee is suspected of committing a serious crime, but where full evidence of this particular crime may be lacking.

As with anything else in the area of human relations, the use of employee folders must be applied equitably and more for constructive purposes than as a weapon of fear. It should be a manifestation of a company's efficiency and interest in each employee — no matter how small or unimportant the job seems. And, with each employee aware of this central file, it is also a measure of the security consciousness of the company. Thus, employee folders become a powerful deterrent force in their own right.

HOW MUCH TO TELL?

In addition to security orientations for new employees, periodic meetings and special training or informational seminars continue to demonstrate the involvement and integration of security into the everyday operations of the company. In such meetings, the fact that management is very much interested in every employee's participation in security should be stressed. Any reward programs for assisting security, along with compensation programs for ongoing use of regular employees in a security capacity, should also be continually detailed.

While one effect of this is a realization on the part of employees of the size, scope and responsibilities of the loss prevention department—the essence of the security umbrella — there is also an appreciation gained for the thorough investigative work on the part of security that follows each and every crime or violation that comes to light. This is another way of demonstrating to the employee that the company is on the ball, constantly alert and aware of what is going on. For the average honest worker this notion is not depressing, but, as noted earlier, actually a morale builder.

Some loss prevention experts feel that security departments should detail their actual exploits as part of a continuing information flow to employees. When serious security violations are uncovered and solved, the entire corporation, in this program, is told in detail what happened. This use of a real example helps security personnel drive home the point that they mean business.

In practice, every company must develop its own particular policies concerning the constant revelation of security apprehensions. In large companies where cases may be numerous, a policy of complete and full disclosure is not only logistically impossible, but in terms of psychology, past a point of "diminishing returns" in terms of deterrent value.

THE AUDITING FUNCTION

Very often, management awareness of serious security problems starts with an unusual change in figures—figures uncovered by audits, inventories, sales comparisons, etc. An established retail store with excellent sales during one quarter, for example, might have a serious profit decline during that same period. Inventories might check out, sales figures might prove accurate, proper markups might have been applied. In short, the entire operation, from the merchandising standpoint, may be performing as expected. A reasonable assumption for such a drop in profits is that a security problem exists.

Since most businesses today are dependent on a paperwork bureaucracy, when a loss is revealed through such documentation, it points to a situation that has probably existed for at least several months. The fact is that few people are caught in the act, with their hands in the till, with cases of goods in cars, or shoplifting some merchandise out of a store, *prior* to the recognition by management of the fact that either a specific or broadly-based security problem exists.

This need to see the forest before examining the trees makes the function of the auditor important in its security applications. Auditors should have the authority to look at any aspect of the company without restraint. As a group, they should not report to any functional branch, including security or loss prevention, but rather directly to the highest level of the company. They should be well versed in business methods and procedures and given the time to pursue leads without hindrance. Activities of auditors should be far-reaching outside the organization itself, to areas including those of vendors, off-site facilities, outside suppliers, etc. They should be allowed to review any records, such as purchase orders placed for materials or services at a vendor, to look for possible criminal activities.

The auditing function thus represents a resource which can make a viable crime prevention team when coupled with the investigative activities of the security department. The auditing unit's ability to make early detection of irregularities, coupled with the ability of the security department to verify the existence of wrong-doing can ultimately result in a strong deterrent effect.

SUMMARY

Every company, large or small, has a security problem which does not always correlate with the size of the company compared to the size of the problem. "Security" as a term embraces not only the prevention and detection of criminal acts, but the overall security of a company. This includes employee safety, customer safety, fire safety. As a result, every employee has some set of security responsibilities and is part of the management security team.

In order to establish formal security departments, retail businesses may employ a string of vendor companies to fashion a complete circle of protection. In companies where growth may be rapid and customer dealings numerous, a permanent, internal security unit reporting directly to top management, and itself part of the management team, is a vital and unavoidable development as part of that growth. Only when security becomes an integrated part of top management does the security umbrella fully open up to both protect a company and help it grow.

Within security departments, a model for relationships and example-setting should be stressed. These examples should have a carryover effect to the company at large. The key is prevention, the underpinnings are good communications and an acceptance of the fact that anyone can breach security rules, via criminal acts or just plain carelessness. Auditing can pinpoint shrinkage losses via intensive review of company and supplier paperwork. Likewise, a documented employee folder can pinpoint a problem in attitude that can produce shrinkage losses.

Thus, the security umbrella must be opened over a company all the time. The need for security is constant.

NOTES

[1] "How Inflation Brings Out the Criminal Urge," **U.S. News & World Report,** September 8, 1980, page 56.

2 INTERNAL THEFT

This chapter will describe:

- **The size of the problem**
- **The "why" of the problem**
- **Basic corporate attitudes**
- **Who the offenders are**
- **The "what, where and how" of internal theft**
- **Prevention techniques: employee screening**
- **Prevention and detection techniques; sources of information**
- **Apprehension, interviewing and disposition**

THE SIZE OF THE PROBLEM

There is no truly accurate way to assess the extent of internal theft in business and industry, particularly in the retail sector. This is not for lack of estimates. The U. S. Department of Commerce, for example, in 1977 pegged employee dishonesty at $18 billion, or $400 million a week. The Department's prior estimate, in 1963, put the annual figure at $3 billion. The Commerce Department further reports that 30% of all business failures are attributable to internal theft.[1]

The National Crime Prevention Institute, taking a "pie chart" approach, states that 60% to 80% of all business and industry losses in 1980 were due to employee theft.[2] Looking at the impact of employee theft in terms of retail prices, *The Christian Science Monitor* in 1978 stated that ". . . by 1983, the prices of American goods can increase by $50-$60 billion a year just to cover employee theft."[3]

Thus, while estimates are worded differently and are impossible to compare directly, there is general agreement that internal theft is by far the largest segment of retail store crime. Respondents to a *Progressive Grocer* poll put employee theft at up to 1% of gross sales in supermarkets,[4] and even this may be conservative since the National Retail Merchants Association figures annual retail store shrinkage from all sources at 3% on a national basis.[5]

If a retail store doing $1 million a year in gross sales loses 1% to internal theft, or $10,000, the loss can be gauged in terms of its impact on net profit, since that $10,000 represents a deduction from the bottom line. It is the equivalent of the cost of merchandise received and paid for, but never sold. The following grid, which can be used as a reference point throughout this text, might be termed the "Theft Make-Up Grid," since it plots the dollar value of sales required to offset a given loss at varying net profit percentages.

THE THEFT MAKE-UP GRID

Net Profit

Dollar Loss	1%	2%	3%	4%	5%	6%
		ADDITIONAL SALES NEED				
$ 2,500	250,000	125,000	83,333	62,500	50,000	41,666
4,800	480,000	240,000	160,000	120,000	96,000	80,000
6,000	600,000	300,000	200,000	150,000	120,000	100,000
10,000	1,000,000	500,000	333,333	250,000	200,000	166,666
15,000	1,500,000	750,000	500,000	375,000	300,000	250,000
18,000	1,800,000	900,000	600,000	450,000	360,000	300,000
25,000	2,500,000	1,250,000	833,333	625,000	500,000	416,666
50,000	5,000,000	2,500,000	1,666,666	1,250,000	1,000,000	833,333
100,000	10,000,000	5,000,000	3,333,333	2,500,000	2,000,000	1,666,666

It is readily apparent that the smaller the net profit, the greater the impact of theft in terms of the additional sales a store would have to make just in order to wipe out the impact of that theft on net profits. In supermarkets, with their traditionally low net profits in the 1% vicinity, that $10,000 theft would necessitate no less than $1 million in extra sales a year.

The extent of employee theft, as compared to other forms of business shrinkage, and the impact of all theft as charted above, provides some appreciation of the size of the internal theft problem. By definition, internal theft includes everything from large scale embezzlement of funds to computer fraud to the taking of a package of cigarettes by a store clerk. Since this text deals with retail store security, the topic of "white-collar crime" will not be covered in order to concentrate primarily on stores and distribution centers. Cases of embezzlement may individually involve vast sums of money, occur over long periods of time, and make sensational newspaper headlines when brought to light. But the relative infrequency of white-collar crime compared to the smaller, steadier, more pervasive forms of internal theft puts the crucial importance of retail store internal theft in its proper perspective.

In the same manner, internal retail store theft can, by far, outweigh the more publicized external shrinkage problems of robbery and burglary, shoplifting and check and credit card losses when measured on a financial basis. Consider that the shoplifter is usually nervous, hurried, limited to what can be taken out of a store in one pass-through, and anxious to get out fast. A passer of bad-checks, the proverbial "paper-hanger," needs only a cooperative manager or cashier to approve what will become the source of a profit loss. But the bad check artist knows that the same store cannot be victimized more than once or twice.

The store's own employees, in sharp contrast, are in the store throughout the work week, know the entire retail setup intimately, and can use their normal assigned duties as the perfect cover to deprive the store of cash income or merchandise. It is a steady, continuing drain on profits that, if anything, will tend to get worse as employees involved become bolder through success.

THE "WHY" OF THE PROBLEM

It is not difficult to see why internal theft is an enormous problem. Understanding the source of the problem, however, is difficult and may require a good deal of soul-searching. Several years ago, *Time* printed a remarkable essay entitled "Larceny in Everyday Life," depicting a situation that gives "plenty of support to those who fear that America is becoming a nation of small-time chiselers."

The major point brought forth in the essay was this: "In freewheeling 19th century America, high-level fraud was far more spectacular than today, when business, trade and politics must function under rigid controls and searching publicity. What has increased [today] is the opportunity for the pettier kinds of cheating, largely because of the growth of communities and population. In the urbanizing world in which crossroads are turning into shopping centers, towns into cities and cities into supercities, nobody knows his neighbor's name—or feels responsible to him. The impersonality of the supermarkets, the super-university, the super-corporation gives the individual a guilt-proof out: 'After all, I'm not hurting anybody in particular.' "[6]

Many psychologists and security experts draw a triangle, with legs labelled "Frustration," "Aggression" and "Opportunity," as one way to approach the question of why internal theft takes place. More recently, the legs of the so-called "theft triangle" have been simplified as "Opportunity," "Need" and "Attitudes." One prominent security firm notes that "The fact that the vast majority of thefts are never detected, and that only a few detected thieves are ever punished, only enhances the opportunity for theft . . . but attitude is the key element of the theft triangle, especially since most employees have regular opportunities to steal, regardless of the precautions taken by the employer."

Many cases of internal theft result from a worker unhappy in a job situation, ready to gain a measure of revenge on the employer. However, a large portion of the internal theft loss, as implied by the *Time* essay, and defined by the "Attitude" leg of the "theft triangle" is uncomfortably innocent in motivation—it's "the thing to do." Compounding the problem is the prevalence of what might be termed "expected dishonesties," such as expense-account padding, or income tax gamesmanship. The ethical line between bending the law and premeditated theft is indeed a fine one.

BASIC CORPORATE OR EMPLOYER ATTITUDES

The question of attitude is a two-way street. Employees come into a firm with their own set of attitudes or beliefs. These may be upheld, modified or changed by the perceived attitudes of the corporation or employer to the employee, to the operating policies of the company, and to the entire question of retail security itself.

Thus, a Small Business Administration management aid pamphlet for retailers states that ". . . it is easy . . . to create an environment in which dishonesty takes root and thrives. Just relax your accounting and inventory control procedures. Nothing deters would-be thieves like the knowledge that inventory is so closely controlled that stolen goods will be missed quickly."[7]

While there is no immutable law stating that lax rules lead inevitably to consistent employee theft, such a policy can help pave the way, saying to the employee in effect: "We're not watching you; we're too big to be hurt by one employee." Modelling or example-setting at close range is also a factor. Small practices apparently condoned by an employer can lead an honest worker into deliberate patterns of theft. A supermarket manager generously allowing his employees to augment their lunches with a candy bar "on the house" may be opening the door to wholesale larceny. In many manufacturing plants or office situations, it is common practice for employees to take supplies from a stockroom without signing for these items or justifying their removal.

A top retail loss prevention director relates one case in which a supermarket manager trainee was once allowed to take a pack of cigarettes gratis by the store manager. The trainee soon made a habit of this, and before long it was not a single pack, but cartons. The employee began to supply friends with cigarettes and eventually the stolen merchandise was being peddled outside the store. Before this employee was apprehended, all kinds of merchandise was being handed by the case out of back doors and side doors, with the store losing hundreds of dollars a week.

Therefore, a retail store operation concerned about internal theft must first approach the situation in broad brush strokes and not ascribe all fault to the guilty parties alone. Simply waiting for employees to steal tends to guarantee that sooner or later it will happen. A set of store policies and procedures that are strict on paper but ignored in practice can be worse than no policies at all. In the final analysis, a retail operation, like any other business, is not a democracy; it needs discipline. Retailers who argue that they run their stores like a big family would have to agree that a family is not a democracy. In fact, the Small Business Administration rates misplaced trust as one of the primary causes of internal theft, and cautions, "One of the first steps in preventing [internal theft] is for the owner-manager to examine the trust he puts in his employees. Is it blind trust that grew from close friendships? Or is it trust that is built on an accountability that reduced opportunities for thefts?"[8]

Communicating to employees a company's attitude toward loss prevention in general and internal theft specifically is prudent to say the least. The sad fact is that in many companies, the policy seems to be that the less employees are made aware of internal theft, the better. A *Progressive Grocer* survey of supermarket chains found that only 20% give new employees manuals spelling out regulations and policies relating to employee dishonesty, and less than half—only 43%—have any kind of *standard* procedure for deterring or detecting theft and pilferage by their own employees.[9] A major East Coast company's security director puts it even more bluntly: ". . . in all my years of experience, the most common situation is one in which companies *never* tell employees that taking merchandise is stealing and that stealing is prohibited. . . . Comments from apprehended employees reveal this condition in a way that is almost comic: 'I was able to take three pounds of sliced ham because I work for the store'. . . . 'I thought they would have no objections'. . . . 'Nobody ever told me not to do it.' "

As the Small Business Administration states: "Let your people know that you care. Make them aware of the stress you place on loss prevention. This point must be driven home again and again. And with every restatement of it—whether by a security check, a change of locks, the testing of alarms, a systems audit, a notice on the bulletin board—you can be assured that you are influencing that moment of decision when an employee is faced with the choice of whether or not to steal."[10]

On an operational basis, one security director describes his company's communications policy this way: "A security orientation is part of the general orientation every new employee receives. Quite simply, we inform them that we have a security program. We say that we believe the employees are basically honest, but that we are here to see that they remain honest. As proof, we ask them to check with veteran co-workers and they'll learn how active security is in every area. We also tell them directly that we're aware of just about any idea for employee pilferage that has been devised."

One payoff to such an up-front program is this: "Our people are now accustomed to seeing us in their stores and will tell us their problems. Manager suspicions are now aired frankly and rapidly. In turn, we've built bridges to employees where we have been even able to help them with security problems outside the work situation. Several cashiers, for example, were receiving threatening calls, which we began to monitor for them, working with the local police."

WHO ARE THE OFFENDERS?

No job classification or level is immune from either the opportunity, need or attitude—the legs of the "theft triangle"—that can make internal theft and pilferage a reality. In a *Progressive Grocer* study,[11] 53% of supermarket executives rated part-time employees and teenagers as the most frequent perpetrators. This has a surface logic in that these younger workers comprise the most transient labor group in the store, may be uninterested in company or industry career opportunities, and are perhaps most apt to be unaffected by the traditional values of "the establishment."

In the same study, 30% rated new employees as the worst source of internal theft. Regular full-time employees were listed in the worst source group by 28% of the companies, while departmental or store managers were included in this category by only 13% of the respondents. Percentages do not total 100% because of multiple category inclusion.

Dishonest employees obviously do not work in a vacuum. Fully 25%

of the stores in the *Progressive Grocer* survey reported cases of collusion between employees and customers, mostly involving cashiers "discounting" purchases of relatives and friends. And 19% reported cases of collusion between employees and vendors or deliverymen—potentially the most serious source of internal theft in terms of value of merchandise stolen.

What percentages in a survey cannot reveal is the "influence value" of one employee on another. There is a good deal of truth in the proverb that one rotten apple can spoil an entire barrel.

The loss prevention department in one large chain reports an investigation of a store where profitability had fallen to such a low ebb that the company was on the verge of closing it down. As all areas of the store's operation were methodically checked, every store employee was interviewed. The security director relates the results this way: ". . . all of these employees were very free in talking about how everybody else was stealing. Regardless of whom we spoke to, we were told instances involving top store management, middle store management, cashiers, receiving area employees, stock clerks—everybody."

"Not one would admit personal guilt. Each pointed an accusing finger at another. The store's problem was simple, however critical: Every worker was stealing a little at a time. Collectively, a vast amount of money or merchandise was being stolen."

THE "WHAT, WHERE AND HOW" OF INTERNAL THEFT

There are three primary areas where internal theft can strike a retail business:

1. Where a cashier handles money or charge accounts. This can be the front end of a supermarket, or the fourth floor of a department store. No matter what the precise location, it is the point where money or credit and merchandise changes hands.
2. The receiving area, or backroom. This is where merchandise coming into a store is received and held, sometimes for minutes, sometimes weeks. It is not only the point where paperwork pertaining to receipt of merchandise is initially processed but also where outside vendors come into contact with employees.
3. Special service areas. This refers to courtesy counters or check cashing booths and non self-service locations. These locations normally house higher priced merchandise requiring sales personnel. Often, in the case of supermarkets, service locations also are the location of the store money safe.

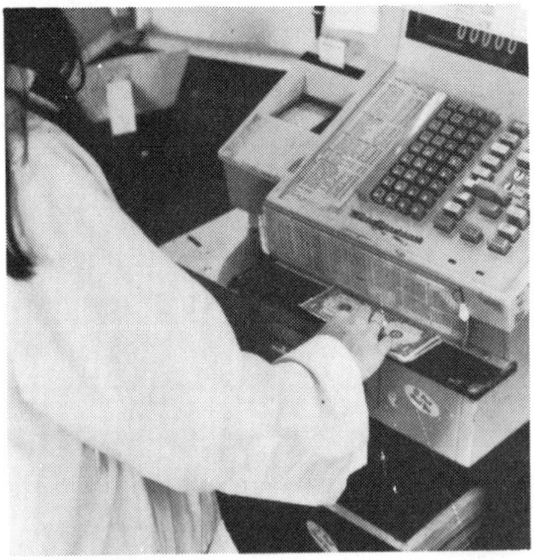

One way cashiers can steal without collusion with customers or fellow employees. Here, the cashier has accepted exact change for a sale, but has not placed the cash in the money drawer, leaving it instead on the ledge above. She will then proceed to handle a number of transactions in the correct manner, until . . .

. . . a good opportunity arises to secret the cash left outside the register. This is done by simply dropping the cash into a waiting handbag below. The cashier now must mentally or physically keep a record of how much cash has been stolen in this manner, and, during the course of the work shift, fail to ring up other exact change transactions that are deposited in the cash drawer so the amount totaled in the register comes out even. This is most easily accomplished on "express" lanes where many transactions are for single items, such as cigarette cartons, milk, bread, etc.

"Bottom of the Cart" theft, particularly serious in supermarkets so dependent on shopping carts, can be accidental or deliberate—a case of collusion between customer and cashier, or shoplifting by the customer against an unobservant cashier. Here, the cashier accepting money for the transaction has overlooked a large size detergent package on the bottom rack. New types of carts now being produced eliminate the possibility of any merchandise placement out of the regular basket.

The Front End

A substantial portion of internal theft occurs at the register. Some estimates hold that as much as 30% of all retail loss can be traced to the front end or checkout stations. Much of that shrinkage involves collusion between cashiers and customers, known as "discounting" or "sweetheart sales," wherein merchandise is rung up at a fraction of the retail price. In supermarkets, bulky merchandise placed on the bottom rack of shopping carts may be innocently or deliberately overlooked.

With the advent of the totally automated front end, featuring optical scanning of all coded merchandise, the potential for cashier theft has not decreased, but actually increased sharply. The reason is that cashiers can easily feign a merchandise scanning motion, but, by manipulating the product so that the Universal Product Code symbol is not scanned, the sale is not registered. A scanning order is processed so rapidly that instances of nonringup are very hard to detect with an accomplished cashier at the equipment. Nonscanned items will not produce the computer "bleeps" that properly scanned items create and front end managers, or even surveillance personnel, can easily become benumbed by the constant clatter of a busy front end of 10 or more working checkstands.

Noncollusion cashier theft can be far more serious than "discounting," since such theft can take place at any time.

The following are some of the more common tactics in front end or checkout crime:

- Selling merchandise to friends and relatives at a discount.
- Accepting manufacturer coupons en masse without product purchase.
- Nonringup of bulky merchandise placed on bottom racks of shopping carts.
- Nonringup or "No Sale" ringup when presented with exact money for a sale.
- Short-changing customers on cash transactions.
- Writing up cash sales as charges and pocketing the cash.
- Issuing false refunds to an accomplice.
- Raising the amount of checks after they have been approved, and pocketing the difference.

Even without loss prevention department personnel on the scene, front end or checkout crime may be signalled by a number of warning signs that should invite closer scrutiny. These danger signals include:

1. Cashiers with chronically long checkout lines vs. other checkstands.

2. Cashiers always checking out the same store employees or customers when they purchase merchandise in the store.
3. Large, bulky sales totaled out for relatively small sums of money.
4. Excessive "No Sale" ringups, particularly on Express Lanes, where a greater proportion of the transactions are paid for by exact change.
5. Small calculators or pads adjacent to cash registers.
6. Blockage of cash register transaction display readout.
7. Cash register drawers remaining open on an unusually frequent basis.
8. Cashiers frequently bending down out of sight or seeming to drop money on the floor.
9. Cashiers who continually enjoy perfect accounting, coming out to the penny at all times.

The Receiving Area

The second primary source of internal theft is the receiving area, or the backroom. Receivers most often do not handle cash, but their role is vital: through the receiving area pours most of the store's merchandise inventory—an inventory of immense value relative to the total business. Receivers in high volume supermarkets can process more than $250,000 worth of merchandise a week, and as a result, receivers are often targets of unscrupulous deliverymen, including outside vendors or chain warehouse truckmen . . . or are themselves someone to "get to" in terms of kickbacks or working in collusion with vendors. The scope of a receiving room theft problem can be appreciated by the realization that a receiver inclined to accept a kickback or work with one deliveryman will undoubtedly work with many.

The following are some of the more common tactics in receiving area crime:

- Checking in merchandise that is not received.
- Removal of merchandise already checked in.
- Allowing vendors or deliverymen free access to store backrooms.
- Collusion between vendors and receivers in return of damaged goods, stales, bottles, etc.

Under these broad headings literally hundreds of specific ploys have been devised—sometimes to meet the peculiarities of one company's operation, or even a single location. Often, collusion is the key. In one classic case, an older downtown store's receiving area was the basement, requiring merchandise to be off-loaded and sent down a conveyor belt into the basement. A beer salesman and a store receiver worked in collusion. The receiver would conveniently disappear for a moment, at which point the beer vendor would reverse the conveyor, sending cases of beer back up from the basement. When the receiver returned, the conveyor was reversed again, and thus cases of beer by the dozens were recounted as received merchandise.

One troubling aspect of internal theft is the addition of outright vendor theft into the overall total. By strict definition, vendor theft in the absence of collusion with store receivers or other store personnel is considered external loss. However, the consistency and frequency of vendor theft, once the pattern begins, places the headache of vendor theft firmly in the realm of employee crime. Adding to the problem is the fact that a good deal of what might prove to be deliberate vendor theft can be upheld as inadvertent error on the part of the vendor, all other things being equal. Here then are some of the more common tactics in vendor theft:

- Failure to give credit for returns, stales, spoils and bottles.
- Adding credits back into sales.
- Adding invoices incorrectly.
- Extending invoices incorrectly.
- Charging the store for undelivered merchandise.
- Holding invoices for re-marking after being checked.
- Delivering "chimney stacked" pallets (cases faced out around a pallet, appearing to be solidly packed, but with a hollow core).
- Theft of other merchandise at the receiving area.

As with front end or checkstand theft, there are a number of danger signs at the receiving area that should flag attention to the existence of possible employee or vendor theft. Among these:

1. Many vendor deliveries during rush hours; receiving area jam-up.
2. Two or more vendors of similar merchandise at the receiving area at the same time.
3. Unsupervised trash removals; unfolded or nonbaled carton removal.
4. Vendor or delivery trucks near employees' personal cars in the parking lot. (To place free merchandise directly into a "partner's" car.)
5. Receivers not "on station" during the entire period of vendor deliveries.
6. Deliverymen, vendors and even chain warehouse drivers breaking truck seals.
7. Newly received merchandise not segregated from regular backroom stock.

Special Service Areas

The third key area where employee theft occurs is the special service area in the store. Theft from security booths, courtesy booths, check-cashing booths and the like can incorporate aspects of both cashier theft—primarily cash loss in one form or another—and outright merchandise theft.

Because the volume of traffic is often so much lighter at these areas than at central or departmental checkouts, theft is far more devious and secretive, although each individual instance may cost the company far more in terms of value than an instance of checkout "discounting." Collusion with friends and relatives in terms of check cashing approval, and with other employees in terms of merchandise theft and undercharging on employee purchases, can rapidly snowball into a huge loss.

The common tactics in service area theft include:

- Direct theft of merchandise, e.g., employee shoplifting.
- Selling merchandise to friends and relatives at a discount.
- Approving checks for friends and relatives without proper acceptance procedures.
- Retaining sales slips and register receipts from legitimate purchases at the service area for use in later theft of merchandise camouflaged as regular purchase. This is a common technique in theft of cartons of cigarettes commonly restricted in sale to courtesy booths. Customers in a hurry may not notice or ask for the sales slip to be stapled to or dropped into the bag with the merchandise. Courtesy booth attendants simply hold these slips for dummy "purchases" at a later time in the day by friends or other store employees.

Some of the warning signs pointing to the possibility of special service area theft include:

1. Clutter and mess around courtesy booth counters and floor spaces.
2. Other store employees continually patronizing the same courtesy booth employees.
3. Personal handbags, shopping bags or small employee tote bags in the courtesy booth or special service area.
4. Store deposit bags or money envelopes within easy grasp of non-authorized personnel.

PREVENTION TECHNIQUES: EMPLOYEE SCREENING

It does not require much elaboration to prove the case for "preventive maintenance" as a key element in reducing retail loss. A good

C SURVEY ITEMS - 1

ANSWER ALL QUESTIONS

FOR EACH QUESTION CHECK THE ONE ANSWER WHICH BEST REFLECTS YOUR OWN OPINION.	(1) Definitely Yes	(2) Probably Yes	(3) Uncertain (?)	(4) Probably No	(5) Definitely No
1. Do you believe that once a person is caught stealing that he should always be watched very closely from then on?	□	□	□	□	□
2. Could you admire a man who was too afraid to physically defend himself?	□	□	□	□	□
3. Do you think that drinking on the job hurts a person's job performance?	□	□	□	□	□
4. Within the last three years, have you ever started a fist-fight (even if only a small one) with a fellow employee?	□	□	□	□	□
5. Do you agree that it is easy to become mentally ill if the conditions are right?	□	□	□	□	□
6. Have you occasionally had ideas and thoughts that you would not like other people to know about?	□	□	□	□	□
7. Do most people let little things bother them more than they should?	□	□	□	□	□
8. Do you often buy magazines or books which tell stories of successful crimes and swindles?	□	□	□	□	□
9. Do most people need help from a psychologist?	□	□	□	□	□
10. Have you ever worried about things you should not have said or done?	□	□	□	□	□
A	(1)	(2)	(3)	(4)	(5)
11. Does everyone steal a little?	□	□	□	□	□
12. Have you ever taken any money (even if only $1.00) from a present or past employer?	□	□	□	□	□
13. Do you believe that good guys come out second best?	□	□	□	□	□
14. Do you agree that low wages will force honest employees to take money from their employers without authorization?	□	□	□	□	□
15. Will everyone steal if the conditions are right?	□	□	□	□	□
16. Is it true that to be human is to be dishonest?	□	□	□	□	□
17. Should a person caught taking small merchandise from his company still be given a promotion which was earned and deserved?	□	□	□	□	□
18. A person regularly borrows money from his company without permission but always repays it at a later date. Do you think that this person is honest?	□	□	□	□	□
19. Have you ever been at least a little tempted to steal something?	□	□	□	□	□
20. Do you believe that an employee who has taken company merchandise just a few times without permission can be trusted in a responsible position having access to money?	□	□	□	□	□
B	(1)	(2)	(3)	(4)	(5)
21. Do you think that once a thief always a thief?	□	□	□	□	□
22. Would you return $100 to its owner if you knew that you would not get a reward?	□	□	□	□	□
23. Do you believe that a person caught stealing should tell on his friends who helped?	□	□	□	□	□
24. Would you say that you are too honest to steal?	□	□	□	□	□
25. If you were caught stealing, would you tell on the people who helped you?	□	□	□	□	□
26. Do you try at all costs to keep out of trouble?	□	□	□	□	□
27. Do you think that it is humanly possible for the average person to be completely honest on the job?	□	□	□	□	□
28. Do you always tell the truth regardless of the circumstances?	□	□	□	□	□
29. Do you agree that honest people are honest because they were raised that way?	□	□	□	□	□
30. If you found a wallet with money, do you honestly think you would return the wallet and money to the owner?	□	□	□	□	□
C	(1)	(2)	(3)	(4)	(5)

3

"Personnel Security Inventory" represents the "state-of-the-art" in attitudinal questionnaires. Essentially it helps determine a job candidate's basic attitudes about personal standards of honesty, overall outlook on work and personal relationships.

deal of what constitutes a systematic approach to loss prevention relates back to basic corporate attitudes discussed earlier in this chapter. Companies which make it obvious to prospective employees that loss prevention is important to the corporation have already taken a number of lengthy steps toward minimizing retail shrinkage.

Pre-employment screening at all levels in retail operations has thus become an important consideration for management. In one recent survey of convenience store chains, for example,[12] 42% of large chains and 36% of small chains reported using polygraph or voice stress analysis (which does not require a physical attachment to a machine) in screening all new employees. An additional 39% of the large chains, and 31% of smaller chains reported using the "lie detector" or PSE analyzer at least in selected situations. A total of 19 states presently have some restrictions on polygraph examinations and/or require polygraph operators to be licensed. State licensing can help avoid unprofessionalism—conduct by examiners "who ask personal questions not germane to security needs, practice intimidating techniques or use faulty equipment"—according to a spokesperson for a polygraphers' association in New York, which is one state that does not presently require licensing.

With the use of the polygraph a growing expense, and with certain states passing laws restricting its use in pre-employment situations, other specialized personnel tests and candidate investigative services have come to the forefront.

One service company specializing in pre-employment investigations, for example, notes that "judicious use of investigations can increase profits by reducing turnover, by spotlighting the alcoholic, the poor "closer," the person who falsifies his/her employment application or educational background, the man or woman who never could do a good job, and the thief. . . . Some people don't get along with their peers, supervisors or those they are supposed to supervise. Someone like that can ruin a store operation in time."[13]

Another investigative firm uses a special scoring system to rate prospective employees based on a detailed background check, and will recommend hiring only those who score 50 or above on the report. The firm contends that "40 people out of 100 will steal from their employers if given the chance; use of a pre-employment report with a bottom level minimum score can reduce this presumptive total to 14 or fewer out of 100."[14]

Background checks alone, as another management consulting firm specializing in pre-employment points out, "do not give any information concerning undetected crime, while pure psychological tests have suffered from low validity coefficients and from the lack of a suitable measurement criterion."[15]

Psychological tests used in the pre-employment context are designed to measure honesty and potential dishonesty . . . in effect, attitudes. Combining such tests, so-called "personnel security inventories," with polygraph tests to validate the results, is a more recent refinement of the pre-employment screening art. One such program consists of a two-part preliminary questionnaire including a personal history and a multiple-choice section measuring attitudes and opinions toward theft, violence, drugs, alcohol and emotional stability. A polygraph session then attempts to confirm the directional trends indicated in the multiple-choice section.

A research scientist for a management consulting firm using this technique notes that "Job applicants who had a high score on the dishonesty scale were very likely to make significant theft-related admissions in a polygraph examination. . . . These people perceive themselves as average people in a dishonest and corrupt world."[16]

All of these services and programs can be costly. Background checks can run to $100 or more per investigation at this point in time. Administration of "personnel security inventory" tests without subsequent polygraph validation can run to $12 or more per test. Polygraphing probably costs in the $30 per test range. Consulting companies allow corporate client personnel departments to administer the test and then forward the test sheet back to them for scoring and written analysis.

While requirements vary widely from industry to industry, the experience of the personnel director in management recruitment for an 1,100-unit restaurant chain is probably quite instructive for firms in the retail area, particularly supermarkets, even if few would go to these lengths:

"An individual goes through some rather heavy screening at our company. We prescreen applications, and about 30% to 40% of the applicants are screened out at this point. After the initial screening, applicants are interviewed by telephone, followed by a preliminary personal interview. If the individual passes these, he is given a 'personnel security inventory' test and then an in-depth personal interview. Another psychological profile follows."

This personnel director adds, "Restaurant management differs from most other styles of management simply because the hours involved are more than they might be elsewhere and because the people in

Security Check Sheet

STORE ______ MANAGER ______ DATE ______ TIME ______

	YES	NO			YES	NO	
			EMPLOYEE APPEARANCE & ATTITUDE	31			Begin with Clear X
1			Proper Uniform	32			Voids Circled & Initialed
2			Name Tag	33			Voided Sales Re-Rung
3			Well Groomed	34			Employee Sign In & Out
4			Eating, Drinking, Smoking	35			Dated & Register No.
5			Friendly & Courteous	36			Bagged by Week
6			Greet Customer				**CASH AUDIT**
7			Busy in Customer Absence	37			N.S.F. Check Amount Proper
8			Use Suggesting Selling	38			N.S.F. Checks Punch Marks
			CASH REGISTER COMPLIANCE	39			Customer Checks Current Date
9			Call Amount Each Item	40			Cash on Hand Proper
10			Move Each Item				**CHARGE CARDS & MONEY ORDERS**
11			Call Total Amount Sale	41			Stored in Safe
12			Call Amount Money Tendered	42			Dated & Filled in Properly
13			Count Customer Change	43			Money Orders No. Sequence
			Issue Receipt	44			Supervisors Report Each 2 Weeks
15			Thank Customer	45			Bank Deposits Balance
			C… REGISTER	46			Sale to Minor Book Used
16							

CANDIDATE BACKGROUND INFORMATION

NAME	DATE OF BIRTH	PLACE OF BIRTH

MAIDEN NAME OR OTHER NAMES USED	MARITAL STATUS	NAME OF SPOUSE, IF MARRIED

MOTHER'S NAME	FATHER'S NAME

SOCIAL SECURITY NUMBER	SEX	HEIGHT	WEIGHT	COLOR EYES	GLASSES?	COLOR HAIR	COMPLEXION

HOME ADDRESSES FOR PAST 20 YEARS

STREET ADDRESS, CITY AND STATE (LIST PRESENT ADDRESS FIRST)	FROM (DATE)	TO (DATE)

ENTIRE EMPLOYMENT HISTORY

… MOST …RST)	FULL ADDRES…	JOB TITLE(S)	NAME OF SUPERVISOR	F… M	TO (DATE)

Ongoing personnel reports maintained by a security or loss prevention department include check sheets designed primarily for cashiers, and basic background reports that become the key documents in an employee's work folder.

restaurant management, particularly chains, are often younger and without the experience of other management training. As such, it's important to select employees who do have the ability to manage large numbers of people and operate businesses which take in large amounts of money."

Possibly the greatest single danger of extensive pre-employment screening is over-reliance on this screening following employment, in terms of a relaxed attitude toward employee conduct. The company may consider this up-front spending on screening and testing as an insurance policy against the possibility of any employee theft.

The setting of role models and the relationship with peers can overcome and override even the most basic attitudes and beliefs of any person. Thus even the most extensive pre-employment screening can only be a necessary first step in a total loss prevention program.

PREVENTION AND DETECTION TECHNIQUES; SOURCES OF INFORMATION

Many of the prevention techniques for internal theft are simply the "danger signals" in the three key areas where such theft occurs—front end, receiving area and special service areas—turned on their heads. If receiving area congestion is an indication that internal theft is occuring, then clearly stated procedural policies restricting the amount of deliveries at any one time should be in effect and scrupulously enforced.

Here, culled from the experiences of many retail organizations, is a roster of operational policies and rules that can work to minimize the occurrence of internal theft:

Preventing Front End Internal Theft

1. Cashier uniforms with no pockets.
2. Pocketbooks or personal bags not allowed at checkouts; use backroom lockers instead.
3. Pencil and paper not allowed at the checkout; this would otherwise permit cashiers to keep separate tallies of overrings and underrings.
4. No mutual checking out of employees, reserving this function for management personnel only. Employees must have a receipt for every purchase.
5. Similarly: Restriction on time allowed for employee purchase and checkout.

6. Register terminal "governors" on maximum and minimum amount rings, termed "HALO" (High Amount Lock-Out) and "LALO" (Low Amount Lock-Out).
7. Publicized use of honesty shoppers—security workers posing as shoppers—to verify accuracy of cashier ringups and also to scan for instances of cashier-customer "discounting" collusion ahead in the checkout line.
8. Periodic head checker verification of finished orders subject to shopper agreement.
9. Uncluttered checkstand area; no blocking of total windows or clutter of boxes and trash on the floor.

Preventing Receiving Area Theft

1. Maintain careful security on price marking devices when not in use.
2. Insistence on eyeballing and counting of all incoming orders. Alert, dishonest vendors can easily spot a receiver who is burying his head in paperwork rather than seeing the merchandise. Vendors must complete and total invoices prior to check-in.
3. Spot check for shortages inside sealed cases.
4. Receive deliveries only one at a time, with schedules arranged and posted to minimize the possibility of jam-ups.
5. Receivers to physically count all merchandise regardless of deliveryman and vendor-submitted records or reports.
6. Spot check of pallet deliveries to verify "solid case" stacking.
7. Receivers to remain "on station" at all times. No interruptions during process of receipt and check-in of incoming merchandise.
8. Only receivers allowed to break truck seals from company's own warehouse.
9. Separate area for newly received merchandise vs. stock in backroom.
10. Sign-in for every salesman or vendor entering the store.
11. Vendors and deliverymen to remove all returns from the store before bringing in new stock.
12. Invoices only allowed in possession of receivers during check-in process. Each must be store-stamped and signed by receiver.
13. Trash disposal supervised by receivers; all cartons baled or knocked down to prevent possibility of outright merchandise theft via use of the trash carton route.

14. No vendor gifts, prizes or merchandise permitted to be given to store employees.
15. No cash payments for deliveries.
16. Check any containers carried by vendors on the way out of the store or backroom.
17. Scanner stores maintain one scanner at the receiving room to scan one of each item incoming to verify that the item is an authorized product and that its scan price correctly compares to the vendor invoice.
18. All back doors remain locked and secured except during actual deliveries.
19. Publicized spot checks on the receiving operation by store management on an irregular but routine basis.
20. Verify that trucks making the last stop at a store on its route are empty of new merchandise . . . especially a chain's own delivery trucks.
21. Check for unusual slits on inside cases of merchandise on pallets. Some vendors will slit open a case of merchandise, remove some of the merchandise, then replace the case on the pallet with the slit side facing in.
22. Use of security receivers: These are store receivers assigned to a store location but who report to a firm's loss prevention department. Such receivers are hired, trained and oriented by the loss prevention department and work strictly as receivers, not as utility workers at the store.

Preventing Special Service Area Theft

1. Authority for markdowns and employee purchase checkout limited to designated management personnel (as for any cashier operation).
2. No personal handbags or tote bags allowed at special service areas.
3. Uniform restrictions identical to those for front end cashiers.
4. Spot checks of check approval by store management.

Information Sources to Detect Employee Theft

According to a *Progressive Grocer* study,[17] the best conduit of information to a company headquarters about employee theft comes through store employees themselves, ranked "best source" by 52% of the respondents. Aware that the entire store, and each employee's job status, can suffer when one or more workers are stealing, many employees will go against the "code of silence," often anonymously, to expose a dishonest co-worker.

Managers are counted as another main source of leads, noted by 43% of stores and headquarters polled. Their overall role in store supervision places them in an ideal position to check, unsuspected by employees, into any area of store operations.

General store gossip—the grapevine—is not to be minimized as a source of leads and, accordingly, is rated as a primary source of information by 42% of those polled. The grapevine, leading up to the manager, offers store employees a way to circumvent pointing a finger directly at a suspected co-worker. Conversely, it also works to tell a dishonest employee that his or her dishonest actions are becoming common knowledge.

Inventory and accounting procedures are listed as a good source of leads on employee pilferage by 27% of the respondents. Figures can tell a fascinating story, but they also serve notice that the amount of pilferage must be steady and quite large to effect a noticeable decline in gross profits. A number of companies will not even investigate shrinkage unless it goes above a certain predetermined percentage of gross sales, perhaps ½%. This attitude may be cost-efficient in one respect, but it also has as a built-in danger: the fact that employees will be quick to recognize a corporate policy that tacitly permits large shrinkage.

Lesser sources of information include customers, mentioned by 23%. These tips normally involve cashiers failing to record sales, or underringing. Employees assigned to security are listed by 17% of the stores as a main source. Even though they are often called in by the company only after employee theft has manifested itself, once they are in the store, they can find more than one guilty party and detect any other internal security breakdown. In this respect, apprehended employees are often a boon in terms of implicating fellow workers involved in internal theft. Lie detector sessions, relatives of employees and store vendors are other occasional sources of information on employee theft.

USE OF UNDERCOVER WORKERS

Some retail organizations have resorted to undercover workers to ferret out employee theft. This is not entirely in the category of security receivers discussed in an earlier section. Security receivers are known security employees and have no "cover" assignments in the store.

True undercover workers in the retail organization are hired as security personnel then subsequently trained as cashiers, stock clerks, night crew workers, etc. Once qualified, they simply go through the motions of applying for a position at the company in question, and subsequently are hired and assigned to the problem store. The store is not informed that a security employee is working in the store, and, naturally, these camouflaged workers are slotted only into stores with serious security problems.

The undercover employees normally are in the stores anywhere from four weeks to four months, and feed the loss prevention department details on the specific problems and on who is involved. Just before the undercover worker leaves a job assignment, loss prevention operatives move in to make the apprehension so that the undercover worker's identity is not compromised.

These "double agents" actually perform their assigned jobs while reporting at the same time to security. Each worker must be appropriate for the job; mature, elderly cashiers will not be assigned as undercover workers to a store where most of the cashiers are young men and women.

What is probably most important in maintaining an effective undercover operation is the tightest possible security. The existence of these personnel should be kept to an absolute minimum number of people within a company. Ideally, this knowledge should be restricted to the one person who interviews and then hires the undercover worker.

Along with undercover workers, the use of special security cameras and observation posts in the store can bring to light instances of internal theft. Employees must become convinced that these observation techniques are being used and monitored during the course of normal work shifts and in closing hours as well for these pieces of equipment or facilities to be of any deterrent value. Various local and state laws may restrict some observational facilities as an invasion of privacy, especially when locker rooms and employee lounges and changing areas are involved.

APPREHENSION, INTERVIEWING AND DISPOSITION

One of the most difficult aspects of employee theft is not the discovery, but the subsequent actions taken by the employer. In the

Progressive Grocer study cited throughout this chapter, respondents were asked how they handled such cases. A full 77% reported discharging such apprehended employees. But a fifth of the apprehensions resulted in no action at all by the respondents, other than a warning. And only 5% of the responding stores and headquarters reported actually ever launching criminal prosecutions.

It is clear that many companies will chalk up one instance of employee theft to momentary temptation. A Midwest chain in its management manual reports that a first offender caught "grazing," or consuming store merchandise, is reprimanded. The second time, the employee is fired. Outright theft brings an automatic dismissal and possible prosecution.

Some companies fine employees or dock them a certain amount of pay when caught. Others may simply document instances of possible dishonesty, such as cashiers who chronically are spotted allowing unpaid-for merchandise to leave the store on the bottom rack of the shopping cart. This at least can allow employers to terminate suspected dishonest employees for incompetence.

Each company must develop its own policies, decide who may apprehend suspected dishonest employees, what publicity to give to such apprehensions, and how to handle these cases. There is no one "best way to go." However, in this era in which "full disclosure" has become the standard of accountability for individuals and governments, it would seem that clearly communicating to employees the policies of the company is something that is becoming more expected. Systems in which employees are more aware of what it takes to avoid legal prosecution, in terms of restitutions, etc., than of the very existence of a company security program, are governed by cynicism and not sound business practices.

Most retail firms permit store managers, assistant managers, night crew chiefs, and of course, security department personnel, to make apprehensions. In many companies, having a loss prevention representative on the premises during an apprehension is preferred to assure compliance with civil liberties.

In cases where a store's gross profit has dropped to the point where an internal theft problem is clear, but the source cannot be readily detected, many companies can investigate by using a simple process of elimination. For example, the loss prevention department will place security personnel in the store's receiving area to check every item of merchandise coming into the store for a period of, perhaps, one month. If, as a result of this check, the store's gross profit comes back up to normal levels, then the problem has been isolated to the receiving area. If the gross margin continues below standard, then the location of the internal theft problem is likely to be at the front end of the store.

If the store's problem is serious enough, a "security blitz" may be called for. This is a saturation of a "disaster" store with loss prevention personnel to cover every vital area. To maintain employee morale in the store, "Inventory Control Audits," or other such terminology may be used in briefing the store employees of the presence of so many "company cops" in the store.

One chain conducting such a blitz discovered a ring of nine dishonest cashiers that had been systematically stealing cash for nearly three years. Up to $20,000 a week was taken at the height of the store's internal problems. Each cashier was discounting 12 to 15 customers plus an additional seven or eight personal friends every weekend.

The majority of internal theft occurrences, however, are less complicated and generally easy to detect if the "danger signals" covered earlier in this chapter, and the proper use of leads from sources such as employees themselves, are carefully followed. Most crime is basically simple in that once a crime is successfully committed, the individual involved will tend to follow the same pattern. A dishonest cashier discounting a relative on a Friday at 2 p.m. is likely to follow this practice every Friday at 2 p.m. This date and hour might coincide with a store manager's or head cashier's break time or along with a routine check of the backroom by the assistant manager; e.g., no management personnel on hand to observe the instance of discounting.

The most successfully employed technique in apprehending front end or checkout theft is the use of honesty shoppers mentioned earlier. These honesty shoppers might be hired from an outside security consulting company or are loss prevention undercover personnel. An honesty shopping team generally includes three people: One shopper to pinpoint the discounting, a second shopper to set up the apprehension, and finally a security supervisor, often initially stationed outside the store, awaiting a signal to come in and make the apprehension.

In instances of cashier theft not involving collusion with a customer—e.g. overringing, or failure to record sales—Honesty Shopper #1 invites an instance of such cashier theft by purchasing a magazine or other checkstand item via exact change after the regular purchase has been totaled and bagged. Right behind in the line is Honesty Shopper #2, in a position to observe what the cashier does with the exact change from the prior purchase. If the cashier does not place the money in the register and ring up the sale, Honesty Shopper #2 signals the security supervisor via prearranged signals. The supervisor may continue to discreetly observe the cashier until the exact change from the sale is moved off the register—possibly to a pocket in the uniform, a shoe—any place other than the cash drawer. When and if this happens, the supervisor makes the formal apprehension.

In instances of cashiers working in collusion with customers, honesty shoppers may also be used, again in a team of three. Surveillance periods are set up to coincide with the time and day of week a cashier suspected of discounting a friend or relative normally commits the theft. When the customer enters the store, two honesty shoppers follow the customer around the store, pretending to shop while they observe carefully. The supervisor again maintains a position outside the store. The honesty shoppers attempt to get as close as possible on the checkout line behind the customer in question. A prearranged signal notifies the supervisor that an instance of discounting has been detected. Ideal timing calls for the supervisor to appear as the register total is being rung up and the tape removed. The customer should not be prevented from leaving the store at this time since there may be no proof of collusion. A sharply differing register total from the original tape and the re-checked order—both store-stamped, dated and coded—should provide sufficient evidence to confront the dishonest employee. Most instances of discounting in a supermarket situation will involve big-ticket purchases like cartons of cigarettes, meat, or large canned goods. Cashiers will either fail to ring the item entirely, or ring a small fraction of the actual retail value.

Some chains will station suspect cashiers at the checkout adjoining the head cashier's office. While the cashier is ringing up an order for a customer, the head cashier will closely observe each item, and ring up the same order, item for item, on a small adding machine. The two tapes can then be compared with action taken as needed.

Interviewing Apprehended Employees

The question of interviewing is a subject in itself and is significant enough to warrant a chapter of its own later in this text. In the area of internal theft, however, when one or more suspected employees are involved, it is important to determine how long a period of time any theft may have been going on, how much the store's losses may be and who else in the operation may be involved. A number of veteran loss prevention directors caution that no attempt be made to intimidate the suspected employee, and that the post-apprehension period not be conducted in the spirit of an interrogation but more as a low-keyed, informal discussion. It might best be considered as a probing exit interview, wherein a good deal of information about other violations of company rules, morale problems, attitude problems, or safety violations can be brought to light.

The goal, generally, in such interviews is not to throw the book at the employee but to appreciate the methods used and to determine how systems might be devised to prevent such occurrences from happening again. As with routine exit interviews, employees might be asked to indicate any job related problems, such as unfair treatment by supervisors, working conditions, sufficient training, sense of adequate pay for the job, and so on, as possibly contributing to the suspected dishonesty.

Finally, some statement should be taken from the employee in cases of admission to allow the employees to write, in their own words, a report of how the store or company was being victimized. Coercion should not be necessary and not be used; loss prevention personnel or store management can use the question of prosecution or non-prosecution as a carrot and stick to encourage a full statement.

The question of prosecution requires case-by-case judgment. It is common sense that extreme policies—either never prosecute or always prosecute—are impractical in their rigidity. As one chain's security manual points out, "The decision whether to prosecute an alleged offender, whether it be an employee, vendor or customer, will have to be made at the time of the alleged offense. After gathering all of the evidence, fully discuss this with your supervisor, and, if necessary, company attorneys or legal advisors. . . . The prime responsibility for each employee, regardless of level of authority, will be to accurately or adequately report each and every incident to his or her immediate superior. The employee shall notify the superior as soon after the incident as is practical, in line with the seriousness of the incident. . . . No two incidents will necessarily require the same action, and/or involvement. The decision to call the police will in some cases require no judgment, but would be assumed. In other cases, good judgment must be used; whenever in doubt, do not hesitate: call for assistance."

A number of retail companies publicize instances of apprehended employee theft. A typical procedure is to have individual store managers call meetings of store personnel to inform them that a named employee or employees has been apprehended for stealing, that the company's security program is continually at work and that the apprehension was made rather quickly. Other stores may also be notified of the apprehension.

Disposition of Apprehended Employees

The proper policy in terms of disposition of apprehended dishonest employees normally is immediate termination for theft at checkouts or in receiving areas and special service areas. Instances of "grazing," as noted earlier, may best be handled by a two-stage policy of a reprimand for one instance and termination thereafter, as noted earlier in this chapter. Consuming or using store merchandise might occur as a result of poor example-setting by supervisors or managers in the store. Such role models are difficult *not* to copy, regardless of any printed company rules and regulations to the contrary.

Company policies on job references following termination of an employee for dishonesty are yet another problem related to employee theft, and as in so many security questions, have no one right answer. One company with an eminently sensible policy issues a statement that the subject's employment was terminated and the former employee would not be rehired. The chain's loss prevention director states, "We do not give the reason why, since we feel this would infringe on the rights of the person involved to earn a livelihood. We do not necessarily believe that a particular person who was making a mistake and was apprehended will continue making such mistakes. Our thought is that they made a mistake in our company, can never be reemployed by us, and that's as far as we go."

The troubling nature of employee theft is perhaps best summed up by the operator of a small group of high-quality, affluent-area supermarkets in a large Midwestern city: "The greatest disappointment any employer has to face is the discovery that one of his employees is dishonest. Yet more often than I want to remember, I have had this knowledge. The sad thing is that my loss is insignificant compared to the loss of the employee involved, in terms of his reputation, job, trust and self-respect."

SUMMARY

Employee theft is clearly the single greatest source of retail store shrinkage or loss, conceivably greater than 1% of all retail store sales. Store and warehouse employees, fully knowledgeable about the company's operations and vulnerabilities, can sap the firm's profits throughout their work shifts; in contrast, shoplifters, bad check artists, burglars and robbers are "hit and run," one-time specialists. Psychologists see internal theft resulting from a triangle of frustration, aggression and opportunity, but it is obvious that the attitudes and actions of the store or company itself are major factors in the extent and severity of internal theft.

Studies seem to indicate that the bulk of internal theft is caused by the most transient segment of the work group in the company—often part-time employees, teenagers working the summer, etc. A good deal of internal theft—perhaps 25%—involves collusion between employees and customers or outside vendors and deliverymen.

The three main areas where employee theft attacks a store are the front end, the receiving room and special service areas. At the store checkouts, the primary source of loss is via "discounting" or underringing merchandise to friends and relatives, or nonringup when presented with exact change. A good deal of loss in receiving room areas results from a chaotic and undisciplined approach to scheduling deliveries, whereabouts of vendors and deliverymen, proper receiving procedures, etc. Special service areas often produce large-scale instances of internal theft via employees underringing other employee purchases.

Improved methods of pre-employment screening may be one answer to combatting internal theft loss. Polygraph or voice stress analyzers and sophisticated honesty-determinant questionnaires—so-called personnel security inventories—are enjoying widespread usage. The danger is that retail companies using such services may then let down their guards, or adopt a generally lax security attitude—with devastating results. Proper loss prevention techniques often are nothing more than adopting enforceable policies that reverse the many "danger signals" of internal theft at the front end, receiving area or special service areas. In addition to loss prevention systems, leads from a number of sources—headed by employees themselves—should be investigated and followed up. Badly hit stores may resort to undercover workers, trained by security but posing as regular store employees, to root out serious cases of internal theft.

The apprehension and subsequent disposition of suspected employees must be treated as a company-by-company question. There is no single right way to catch employees in the act, and there are at the same time a number of legal pitfalls to avoid. Possibly the best all-purpose policy for store management is to call for assistance when in doubt, attempting to utilize a company's own loss prevention personnel whenever possible to make any necessary apprehensions.

NOTES

[1] **Crime in Retailing**, U.S. Department of Commerce, U.S. Government Printing Office, Washington, D.C. 20402, August 1977, p. 5.

[2] Cited in "The Ins and Outs of Internal Security," **Convenience Stores**, May/June 1980, p. 45.

[3] "We Must Combat Employee Dishonesty," **The Christian Science Monitor**, July 17, 1978, p. 23.

[4] "Employee Theft: It Hurts the Worst," **Progressive Grocer**, November 1970, p.42.

[5] Cited in "The Ins and Outs of Internal Security," **op. cit.**, p. 45.

[6] "Larceny in Everyday Life," **Time Magazine**, September 9, 1966, pp. 26-27.

[7] **Preventing Employee Pilferage**, Small Business Administration Management Aids #209, January 1977, pp. 2-3.

[8] **Ibid.**, p. 2.

[9] "Employee Theft: It Hurts the Worst," **op. cit.**, p. 44.

[10] **Preventing Employee Pilferage, op. cit.**, p. 3.

[11] "Employee Theft: It Hurts the Worst," **op. cit.**, p. 45.

[12] "Security, It's an Inside Job," **Convenience Stores**, March/April 1978, p. 68.

[13] Jeremiah P. McAward, "Information via Pre-Employment Investigations Cuts Turnover," **Convenience Store News**, February 1, 1979, p. 1.

[14] "The Search for an Honest Employee," **The Reid Reports** (introductory brochure), unpaginated. John E. Reid & Associates, 215 N. Dearborn St., Chicago, IL 60601. (Also cited in "Are Super Market Employees Honest? Here's A Test to Find Out," **Progressive Grocer,** June 1977, pp. 67-68.)

[15] "New Research Shows Importance of Employee Theft," **London House Management Journal**, August 1979, p. 1.

[16] **Ibid.**, p. 2.

[17] "Employee Theft: It Hurts the Worst," **op. cit.**, p. 45.

3 SHOPLIFTING

This chapter will describe:

- **The size of the problem**
- **Who is involved and why**
- **What is being taken**
- **Methods used in shoplifting, the prevalent times, etc.**
- **Observing potential shoplifters**
- **Apprehensions, interviews and admissions**
- **Disposition of cases, prosecution, juvenile offenders**
- **Employee training and preventive techniques**
- **Preventive devices and equipment**
- **The question of publicity**

THE SIZE OF THE PROBLEM

If internal theft is the most serious cause of retail business loss, then shoplifting is easily the most publicized, and in terms of sheer instances, certainly the most frequently committed crime against business.

There are many ways to view the magnitude of the problem. A survey of more than 6,000 discount department stores conducted by the Mass Retailing Institute[1] revealed that an estimated 900,000 shoplifters were apprehended for theft in 1972. In the same study, a total of 18,000 employees were reportedly apprehended. In the study, the number of shoplifters apprehended averaged 125 per store, with one store reporting no fewer than 512 apprehensions.

A more recent estimate puts the annual loss to merchants from shoplifting at a figure approaching $16 billion a year. The same study also indicates that overall retail security costs add an average of 2% to 3% to prices of goods sold by major department stores and grocery and drug chains.

Still another insight into the problem is seen in a figure from a study by an economist of West Virginia College of Graduate Studies. This researcher found that the typical professional shoplifter, in terms of 1979 dollars, was walking off with more than $53,000 worth of merchandise a year. The same study indicated that only one of 1,250 shoplifters ever sees the inside of a jail cell.[2]

A menswear retail publication in 1972 estimated that shoplifting losses ranged up to $100,000 per store . . . a figure that would be significantly higher today even if the rate of shoplifting was precisely the same now as then. The Federal Bureau of Investigation has gathered figures which indicate that shoplifting increased 93% over a six year period to the present, and that only one other form of crime—daytime robbery—showed a higher growth rate during the same period. In the period 1974-1975 alone, shoplifting arrests increased 32%. A *Progressive Grocer* survey concluded that each store detects some nine instances of shoplifting in a given week.[3] Using the traditional yardstick of 20 shoplifting events undetected for each detected instance, the total weekly count would average 180 instances per store. If the average value of stolen items is $4.00 for supermarkets (a very conservative figure), then each store loses $720 per week to shoplifters, or $37,440 per year. Using the "Theft Make-Up Grid" table presented in Chapter 2, an operation working on a 1% gross profit would have to ringup nearly $4 million more to offset the shoplifting loss. It is therefore close to the mark to say that shoplifting may outweigh the total profit in high-volume, low-margin operations. Supermarkets, with their huge merchandise assortments, free access to almost all items, relative shortage of personal service and high traffic density, are probably the retail operations most consistently victimized by shoplifters. But all retail businesses are being hit. What's more, shoplifting defies localization to large cities, or inner city ghetto areas. U.S. Department of Commerce statistics indicate that shoplifting occurs with the same frequency in cities of 25,000 as it does in population centers of more than a million. In low income areas, shoplifting can be extremely serious, particularly in drugstores. Many inner city stores are more easily victimized because such stores are often older units, with floor plans never conceived for prevention or minimization of shoplifting in mind.

Essentially, shoplifting is the unlawful taking of merchandise, secreting it on one's person, and not paying for it. In most states, the laws dealing with shoplifting do not necessarily require the perpetrators to leave the premises with the merchandise in order to have committed the crime. The key operating factor is "intent." Thus, a professional shoplifter caught in the act prior to leaving the store premises, with merchandise concealed in a special accessory or prop has demonstrated intent rather dramatically. The amateur shoplifter who simply places an item in his pocket, or in her bra, etc., is operating in a much grayer area as far as proof of intent is concerned. Because of this, many operations routinely follow a procedure of shoplifting apprehensions made beyond the checkouts, or outside the store premises itself.

WHO ARE THE SHOPLIFTERS?

According to the U.S. Department of Commerce, "People shoplift for a variety of reasons. The true kleptomaniac, an individual with an uncontrollable impulse to steal, is very rare. Others may be classified as either amateur or professional shoplifters, with amateurs being the larger group.

"Professional shoplifters earn their livelihoods through frequent thefts. They steal in order to resell their loot for cash and take goods in higher aggregate value than the amateurs. Most professionals have standing arrangements with 'fences,' and will often specialize in a specific type of merchandise or particular type of store. They are hard to detect in operation because of their smooth and efficient techniques.

"Amateur shoplifters, on the other hand, include many different types stealing for widely divergent reasons. The most unpredictable types are the desperate shoplifters, whether they are drug addicts, vagrants or others in dire need of money. They steal goods for resale to support drug addiction, alcoholic addiction or to pay off loan shark commitments. Their methods are often crude, and more are the result of opportunity than of planning and finesse. With such crude methods their thefts depend on surprise and speed. Since they steal out of desperation, they can be dangerous when stopped in the act.

"Amateurs who do not fall in the category of desperation are very difficult to classify. They may steal on impulse or because of a real or imagined grievance against the store or its employees. It may be that the shoplifter needs the item but is unable or unwilling to pay the price marked. Or, as with youthful shoplifters, they may steal for the thrill of it or because of peer pressure. Their actions are sometimes a bid for attention and are difficult to understand."[4]

There is a good deal of agreement among security experts that the bulk of shoplifting is committed by amateurs—and young people at

Blister-packaged and pegged items, especially drugs and cosmetics, are strong candidates for shoplifting. Removing the item from the package as the eye makeup in this photo is normally a sign of an amateur shoplifter. The pros normally take the entire package, since they arrive at the store fully equipped with "booster boxes" or other paraphernalia to accommodate large quantities of goods.

A loaded shopping cart abandoned in mid-aisle is another giveaway that a shoplifter has been at work—in this case most likely a pro. Amateurs generally steal on impulse, shoplifting merchandise during a normal shopping visit; thus most of the items they leave the store with are paid for. The pro makes this his business, and uses a shopping cart merely to blend in with the other shoppers. Once he or she has all that he can handle, the "cover" is dropped and the shoplifter rapidly leaves.

that. The *Progressive Grocer* study mentioned earlier indicated that teens—boys and girls—are the worst offenders, and subteen children are noted as worst offenders by 29% of store operators interviewed. Professional shoplifters are mentioned by only 7% of store operators as the worst offenders.

Roger K. Griffin of Commercial Service Systems (CSS), Van Nuys, California, one of the veteran analysts of shoplifting loss, notes in the firm's most recent study, "It is most significant . . . that 67% of all shoplifters reported were under 30 years of age. There is an inherent challenge to society in these figures: 6.2% of all shoplifters were under 12 years of age . . . 27% of all shoplifters were between 12 and 17 years . . . 34% of all shoplifters were between 18 and 29 years. The challenge would seem to lie in the belief that the young are impressionable and can be taught. . .These figures indicate that the lower grades of primary school is the place to begin."[5]

Griffin's Commercial Service Systems data, further refined, weighted the incidence of shoplifting in a particular age group to that group's overall share of the general population, with results that show clearly the juvenile or teenage aspects of the problem.

1979

Age Group	**% of Age Group Estimated Within the General Population**	**% of Total Shoplifters Reported Within the Age Group**
12-17 years	10.6	26.7
18-29	21.7	33.7
30-39	13.7	12.8
40-49	10.3	7.0
50-59	10.5	5.4
60 and over	15.4	7.1

Thus the 12 to 17 group was the most troublesome relative to its size within the general population. Accounts of shoplifting gangs—"steal for fun" clubs—are numerous. Members of this age group were apprehended approximately 2½ times the rate one might expect, based on their actual numbers. This data, from the CSS 1979 survey, should be regarded as the tip of the iceberg in that it is based on shoplifting apprehensions—not including undetected cases. The full results of the Commercial Service Systems study are presented in Appendix A.

Most teen offenders, according to Griffin's study, are male; in the adult group, the male/female apprehension ratio is evenly balanced.

The earlier *Progressive Grocer* study indicated that 61% of the respondents felt women were the most frequently detected shoplifters.

Thus the shoplifter can be anybody and everybody — a "booster" (professional) or a "snitch" (amateur). Written accounts of shoplifting date to 1597, where the activities of a professional troupe consisting of a "clout" and two "covers" were detailed in annals from Elizabethan England.

WHAT IS BEING TAKEN

A serious error often committed by store management is the placement of high-ticket, high-profit merchandise in a location where the possibility exists that no store employee is watching the area 100% of the time. A drugstore, recently opened, was almost immediately saddled with a huge shrinkage problem, which was analyzed in terms of merchandise display. The analysis showed that expensive items, including perfumes, watches, costume jewelry and other valuables were all placed in a corner in the rear of the store. They were also shielded from the view of store personnel. Shoplifters attacked this vulnerable area so heavily that the store very nearly closed before it had even gotten past its grand opening.

Shoplifters can and will take anything and everything. But in supermarkets, as in other high-volume retail stores, not every item in the store is a *prime* target. A *Progressive Grocer* survey of supermarkets disclosed the following ranking of categories mentioned by store managers as key sources of shoplifting loss:

Health and beauty aids	77.7%
Meats	63.3%
Tobacco	61.9%
Candy	47.0%
Cosmetics	19.1%
Hosiery	13.0%
Soft goods	13.0%
Records	6.5%
Toys	6.0%
Gourmet foods	4.2%

Other categories of critical importance, especially in today's tight budget economy, include canned fish, light bulbs, and greeting cards.

Another survey of stores—this one from the West Coast—produced this ranking of most frequently taken food store items:

	% of total items
Drugs and sundries	9.6%
Fresh meat	9.8%
Delicatessen	7.7%
Clothing	7.0%
Cigarettes	3.9%
Liquor	5.4%
Vitamins	1.2%
Other nonfood items	36.3%
Other food items	19.1%

Veteran security directors note that bands of youngsters in a store may tend to go after gum, candy, or records. Women will zero in on health and beauty aids, cosmetics, and pantyhose. Men will gravitate toward auto parts, film and camera supplies, razor blades and shaving equipment. Theft of garments in the fitting rooms of clothing stores is also a critical problem related directly to shoplifting. In many cases, the "priority" merchandise in terms of shoplifter vulnerability are impulse items, or high-demand goods. For the most part easily concealed, many have good resale value. Unfortunately, these categories are most often among the higher profit items in the store. Pilferage in these categories, then, has an impact even greater than the surface dollar loss alone. Loss prevention experts often talk in terms of a "value-to-size" ratio to assess the appeal of particular items to shoplifters. This can become critical in determining the severity of an instance of shoplifting from the legal standpoint, since many state laws move shoplifting into the area of grand larceny when retail value climbs above a certain amount.

HOW SHOPLIFTERS OPERATE

A completely detailed enumeration of amateur and professional shoplifters' methods could fill several volumes. Probably the largest statistical study of methods used is Commercial Service Systems' annual survey.[7] Current data breaks out these major methods of concealment in supermarkets, drugstores and discount stores:

If You See This . . . GET SUSPICIOUS!

Bulging pizza boxes—
or record sleeves,
magazines, etc.

Items disappearing into
paper towel roll

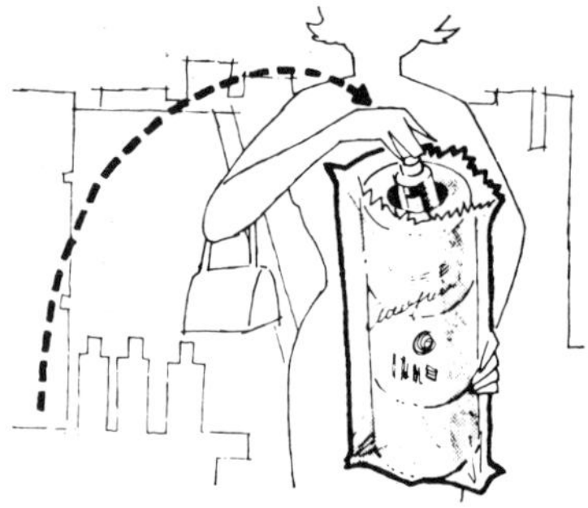

Kids grouped around displays

Loitering customers
making no attempt to buy

Primping in the store—
another version of the
free-samples gambit

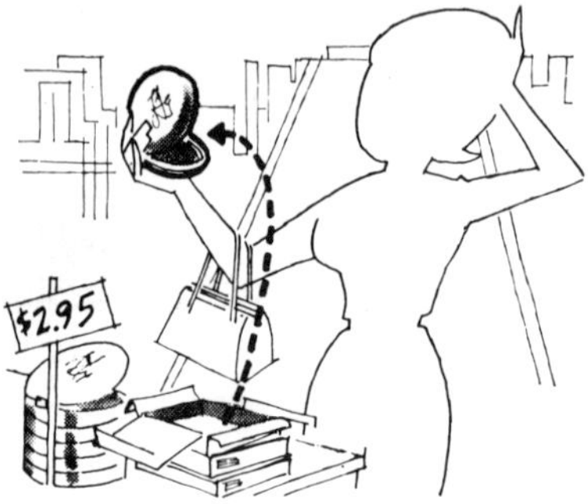

The forgotten bottom
rack of the cart

Low-price label
en route to
high-price item

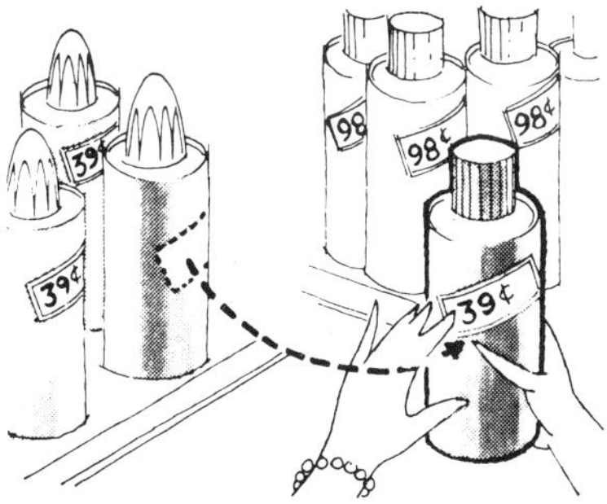

Same-size item into
less expensive box

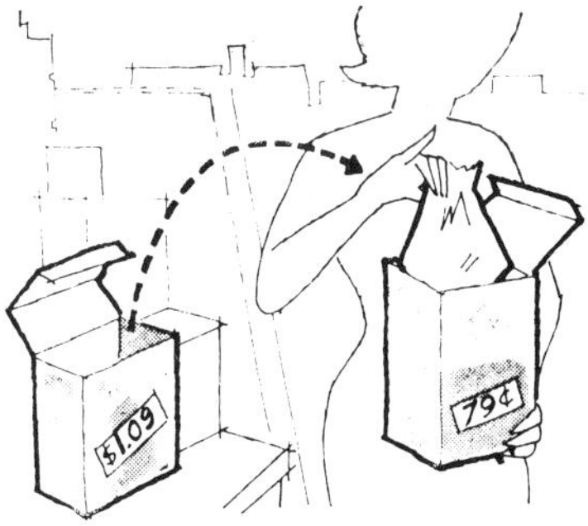

Gift-wrapped boxes

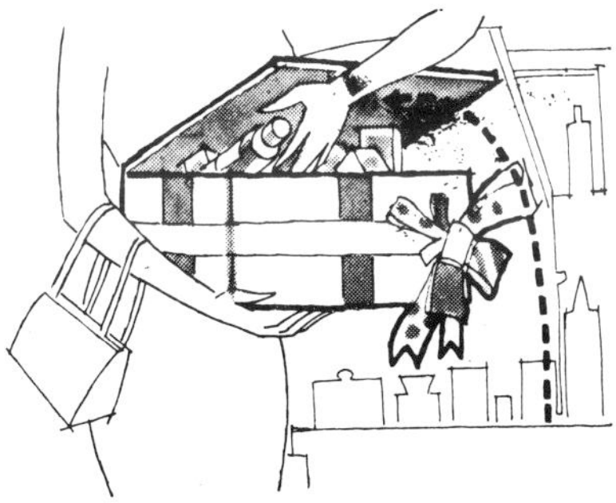

Oversized handbags,
briefcases, etc.

Wallet in hands (so handbag
doesn't have to be
opened at checkout)

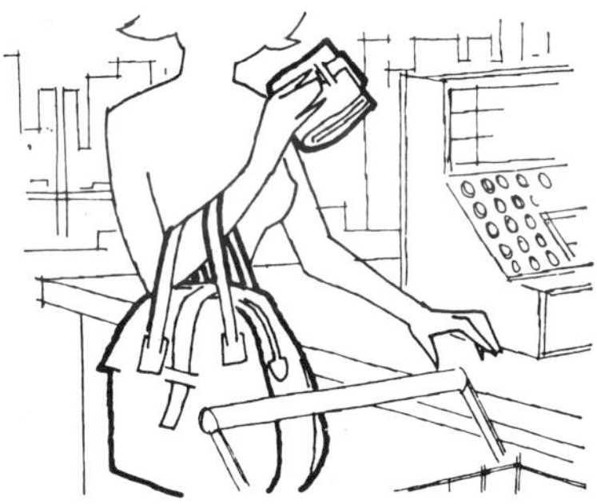

Free-samplers leaving a
trail of empty boxes

Open umbrellas—
especially on sunny days

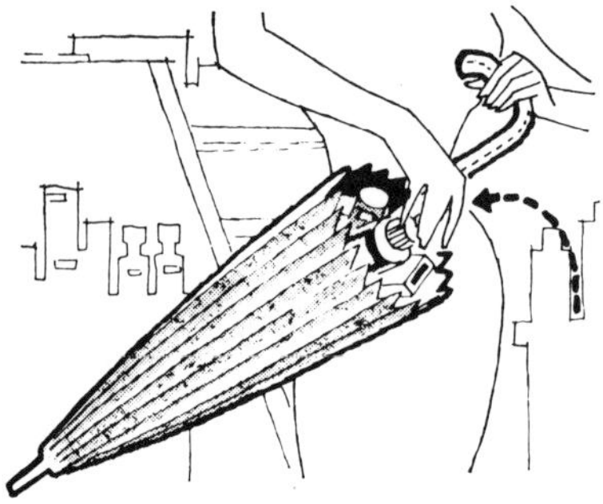

The ubiquitous
shopping bag in a
shopping cart

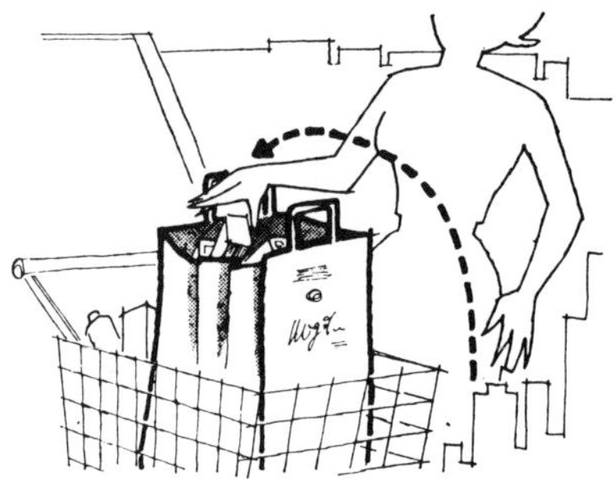

Open packages from other stores

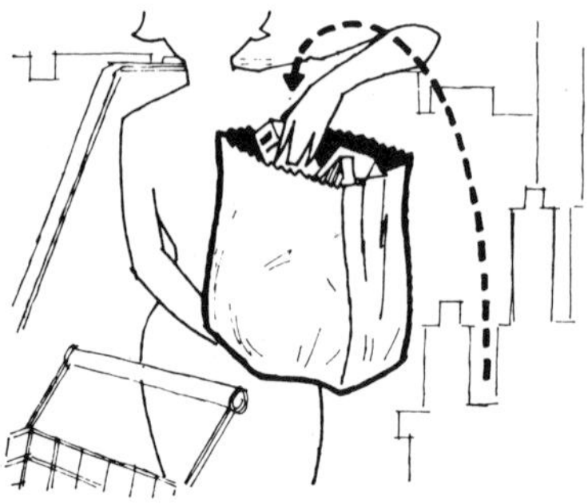

Heavy clothing in mild weather

Ducking down to
avoid observation

The complete
do-it-yourself
produce-marking kit

	Supermarkets	Drugstores	Discount Stores
In purse	30.6%	24.0%	29.6%
Shopping bag	2.8	4.3	15.9
Other bag	3.3	4.5	2.7
Professional	.5	.3	1.4
In pocket	21.8	29.5	15.6
Label switcher	1.9	2.5	5.6
Accomplice	2.7	3.4	4.9
Under clothing	25.6	13.7	9.8
Other method	7.9	12.8	11.9
Not indicated	3.0	5.0	2.6

The professional shoplifter generally works when the store is busy, so movement is less easily noticed. Professionals are methodical, use many tools or props to help them in their work, and tend to hit stores during the busiest hours and days of the week. A *Progressive Grocer* survey of 2,000 stores indicated that, ranked in order, the worst hours, days and months of the year for shoplifting occurrences are: 1) December—Friday—3-6 p.m. 2) January—Saturday—4-6 p.m. 3) November—Thursday—5-6 p.m. This tends to indicate that amateurs as well as professionals are as one in terms of when they operate. Clearly the major holiday periods of the year, the end-of-week rush, and the after-school hours when store traffic is heavy and children are on their way home from school, is "Zero Hour" for shoplifting frequency.

Professionals may use the following props or physical attributes:

Booster Box—This is simply an empty box camouflaged to look like an ordinary package. The box is carried by the shoplifter and used to boost, or steal, merchandise. Generally, one end of the container is open, or can be opened on a spring-action so sensitive that a flick of the finger can push it in. Releasing pressure on the panel causes it to instantly snap shut. When properly used by a professional shoplifter, the illusion is almost that of a sleight-of-hand magician; the merchandise goes from shelf to booster box so rapidly and deftly that it simply seems to disappear. Professionals using the booster box have been known to talk directly to store employees while stealing merchandise from the store.

With a good deal of shoplifting taking place during holiday seasons, many professional shoplifters disguise booster boxes as gift-wrapped packages. Or, they may design the boxes to resemble mail parcels in brown paper tied with heavy cord. Sometimes wraps from other stores are used to create more authenticity. None of this should divert store employees from instantly giving extra attention to any box or box-like object being carried around in a packaged product/self-service environment.

Booster Bloomers—These are special underpants that are four and five times normal size, and can hold a large amount of merchandise. Most often, two professional women shoplifters working together make use of this prop. The bloomers are constructed so that they can be tied tightly around the thighs to prevent the apparatus from slipping down the wearer's legs. The top band is made of elastic so that it can fit snugly around the waist of the shoplifter, yet easily stretch and reclose around dropped-in items. The principle is that of a booster box worn on the person.

Lingerie, gloves, even handbags can very easily be concealed inside booster bloomers. The user may wear it under a flared skirt, allowing even more unnoticed room underneath the skirt for the bloomers to balloon with stolen merchandise. When used by a professional team, one shoplifter may stand back to back with another so that two pairs of eyes effectively cover the entire horizon, while the hands are stuffing merchandise into the bloomers.

Booster Belts—These are belts fitted with hooks, and worn over a pair of pants. The shoplifter wears a booster belt in conjunction with a raincoat or overcoat, frequently with pockets that may open up inside the coat. The hooks on the belt can hold a large number of smaller items (but often expensive merchandise like jewelry) that can quickly be taken from a countertop, rammed into the coat pocket, through the inside of the coat, and onto one of the hooks on the belt.

Other Props—The professional shoplifters—and some adept amateurs—also use many seemingly innocent, normally innocuous items as props to assist them in their crime. Some of the more frequently used include umbrellas and raincoats. A man or a woman in a store carrying an umbrella and/or wearing a raincoat on a warm, sunny day should be suspected immediately. When an umbrella is loosely opened at the top, and placed alongside a counter, merchandise can easily be slid off the counter into the large pleated interior of the unopened umbrella. Coats can be used as diversionary devices. A shopper removing his or her coat in the store and leaving it atop a bin of merchandise can steal a number of items *below* the coat when he or she scoops up the coat to leave.

Baby carriages are also an excellent prop, especially when shoplifters create a large camouflaged hiding place under the seat of the carriage. Large books carried by teenagers and hollowed out to absorb a number of smaller items are fairly common. Phony bandages or casts on arms or legs are also good ways to conceal shoplifted merchandise.

Development of the Legs—By practicing and perfecting control of the thigh muscles, professional women shoplifters can place an item as large and heavy as a typewriter, or even a small portable TV, between their legs and proceed to walk out of the store with a normal appearance. These "crotch workers" normally are solo acts. A "ready to steal" item like a man's suit—hanger and all—woman's dress, several cartons of cigarettes, or a dozen steaks, are carried to a dimly lit blind spot in the store. Satisfied that no one is observing, the shoplifter lifts up her flared dress, slips the items between her legs, and slowly walks out the front door, right past the checkouts. Top shoplifting pros can actually run at top speed with bulky items between their legs, and neither drop the stolen merchandise, nor miss a beat while running.

Other props include record album jackets—relatively large sleeves which can hold thinly folded goods like hosiery, greeting cards, magazines, stationery items, and, naturally, other records. Large boxes such as family pack cold cereal may be carefully slit open, the contents dumped behind a shelf or counter, and the empty box now filled with more valuable cartons of cigarettes, and resealed. The box, with its cereal price tag intact, is simply checked out with the shoplifter's legitimate purchases in the store. In like manner, frozen pie boxes or frozen pizza boxes are ideal and commodious storage bins for shoplifters. Paper towel cores are yet another easily accessed hiding place for small valuables.

The amateur shoplifters, while a more serious problem in retail pilferage loss than the professional because of the potential numbers of people involved, rarely use sophisticated techniques in shoplifting. Most often, they steal on impulse, simply jamming the merchandise into their pockets or handbags. If amateurs are cleared through a checkout via cashier error with unpaid items on the bottom rack of the carts, these shoplifters will attempt this again and again, knowing they can never be proven guilty of any crime even if this merchandise is finally spotted by a checkout clerk. Amateurs often do carry extra shopping bags or large handbags with them when they go shopping to facilitate their crime. Some women habitually carry their wallets in their hands rather than leaving them in their handbags. The reason for this is so that the handbag, which may be hiding some stolen merchandise, need not be opened when the customer checks out her legitimate purchases in the store.

Professionals may feign shopping within the store. Rarely do they ever make a real purchase. Therefore, finding half-filled shopping carts abandoned in a supermarket aisle, for example, is often a sign that a pro has been at work. Amateur shoplifters almost always steal during normal shopping trips to the store. Once they arrive at the checkouts, they properly check out anything visible that they wish to purchase.

While the professionals may seek crowds, the amateurs seek isolation. They are constantly looking, constantly on the alert, and will place an item in a secreted place only when they feel they are not being observed, when store activity is low and the lighting level is dim.

Amateurs who steal frequently will develop their own tricks and specialties—a fact that sometimes makes distinguishing between the amateur and the professional difficult in practice. Over-the-shoulder handbags are especially popular with younger female shoplifters. Male shoplifters taking cigarettes and cigars often blatantly place them in their pockets, partially exposed for all the world to see. It is almost impossible to prove the theft of such merchandise—even if what is in the pocket is a new, unopened pack of cigarettes—without an eyewitness or a videotape recording. Even then, a shopper can always innocently state he had forgotten he had put the item there.

While an abandoned shopping cart in an aisle may be a giveaway clue that a professional shoplifter has visited a store, discovery of ripped-open blister-pack packages is generally a sign that an amateur has been at work. A professional, depending on speed and large-volume booster equipment, takes the entire item, pack and all. The amateur, even though blister packs may be quite difficult to open, tends to go for the item only.

The Larger Issue of Product Packaging

One of the principal reasons for the development of blister-packing was the advantageous display of merchandise in a secure, relatively theft-proof container. This development begs the entire question of packaging—particularly that of highly vulnerable packaged products in the food and drugstore environment—as a source of pilferage trouble.

In one study of food store operators, 78% felt that customers do tend to break open certain kinds of packages to look inside. In most instances, this renders the item unsaleable if it isn't then purchased. Mentioned as most susceptible to break-ins were the following:

Mention of Break-ins by Retailers

Cookies	50%
Candy	28
Drugs	16
Produce	12
Cereals	12
Dried fruits	10
Crackers	10

Other than protective packaging, checker scrutiny or on-the-spot detection and apprehension, not much can be done to stop the shopper who sees nothing wrong with quieting a balky child with samples of cookies or candies, and leaving partially empty bags or boxes discarded on the shelves. The same dilemma holds true in cases of theft by more deliberate shoplifters who switch packages to cover up items stowed within (cartons of cigarettes inside cereal boxes, etc.) or break into packages to extract high-value coupons, prizes or proofs-of-purchase for merchandise offers.

In the area of produce, breakthroughs have been achieved in prepackaging, but pilferage is still relatively easy in stores that offer produce in loose form. It is normally not the produce itself that gets hit, but other items that can fit inconspicuously in opaque produce bags. These, pencil-priced by a produce clerk and sealed at the scale, are generally not rechecked by a cashier. The development of clear plastic bags on bulk rolls for customer selection of produce has been quite effective in holding down this source of loss, even though they remain more expensive than paper bagging. Not only do they reveal all merchandise, they have the advantage of leakproof, airtight handling of produce from store to shopper's refrigerator.

Shoplifting Teams in Action

While amateur shoplifters, with the exception of teenage theft rings, almost always work alone, professionals, as noted earlier, sometimes work in pairs, and even in larger "wolf packs." Security professionals have described accounts where stores were witnessed to be literally invaded by professional groups numbering eight or more. In one drugstore such a pack entered the store in pairs of husband-and-wife teams, creating utter chaos. The three sales people on duty were completely unable to keep up with the demands of all of the shoplifters, who peppered the clerks with demands to see items that were out of reach, or locked up in jewelry and perfume counters. Since this group had been witnessed, police were summoned to the scene, and four of the eight professionals were apprehended while still in the store, carrying more than $300 worth of merchandise. This all took place in a matter of less than seven minutes.

Professionals working alone can accomplish with stealth and good props what large wolf packs do with misdirection and diversion. A loss prevention director relates witnessing a professional shoplifter working a drugstore and wearing what was eventually discovered to be a coat with false arms realistically arranged in the pockets. The coat was rigged and buttoned so that it was almost impossible to notice that the shoplifter's real arms were underneath the coat and free to maneuver. Approaching a jewelry counter, the thief's arms were placed right through the coat, removing items from the counter and placing them in an inside pocket. The shoplifter was nonchalant, never looked around but constantly peered straight ahead.

This retail security director approached the shoplifter and took hold of one of the bogus arms, which immediately came away from the pocket. The suspect immediately began to unbutton his coat and flee at the same time, but was quickly caught, restrained and placed under arrest. During questioning, the shoplifter admitted that he had used this ploy for some 15 years, had been arrested only once previously, and was stealing anywhere from $400 to $700 a week in merchandise, tax free. In today's inflated dollar terms, this professional's take could amount to $1,000 a week or more.

The Effect of Store Layout on Shoplifting

Part of the prevalence of shoplifting is due to the ease with which the act can occur, evidenced by some of the cases described above. The fact that a retail store may have dozens of employees on the scene at any given moment does not seem to have much influence on occurrence or frequency. The consensus that shoplifting peaks during the busiest store times of the day/week/year—times when store work crews are at maximum strength—should provide ample proof that many potential eyes on the customers may not achieve 100% protection.

Contributing to this is the fact that many stores are planned and built with everything in mind but the reduction of shoplifting. The same factors that can make a store a sales powerhouse—specialty department alcoves, massive, high-stacked displays, complete self-service in meats and produce, huge assortments and a "one-stop shopping" inventory of food, household items, drugs, sundries, even small appliances—can work in favor of the shoplifter.

For retailers, any sudden change in a store's merchandising, display or even overall layout (in the event of a major remodel) that also coincides with an increase in shoplifting, is almost certainly a major cause of that increase, and could indicate a prior store display or fixturing plan that, whatever its shortcomings, at least served to keep shoplifting down to a lower level.

OBSERVATION OF POTENTIAL SHOPLIFTERS

Since eyewitnessing acts of shoplifting may be crucial to proper apprehensions and prosecutions, observation of potential or presumed shoplifters is something that most sales floor managers and employees should be aware of. Here is a fairly strong set procedure for retail employees to make the visual "catch":

1. The employee must actually see the suspect take and hide the item in a location that is abnormal. A pack of cigarettes in a trousers pocket, for example; a tube of lipstick in a bra; a steak under a jacket; a pair of pantyhose into a pocketbook which is then snapped shut.
2. Once an observation has been made, the employee should constantly watch the suspect to assure that the secreted item has not been moved—or removed—before the suspect is approached by security or management. Eyes must be riveted on the presumably stolen item—or the suspect's hands—without wandering for one second.
3. The employee must follow some pre-established signal system adopted by the store to alert other employees or management that a shoplifter has been spotted in such-and-such an area. Prior to loss prevention personnel or store management approaching the suspect, verification must be obtained from the observant employee that the suspect still has the item or items in question in his or her

possession at the critical point where the merchandise has not been paid for.

4. At this point, management can approach the suspect. A low-keyed approach may be in the form of a request that the item in question either be returned to the shelf or paid for.

To summarize the four main pre-apprehension requisites in cases of shoplifting: The witness must *see the item being taken, see the item being concealed, see that the item has not been replaced on the shelf* and *see that the item has not been paid for.* An apprehension can now take place.

APPREHENSIONS, INTERVIEWS AND ADMISSIONS

General points about retail security apprehensions and interviews are covered in a later chapter. It is important that retail employees be familiar with the state laws pertaining to shoplifting. Most states require a combination of "probable cause" to steal and "willful concealment" as factors permitting an apprehension. In addition, few states restrict the place of an apprehension, although as a matter of policy many companies voluntarily restrict their apprehensions to out-of-store locations in order to allow the suspect to go that much further in establishing true intent to steal.

A typical law is that of the State of Illinois which specifically, in its Criminal Code revised in 1973, gives "a merchant, his agents and his employees power to detain suspected shoplifters without incurring civil or criminal liability under certain conditions."

The law itself reads as follows: "Any merchant, his agent or employee, who has probable cause to believe that a person has wrongfully taken possession of and is about to wrongfully take merchandise from a mercantile establishment may detain such person in reasonable manner and for a reasonable length of time for the purpose of investigating the ownership of such merchandise." In addition, "such reasonable detention shall not constitute an arrest, nor an unlawful restraint, nor shall it render the merchant, his agent or employee liable to the person detained."

Thus the requirement of "probable cause" is not satisfied if a retailer detains an individual on mere suspicion. Such detention must consist of facts and circumstances which would lead any reasonable person to believe that store merchandise has been taken by someone who does not intend to pay for it.

While apprehension and detention is permitted, searching the suspect may fall into the area of "unconsented touching" or battery, and incur the risk of civil liability. In the State of Illinois, therefore, it is suggested that merchandise evidencing the shoplifting that is visible without a search may be taken from a suspect. Additionally, these common sense procedures are suggested:

- If there is no merchandise visible, the suspect can be asked to voluntarily surrender the goods or to open a briefcase, pocketbook, etc.
- If the suspect refuses to cooperate voluntarily, no further action is permissible unless the requirements for a lawful arrest are present.
- If there is a possibility that stolen goods have been carried out to a car, an employee should be detailed to watch the car until police arrive and make sure nothing is removed from it by accomplices.
- The suspect should be watched closely to prevent the destruction or discarding of evidence.
- All evidence obtained from a shoplifter should be labeled and given to the police, not simply put back on the shelves.

The essentials of newer shoplifting laws in a number of states are covered in Appendix B. Since provisions vary somewhat from state to state, it cannot be emphasized more strongly that a shoplifting plan of arrest for each store be part of employee training, and that such training concentrate on the establishment of legality and the prevention of physical injury.

Most loss prevention experts warn that if an apprehended shoplifter attempts to run, or pushes employees aside in a rush to get out of the store, it is better not to pursue the suspect, or restrain the suspect in any way, even though this may be contrary to human nature. It is urged that only qualified law enforcement agents should be used to physically restrain anyone in a retail business. If such law officers cannot be quickly produced, it may be necessary to let the apprehended shoplifter go. Many errors have been made not only by impulsive store management or employees who want to "play cop," but even by incompetent security people.

Physical restraint can bring about confrontations resulting in enormous harm to the company. Trying to restrain a suspect by placing a hand on the individual can easily lead to a ripping of clothes, a fistfight, or even appearance of a weapon. Current civil law makes it difficult even for duly appointed police officers to take physical action without careful consideration of all the legalities involved; this burden and responsibility should definitely not be made to rest on the shoulders of a retail business.

Thus, a good list of training points in the apprehension of shoplifters and taking them into custody would include these points:

1. Be sure, firm and positive in the apprehension.
2. The person apprehending the shoplifter should identify himself or herself by name as a store employee.
3. One or more employees should be along at the point of apprehension, to provide a margin of physical safety and act as corroborating witnesses.
4. The suspect should be addressed politely and directly, along the following lines: "Madam, I am the store manager. You have a can of our hair spray in your purse which you did not pay for. Please come back into the store with me so that we can straighten this out."
5. Even though reasonable force may be employed if the suspect refuses to cooperate, with safety and legality foremost in mind, the suspect may be released if he or she starts to run or puts up a fight.
6. The employees backing up the apprehender should follow to see that the shoplifter does not destroy or discard stolen merchandise.
7. At least one item should be recovered prior to taking the shoplifter back into the store.
8. An attitude of confidence and self assurance is critical to gaining the cooperation of the suspect. Any doubt or indecision may be sensed by the suspect and exploited to the disadvantage of the store.
9. If the suspect escapes or is allowed to run to prevent physical injury to store employees and customers, police should be notified. A description of the suspect, any automobile involved and its license number are vital pieces of information. Police should also be notified whether or not the stolen merchandise was recovered prior to the suspect escaping the scene—this may result only in filing an advisory report with the police, not a formal police pursuit and apprehension.
10. Never leave a suspect alone.
11. If a decision to prosecute is made, call appropriate law enforcement agencies as soon as possible, noting in a written report the time of the call to police and the time of arrival.

The success of a store's anti-shoplifting program is probably more dependent on knowing local laws and correct apprehension procedures than on any other single factor. Assuming that a proper apprehension has been made, with the store now in custody of a suspect who has either admitted concealment of merchandise or turned over such merchandise to employees or loss prevention personnel, the next step is the taking of a statement, following the questioning of the suspect. The purpose of the procedure is to recover all of the stolen merchandise, to obtain an admission of theft from the suspect, and to get the suspect to sign a form releasing the store and all parties involved in the apprehension from a civil liability suit.

This questioning procedure should be conducted in a private room or office off the sales floor. Suspects should be ushered to these offices with a minimum of physical contact—something that is not only legally, but also psychologically necessary. A witness should always be present. If the shoplifter is a female, a female witness should be present. The reason for this is obvious, and relates to instances of concealment taking place in such areas as department store dressing rooms or fitting rooms. This is one of the most critical areas related to shoplifting in department stores because it has a built-in concealment factor.

Many stores have adopted two-way viewing mirrors and viewing ports to maintain surveillance over dressing rooms. Some privacy violation cases have resulted, but in any event, it is mandatory that female observers, if used at all, must be used for women's dressing rooms, and male employees for men's fitting rooms. Witnesses of the same sex should be on hand during shoplifting interviews to forestall any possibility of sexual discrimination or invasion of privacy.

In questioning, being able to name the item and the place of concealment will go a long way in convincing the shoplifter that he or she has been caught red-handed. Shoplifters should then be instructed to place all of the items they have not paid for on a table or desk. An unproductive approach in this questioning is to ask "Did you steal this item?" A more effective approach would be to state, "When you took this item, were you interested in taking others like this, or is this the only one you took?" Or, "Why did you take only one of these? What use do you have for this particular item?"

Any answers to these questions are further admissions that the suspect took the items in question with intent to steal, making the retailer's case more binding in court.

A positive attitude and persistence will generally produce results in such interviews. Suspects may distract the interviewer or stall by asking for cigarettes, water and the like. Reasonable requests should be granted; requests for cigarettes can profitably be deferred following the formal statement of admission. If shoplifting suspects refuse to produce stolen merchandise, the police may be called at this point for assistance.

Many shoplifting suspects will appear to cooperate because their main interest is in getting out of their predicament with minimum problems. And most will claim that the theft is their first time ever. A skilled interviewer, as implied above, can subtly draw the suspect out. "Yes, I took the steak. We are poor and we haven't had meat for quite a while now." Or, "I really don't know why I took this lipstick. It's not a flattering shade," can lend a good deal of credence to a company's case, while demonstrating the essential fairness and truthfulness in prosecuting a suspect. The key here is that questioning and actions should be taken as if every case were going to court.

The Question of Restitutions

After eliciting a properly witnessed verbal statement from a suspect, it is suggested that the suspect repeat the statement on paper, using a blank legal-size pad in preference to a preprinted form. Any statement should release the retail business from civil liability.

At this point, suspects often offer to make restitution for the stolen merchandise. It is not recommended that restitutions offered by the subject should be taken at this time; the courts are the place for this type of decision. Such restitution may be accepted at a later time with proper handling on both sides to prevent any possibility of a claim of extortion.

Some retail operations can fall into a kind of game involving restitutions, using the possibility as a carrot to dangle before a shoplifting suspect. It is a fact that security personnel, management personnel and store personnel have been arrested for what these people described as "collecting restitutions" and a district attorney's office has described as "extortion."

The line drawn between collecting restitutions for a small pilfered item at the time the crime was committed, and collecting restitutions for a crime that is not committed in the presence of the interviewer is important. For example, an individual is apprehended for stealing $15 worth of merchandise, and in the course of questioning admits that over the past two years, about $9,000 worth of other merchandise has been stolen from the store. At this point, entering into a contract with this suspect for restitutions based on admission of prior crimes is illegal. A proper course would be to proceed directly to the district attorney, prosecutor or the courts, or have the subject arrested, letting the full story develop during trial proceedings.

Several cases are on record that followed this development: Professional thieves went into a store, were caught committing a crime, and made admissions to the tune of $12,000. When management offered a deal to make restitutions, the thieves went to the district attorney's office, stated that they had no prior police record, had gone into a store, taken an item and innocently forgot to pay for it and were then told they had to pay anywhere from $9,000 to $12,000 back. The D.A. construed this as extortion by store management—something illegal in itself and certainly not permissible in a case of grand larceny, where court action must be taken regardless of restitutions.

Often, it comes down to a matter of perspective. Payback for a single small item is one thing; payback for large amounts is something totally different. Unscrupulous store managers have been known to demand two and three times the value of an item taken as the price of not prosecuting, and as a warning to the suspect never to come into the store again. There is also the perspective of nature of crime. If a thief came into a store and held it up at gunpoint, obtaining $1,500, there would normally be no thought of contracting with the thief for the return of the money. If the same amount were embezzled or shoplifted from the company, an option would then exist as to restitutions. Large scale restitutions should be left to the courts, because a professional thief with a shrewd lawyer can convince a court that said thief was shaken down while under duress. As a result, the company, not the thief, could end up as a defendant.

At present, courts do not *require* private citizens or private loss prevention personnel to give so-called "Miranda" warnings to suspected shoplifters. Such warnings are required only during interrogation upon arrest by police officers. A technicality might arise where store security guards might be working part time, holding down full-time positions as regular police officers. In such cases, Miranda warnings should be given. These are:

1. You do not have to make a statement and have the right to remain silent.
2. Anything you say can and will be used against you in a court of law.
3. You are entitled to consult with an attorney before interrogation and to have an attorney present during interrogation.
4. If you cannot afford an attorney, one will be appointed for you. Suspects should then be asked whether they understand the Mi-

WHEN APPREHENDING A SHOPLIFTER, IT IS DESIRABLE TO READ THEM THE FOLLOWING RIGHTS:

1. You have the right to remain silent.
2. Anything you say can and will be used against you in a court of law.
3. You have the right to talk to a lawyer and have him present with you while you are being questioned.
4. If you cannot afford to hire a lawyer, one will be appointed to represent you before any questioning, if you wish one.

DO YOU UNDERSTAND EACH OF THESE RIGHTS I HAVE JUST READ TO YOU? Yes No

HAVING THESE RIGHTS IN MIND, DO YOU WISH TO TALK TO US NOW? Yes No

Signed by the one the rights were read to: X ______________________________

The following is a suggested form for your use in recording information about the shoplifter, a description of the incident and the shoplifters signature.

STORE ADDRESS		CITY		STATE	
DATE		TIME OF DAY		A.M.	P.M.

NAME — LAST	FIRST	MIDDLE	TELEPHONE

ADDRESS — If P. O.Box list actual street and number	CITY	STATE

MOTHERS NAME AND OCCUPATION	FATHERS NAME AND OCCUPATION

MAIDEN NAME IF MARRIED OR DIVORCED ______________________________

DRIVERS LICENSE NUMBER	STATE	SOCIAL SECURITY NUMBER IF DIFFERENT

DATE OF BIRTH	AGE	HEIGHT	WEIGHT	HAIR	EYES

INCIDENT DESCRIPTION ______________________________

____

____

____

____

SIGNATURE OF PERSON DETAINING SUSPECT

____

SIGNATURE OF WITNESSES

____

____

I ______________________________ do voluntarily admit and state that the following items listed below were taken from the premises of ______________________________ without being paid for.

____________________ • __________ ____________________ • __________

____________________ • __________ ____________________ • __________

____________________ • __________ ____________________ • __________

TOTAL NUMBER OF ITEMS ____________________ TOTAL VALUE WITHOUT TAX ____________________

I, the undersigned, in signing this statement and surrendering the aforementioned items, do so voluntarily and of my own free will and without threats or promises of immunity from criminal prosecution, that with the signing of the document I fully release the above mentioned store, or company, and all agencies and representatives and individually from all civil liability.

SIGNED ______________________________

SUBJECT RELEASED TO: POLICE __________ PARENTS __________ SELF __________

EVIDENCE RELEASED TO: POLICE __________ ____________________

An extensive and detailed form for retailers to use in instances of shoplifting is suggested by one of the state retailers associations. The information on the form is vital to obtain, but many loss prevention experts recommend statements by suspects written completely in their own words on blank legal pad paper.

randa rights and are willing to waive them and talk about the incident.

When the questioning is done by store personnel or loss prevention department officials, as noted above, the Miranda rights need not be given, and following admissions, the suspects should complete a written admission/release statement.

Statements—Written and Preprinted

The statement of the facts should be in the suspect's own handwriting, and could yield a good deal more information if the suspect is simply handed a blank legal-size pad. If preprinted forms are used, the shoplifting suspect should be asked to re-read the filled out form aloud, and then sign it in the presence of witnesses. If the suspects are reluctant to sign because they do not want to admit in writing that they stole something, the statement may be described not as an admission of guilt but rather an agreement that they did leave the store without paying and that it was reasonable for the store to recover its merchandise.

Having the shoplifting suspect sign a written release is important if the suspect is not going to be prosecuted. If the company decides to prosecute, signed release forms become somewhat less important. In any event, prosecutions should only be done if all of the elements required to prove intent clearly exist and that the case is a strong one, not likely to result in acquittal.

DISPOSITION OF SHOPLIFTING CASES

Every case should be judged according to its special circumstances. Most retail organizations are not inhuman. Very old or very young offenders, obviously sick people, or those who are known personally to store employees, may get special handling (which does not mean that all should go unpunished). Consistent policies are not easy to hammer out. Respondents to the *Progressive Grocer* shoplifting[10] study are divided over how often, if ever, to actually bring an apprehended shoplifter to trial: 21.8% say "always," 34% report "occasionally," 27% say "seldom" and 17.2% of the composite group admit "never."

Adding to the problem, 47.6% of the respondents feel that their state's shoplifting law is too weak. Prosecution is costly—ironically almost always more costly than the value of the pilfered goods in a food or drugstore. Prosecution is also time and labor consuming, while equally often frustrating since shoplifting laws often tread very softly, even on those repeatedly convicted. False arrest suits are always a possibility if the company has not followed good procedures in apprehensions and obtaining admissions.

Individual respondents to the *Progressive Grocer* survey report all manner of policies, including the prosecution of one case in five to prosecuting 75% of the time. Some companies won't prosecute if the goods stolen amount to $10 or less, some only when whiskey or cigarettes are involved. Many stores repeat a similar tale: "We used to prosecute, but the judges dismissed the cases," or the courts "let the shoplifters off with a warning." A recent study in California, however, indicates that 45% of convicted shoplifters there do time in jail. It's not hard to understand why. When retailers were asked in this study how they would improve their state's handling of shoplifting cases, 66.7% of the respondents indicated that increased penalties would be the first priority. A large percentage—48%—felt that elimination of all false arrest liability would be important, while 41% felt that classifying all shoplifting offenses as felonies rather than misdemeanors or larcenies would add to the seriousness of the crime. Nearly a third mentioned a provision that would specifically allow arrest and detention within the store. In general, the retailers also mentioned a quicker judicial process, a less apathetic attitude by the court, and certain special treatments; for example, mandatory 24-hour jail lockups for all convicted teenagers.

Consideration for prosecution should be given if the suspect has no identification, if the suspect resists or attacks store employees, appears to be drunk or under the influence of drugs, has taken a significant amount/value of merchandise, is using props that are those of a professional shoplifter, etc.

When retail companies do not have sufficient evidence to win a court case, shoplifting suspects should be released. This means elements required to prove intent to steal may be missing, that observations of witnesses may be relatively weak, or that some doubt about the suspect's intent to steal does exist. In cases where the suspects are senile, pregnant, or obviously abashed and cooperative following apprehension, it may be sensible not to go to prosecution. Often, accomplices are caught but not the shoplifters themselves. Cases against accomplices alone may be at best difficult to prove.

Handling Juvenile Offenders

There is also the special problem of shoplifters under 18 years old—the juveniles. Most studies indicate that at least a third of all detected instances of shoplifting in high-volume food, drug and discount stores are under 18, and in some stores juveniles make up at least half of the shoplifting problem. In the grocery industry, convenience stores are particularly hard hit by young children.

Regardless of this degree of seriousness, many companies are content with simply getting their merchandise back and throwing apprehended juvenile shoplifters out of the store, but as one loss prevention expert notes, it makes no impression on either the shoplifter or his family when a store does not treat the case in an "official" manner. This expert recommends the following procedure:

1. The portion of the release form which contains identifying information should be completely filled out in each case.
2. The juvenile should be released only to parents or to a local police agency. There, juvenile officers may interview the suspect and check their files for prior problems.
3. The subject should sign the official release form.

Another supermarket security director notes that, "In the case of juvenile offenders, it is almost mandatory to notify their parents, and if the parents are not cooperative, it is also a good idea to notify the juvenile authorities, especially if this is not a first-time offense. A statement should be sought from the parents when a child is released in their custody, stating either that the child did commit the crime or admitted so to the parent, and that they will see to it that the child is kept off the company's premises. Parents should be told in no uncertain terms that if their child is apprehended again, juvenile authorities will definitely be brought into the case."

PREVENTIVE MAINTENANCE FOR SHOPLIFTING

Shoplifting is a very old "business"—for professionals and amateurs alike, it can be a very good and profitable business. Penalties against convicted shoplifters handed down by courts are most often lenient. Anyone who has a tough hide, can take the shame of being caught stealing and marched unceremoniously into a store office from time to time, makes a perfect shoplifter candidate. The number of apprehensions and prosecutions, huge as it may be, is dwarfed by the sheer number of *attempts* per week, per day, and even per hour.

Against this pessimistic picture, anything a company can do to minimize or alleviate the problem can pay profit dividends. A good anti-shoplifting program starts with a company's own employees from the moment they are hired. While most employees understand that profitability is the key to retail success, even corporate management often fails to fully grasp the relationship between security *training* and profits. Any employee can make a better contribution to profits if an introduction to security from the standpoint of saving profits is part of every orientation.

Workers who are aware of what to look for in a store and how to recognize an illegal act as it is happening are making a definite profit contribution. It is the responsibility of store employees to try to protect merchandise from theft and each employee should be trained to take some specific action when a theft is observed. This training might consist of how to observe and whom to contact, following procedures clearly and carefully outlined in briefings and training sessions.

Obviously, no store employees should take any action in apprehensions that could bring harm to themselves, other employees or customers. As is so often the case, common sense may be the best policy; it is far better to take no action until it is *certain* that someone has stolen something in the store.

Key tips for employees in spotting shoplifters:

1. Be alert to switched bottle caps and easily removable/restickable price tags.
2. Be suspicious of customers loitering in an area but making no attempt to purchase items.
3. Be especially wary of loiterers in high-ticket areas such as jewelry, tobacco, health and beauty aids, giftware, and auto supplies.
4. Be alert to customers nervously handling an item for an inordinate length of time.
5. Be alert to shoppers with large handbags in sections with many small items.
6. Become adept in watching shoppers' eyes. A shoplifter might seem to be staring fixedly at an item in his or her hands, but more often than not, the eyes will be in constant motion.
7. Be suspicious of a group of young people gathered around a display.
8. Be suspicious of a customer who distracts a salesperson several times when leading up to a purchase, but who never buys.
9. Be wary of a person with additional items in his or her hands,

such as gloves or handkerchiefs, while they are handling merchandise.
10. Question all customers entering "no admittance" areas, especially those asking directions in such off-limits areas.
11. Be suspicious of customers who suddenly leave a loaded shopping cart in mid-aisle and head for the store exit.

Beyond the scope and degree of employee training, retail organizations have a myriad of options in store construction and operations that can serve to minimize the occurrence of shoplifting. In the area of store planning and layout, a store designed to permit maximum observation of shoppers would have:

- No cross-aisles.
- Low displays.
- Pilferage-prone items within eyesight of checkouts.
- Valuables in a locked showcase.
- Good housekeeping on display areas and shelves.
- Manager's office or courtesy booth on an elevated platform.
- Warning signs posted prominently around the store.
- Proper lighting to eliminate shadowy areas.
- Arrangement that restricts movement of persons exiting the store.

Special equipment such as angled mirrors, real and dummy TV cameras, and camouflaged viewing ports are used by many retail operations. Mirrors, in fact, are used so frequently that customers expect to see them in the stores. Still in an early stage of development after many years of slow progress, the micro-dot, an electronic relay affixed to merchandise that must be desensitized at checkouts or else noise or silent alarms will be triggered, may be the anti-shoplifting device of the future. While cost-effective for super high-ticket goods, such as expensive furs and jewelry, it is still a long way from being completely acceptable in the 15,000-item low-margin conventional supermarket of today. (See information on these systems in Chapter 8.)

In many department stores and supermarkets badly hit by shoplifting, uniformed guards may be used. The purpose here is clearly more for deterrence than apprehension. Plainclothes guards, either in conjunction with uniformed guards or working alone, actually make apprehensions. The plainclothes guards can also assist in training store employees in detection and apprehension techniques. Uniformed guards are additionally useful in areas where money is counted or safes opened.

Despite the availability of equipment and services to aid in observing/deterring shoplifters, the single most widespread technique is the relocation or revised handling of specific problem categories or items. In the *Progressive Grocer* study,[11] 73% of the responding stores reported relocating categories to permit better surveillance. Here are some of the specific steps respondents took:

- Relocated drugs in view of checkouts.
- Put all drugs over $3.98 in view of the pharmacy checkout.
- Put cigarettes in view of checkouts.
- Put cigarette single packs into vending machines only.
- Moved all cigarettes into the courtesy booth only.
- Relocated whiskey and cigarettes.
- Moved the wine and liquor department to an "outside aisle."
- Moved record albums and health and beauty aids out of alcove departments.
- Put film at checkouts.
- Put sunglasses at checkouts.
- Closed all cross-aisles.

It is clear that if prevention of shoplifting were the only retail criterion, stores would return to a completely serviced "general store" operating mode, reversing more than 50 years of streamlined, efficient self-service development.

The Question of Publicity

Most shoplifters, as amateurs, fear being caught far more than the punishment itself. For this reason, many security experts advocate the use of publicity in the case of apprehended shoplifters as a potential deterrent to other customers who might be tempted. Some chains have gone on widespread campaigns in all stores, using local newspapers and in-store photographs of apprehended customers.

Any judgement on the use of publicity should be tempered with consideration for possible repercussions against a store or a company. In a small community where everyone knows everyone else, the use of publicity may boomerang on a store, for all its good intentions. In larger towns and cities, possible backlash problems may be less of a factor, and therefore publicity could serve as a powerful deterrent, especially to the amateur shoplifter who lives in the community and shops in local stores. Any publicity gained should embrace not only external newspapers directed to the community at large, but also within the company, so that the firm's employees are kept aware of the company's consistency and success in pursuing crime.

Various pamphlets aimed at retailers, customers and parents are available to assist in minimizing the shoplifting problem. Some retailer associations even run shoplifting warning ads in newspapers prior to major selling seasons.

Often the single best policy in deterring shoplifting is one that retail companies should attempt to develop in *all* employees at *all* times: Friendliness and a spirit of service. Smiling at shoppers, greeting them as they come into a store or weave through the aisles, asking them if they need help if they seem to be hesitant and nervous—all of this is nothing more than good retail sales training, and at the same time is also good preventive maintenance for shoplifting. It pleases the honest customer, while it says to the potential shoplifter: "They are watching me."

SUMMARY

Shoplifting is without doubt the most frequently committed crime against retail businesses, costing merchants perhaps as much as $16 billion a year. Although there are a number of statistical studies to determine shoplifters by age, sex and other demographic figures, there are essentially only two types: professionals and amateurs, with the amateur shoplifters in the overwhelming majority. Highly troubling is the fact that a sizeable portion of apprehended amateur shoplifters are youngsters under the age of 18.

In high-volume retail stores, departments prominently hit by shoplifters include health and beauty aids, cosmetics, candy, tobacco and meat. These are the high-profit, high resale-value items in the store, and because of their profitability, can be an acute problem for a severely hit operation.

Professional shoplifters come equipped with an arsenal of props and gadgets from trick boxes and pants to special overcoats with false arms. Amateurs may often develop favorite props and routines, but most commonly simply stuff a pilfered item into a handbag or pants pocket. Studies indicate that the busiest shopping times of the year are generally the peak shoplifting periods. Since youngsters are so heavily involved, after school hours are always worse shoplifting times than any others.

The rise of self-service retail stores made shoplifting a reality. The continued sophistication of modern superstores, with huge displays of merchandise, mammoth total floor space, and complete self-service, has served to make shoplifting even more of a temptation. Cynicism as to the kid gloves attitude of the legal system toward the shoplifter (vs. crimes of greater cost, and crimes of violence) is surely another factor in the continued growth of shoplifting.

Employees must be trained to observe customers and detect instances of shoplifting. Intent to steal and the deliberate concealment of stolen merchandise, properly eyewitnessed, are the basic requisites to consider an apprehension, which most companies suggest should be made outside the store premises or at least beyond the store checkouts. Statements should be taken from apprehended shoplifters and release forms signed to protect the store from false arrest or damages suits. Restitutions carry with them the possibility of criminal suits against a company for extortion; in restitution, a policy of common sense and perspective should be applied.

The question of whether or not to prosecute admitted shoplifters also requires the exercise of common sense. Extremes of never prosecuting or always prosecuting are each overly rigid and harmful in their own ways, although most retailers would like to see penalties for convicted shoplifters increased.

Preventive maintenance in the retail business includes good employee orientations and continuing training, the use (not merely the *existence*) of devices such as convex mirrors, closed circuit TV cameras and two-way mirrors or viewing ports, and physical changes when necessary in departmental or item location and store fixturing.

Publicity of apprehended shoplifters via store signs or even retail newspaper ads may be of deterrent value but could backfire in small town stores. It also fails to appreciate any psychological, economic or emotional problems that make shoplifters commit thefts. Offsetting the impersonal self-service image of the modern retail store with friendly employees who are alert while in the aisles, may be the best deterrent any store can have against shoplifting . . . and it is also good business practice as well.

NOTES

[1] Cited in "The High Cost of Shoplifting," **Nation's Business**, November 1978, p. 44; Also **Crime in Retailing**, U.S. Dept. of Commerce, August 1975, p. 4.

[2] Cited in "How Shoplifting is Draining the Economy," **Business Week**, October 15, 1979, p. 119.

[3] "Your Profit May Be in the Customer's Pocket," **Progressive Grocer**, September 1968, p. 54.

[4] **Crime in Retailing**, U.S. Department of Commerce, U.S. Government Printing Office, August 1975, pp. 4-5.

[5] **Seventeenth Annual Survey of Shoplifting**, Commercial Service Systems, Inc., Van Nuys, CA, p. 7.
[6] "Your Profit May Be in the Customer's Pocket," **op. cit.**, p. 56.
[7] **Seventeenth Annual Survey, op. cit.**, Table D.
[8] "Your Profit May Be in the Customer's Pocket," **op. cit.**, p. 54.
[9] **Ibid.**, p. 59.
[10] **Ibid.**, p. 55.
[11] **Ibid.**, p. 57.

4 APPREHENSION, FALSE ARREST AND INTERVIEWS

This chapter will describe:

- **The need for positive evidence in apprehensions**
- **Basic approaches to suspected shoplifters**
- **Apprehension of employees**
- **Interviewing suspects**
- **Nuts and bolts of statements of admission**
- **Guidelines for courtroom procedures and publicity procedures**

Because company managements, including security departments, are not officially sanctioned public law enforcement agencies, the apprehension and subsequent interviewing of suspected employees or customers must be handled with extreme caution. There are many cases in which an executive of a company opened the morning mail and discovered that the company was being sued for false arrest, false imprisonment, libel, slander or defamation. The most common cause of this is a wrongful action taken by employees of the company against the plaintiff.

Any procedures recommended in apprehensions of customers or employees can stand only as *rough guides*, since each company is bound by its own set of local, municipal and state laws and its own security philosophy, which can range from prosecuting all violators to maximum forgiveness and understanding.

False arrest is a trap that many companies needlessly fall into. Yet, at the same time, no company should become paranoid concerning the possibility of false arrest to the point where no one is ever apprehended. The fact that many people may threaten to sue or call lawyers does not necessarily mean that if the case came to court the retailer would be found liable. False arrest and false imprisonment *convictions* are actually rare, because intent to falsely arrest or imprison someone must be proven. False arrest due to an accident or honest error, unfortunate though this may be, is not a convictable offense. In short, no company should allow the specter of false arrest to interfere with its security duties. For the professional shoplifter, making false arrest threats is almost standard operating procedure when apprehended.

At the same time, many accomplished confidence artists use false arrest and libel as a way to "shake down" the unsuspecting businessman. One classic instance occurred at a supermarket where a man was found lying on the ground directly in front of the store with a crowd of 70 to 80 people around him. The store manager was standing beside the man demanding that he be arrested for shoplifting. The horizontal suspect, on the other hand, was demanding an ambulance.

Through subsequent investigation, the following story emerged: The accused suspect had entered the store and proceeded to act in a deliberately suspicious manner, hoping that some alert employee would take action. Sure enough, a stock boy signaled the store manager as the suspect was in the meat department. The manager then kept the suspect under constant surveillance.

Making sure that he was being watched, the suspect reached over and very obviously took a steak and tucked it inside his jacket, under his arm. This allowed him to hold the meat tightly, leaving his hands free to handle other merchandise. Realizing the store manager was now watching him, he continued to act in a devious manner, and made his way to the frozen food aisle. Reaching over the low frozens case to select an item from the non-refrigerated shelves above the frozen foods, he allowed the steak under his jacket to slide down into the frozen food case, unseen by the store manager. All the while he continued to hold his arm as if he still had the steak wedged under his jacket.

At this point, he looked around rapidly several times, then began to make his way out of the store. The manager followed him outside the door and, once out in the street, placed his hand on the suspect's shoulder, told the man he was under arrest, and demanded the steak hidden under his jacket. At that moment, the suspect fell to the ground.

After local police had arrived, the manager insisted he had constantly observed the suspect, had seen him take the meat and place it under his jacket. When the suspect was brought to his feet, he demonstrated that there indeed was nothing hidden underneath. The manager was completely surprised and embarrassed, and he publicly regretted that he had threatened arrest. The suspect in turn demanded that the manager be arrested for illegal detention and false accusation. The confidence man's next step would have been to make a cash settlement with the store.

This case points up the seriousness of accusations and apprehensions. While false arrest or slander is rare because intent must be proved, a business concern must still be very sure of its actions. Accusations cannot be made haphazardly and then passed off very lightly. In essence the company which falsely accuses deprives suspects of their liberty. As the U.S. Department of Commerce states: "It is essential that apprehension of suspects be carried out in strict accordance with the law. Disregard or ignorance of proper legal procedures can result in unsuccessful prosecution efforts or even false arrest suits. It is therefore imperative that security personnel be thoroughly familiar with regulations, and although sales people do not ordinarily make arrests, they should have an understanding of the procedure. These arrest procedures should be developed fully by an attorney completely familiar with the local statutes pertaining to retail crime and arrests."[1]

NEED FOR POSITIVE EVIDENCE

Any actions taken that pertain to an apprehension must be based on definite, factual evidence. A store manager, for example, is told by a well-meaning employee that he observed a woman place an item in her bra as she left the jewelry counter. In actuality, what he could have seen was the woman adjusting her bra; an apprehension thus based on mere belief can clearly cause difficulties. No employee of a retail company can afford to jump the gun, nor should any employee forget realism and the need to adopt a good measure of expediency, despite thoroughly understandable outrage. The best single policy may well be, "When in doubt, let them out!" It is preferable for a manager to allow 10 people to escape arrest because there is no hard evidence, rather than arrest one person with insufficient evidence, become involved in a lawsuit, or at the least, have the company publicly embarrassed.

In cases of shoplifting or internal theft, then, the following rules are suggested:

1. An illegal action must actually have been seen taking place, either personally or reported by a witness representing the company or place of business.
2. What has been seen must have been a definite, overt act: "I saw the suspect take a carton of cigarettes, place it under his jacket and push it up under the armpit."

3. The witness must not lose sight of the suspect, even for the moment it takes to alert store management or loss prevention personnel.

When these conditions are met in observing a case of store theft, it may not be necessary, as many security consultants continue to advise, to wait until the suspect leaves the premises prior to making an apprehension. Again, state, local and municipal statutes apply. Generally, the suspect may be approached immediately by management or security, along with the witness/employee. The approach should be positive, asking specifically for the item or items the eyewitness actually saw taken: "Sir, may I please have the cigarettes you have under your jacket . . . Would you care to pay for them?"

Note that a form of subterfuge is inherent in the statement to the suspect, raising the possibility of allowing the suspect to make restitution by paying for the merchandise, where the intent of the phrase is to encourage an admission by the suspect. There is nothing to reproach a bit of bluff in apprehending or questioning a suspect. The basic approach should be to make it easy for the suspect to partly or fully admit to an illegal act.

At the same time, it is not wise to lie to a suspect by threatening arrest or promising non-arrest or taking no action. Case in point: A suspect has been observed taking several expensive, handrolled handkerchiefs from a display and tucking them inside the top of his pants. A good, tactical approach to this suspect would be: "Sir, would you like to pay for those handkerchiefs now or on your way out?" The reckless, dangerous approach would produce a statement such as: "Sir, for those handkerchiefs you stole and put in your pants, you are going to be arrested." This immediately backs the customer into a corner. The suspect may force the issue by saying, "I don't know what you're talking about." Or he may make a dash for the door.

BASIC APPROACHES TO SUSPECTED SHOPLIFTERS

The common sense approach represented by the first statement in the case above may often elicit a response such as "Oh, I meant to pay for them," and the suspect may actually produce the handkerchiefs on the spot. Once this happens, the suspect may then be asked to proceed to the store office. The suspect has not been promised non-arrest, but the wording of the question has given him an out. He has not been immediately threatened with arrest and therefore feels relatively safe. Once the hidden merchandise has been produced, along with whatever exotic reason the suspect believes will satisfy management or store security, the entire issue becomes academic. The suspect has effectively admitted to a theft without ever uttering the words "theft," "steal," or "shoplifting." From that point, further questioning becomes relatively easy, and a full admission can be obtained.

In some cases, the approach must even be more subtle. For example, a man takes a package of cigars and places it in his shirt pocket during the shopping trip. While such placement prior to purchase is a suspicious act, it does not yet offer solid evidence of intent to steal that particular item, simply because a shirt pocket is where most cigar smokers would normally carry their cigars. As long as the customer remains in the store, especially if he appears to be making other purchases with full intent to pay, he may indeed remember the cigars in his shirt pocket and pay for them at the checkout, obviously having placed the package in his pocket out of force of habit. In such cases, the best policy is often to allow the suspect to check out all purchases while a witness constantly observes, then approach the suspect on his way out of the store, and say, "Sir, I believe you forgot to pay for the cigars."

Actions Based on Abnormality

Another way to look at the question of whether or not to take action is to base such action on suspicious handling of a given item of merchandise. Many women, for example, when buying greeting cards in a supermarket or drugstore, will place the cards in their handbags instead of the shopping cart. The reason is that the cards may become creased or soiled by food items placed on top of the cards as they sit in the cart. In most cases, the women will have the cards clearly visible in the bag. As they complete their shopping tour and check out their merchandise, they may honestly forget to take out the cards and pay for them; at the same time, the cashier may not notice it. In such cases, management or loss prevention personnel observing the unfolding scenario can approach the customer and say, "Madam, I believe you forgot to pay for the greeting cards in your handbag."

However, if the same woman places cosmetics, health and beauty aids, or other small, relatively expensive items directly into her handbag, the chances for honest error on the part of the customer are small indeed. A positive, more forceful approach, assuming intent to steal, can be made, providing the acts have been witnessed and the customer observed at all times.

In cases where there is any doubt, because of lack of constant observation or lack of direct observation of the concealment of merchandise with intent to steal, the wisest policy, as noted earlier, is normally to let the suspect go. It may also be expedient to let a suspect go if he or she either starts to fight or starts to run. If the observed theft is serious enough, local police may be contacted. If not, common sense should take over. In a confrontation, the chances for injury are great. Even though the company may be legally within its rights in using force when a suspect resists apprehension, at the same time it leaves itself open for possible assault charges lodged by the suspect—even if the suspect admits to the theft, is prosecuted and convicted.

The Importance of Constant Observation

In the case of the "phony" shoplifting of meat described earlier in the chapter, it was apparent that the whole procedure was a deliberate ruse to draw store management into a false arrest liability and to then "shake down" the store. Accomplished shoplifters are very sensitive to the possibility of observation, and often, if they believe they are being watched, will attempt to get the concealed merchandise out of their possession and back onto a shelf. They will normally do this in the same surreptitious manner they used when lifting and concealing the merchandise in the first place. This is why constant observation becomes so important in making a shoplifting apprehension. If the suspect sees store personnel converging from a number of directions, then stopping to discuss their plan of action—averting their eyes for a moment—the shoplifter has all the time he/she needs to get rid of the goods. False arrest will then be threatened by the suddenly overly-righteous suspect. Although few false arrest suits are ultimately judged against a business which has acted honestly on its beliefs, repeated instances of false arrest suits coming before the same court, involving the same company time and again, may produce a conviction for harassment. Courts often do this to force businesses to learn to use proper procedures in making apprehensions.

APPREHENSION OF EMPLOYEES

Apprehending shoplifters is a process of obtaining witnesses, obtaining evidence, and gaining a statement of admission. In apprehending employees for dishonesty, the basic rules are very similar. The most common instance at the retail level is that of a cashier discounting the merchandise he/she is ringing up, as described in an earlier chapter. Normally, the discount is at least half of the total merchandise value, sometimes even more. In giving this "discount," the cashier is working with a customer who may be a friend or a relative. As with shoplifting occurrences, the discounting itself must be constantly observed by a witness; the evidence is the cash register tape itself, and both cashier and "working partner" should be apprehended if possible.

In the case of a cashier simply taking money from the register, the theft must be observed, and most importantly, the company must be able to identify the cash as belonging to the company. Such an arrest or apprehension can be tricky because once the cash gets into a personal billfold or handbag, no search is possible without an arrest by a law enforcement officer. Even if a sum of money is visible in the bag, and this exactly correlates with the sum of money missing from the register, the evidence remains circumstantial. In such instances, when direct observation has been made, and the suspect has been observed alone at the register where no one else had access to the cash box, it may be advisable to call the police and have them make the apprehension.

An alternative practice is the planting of "marked" money or recorded money in the register of a suspected cashier. Serial numbers of the planted cash should be noted on a sheet and witnessed by another employee. In this manner, if it is necessary for a police officer to make an arrest and a search, the evidence of the theft is clearly indicated by matching the serial numbers.

Proper questioning procedures, as detailed later, can produce admissions from employees just as it can from customers. In the case of employees, when this route is followed, the evidence must be gathered, but a formal apprehension need not be made all the time if the company has adhered to proper questioning methods. It is only human nature to try to catch criminals red-handed. Indeed, in many instances the needed evidence to prosecute a customer or employee can only be gathered in a manner which would yield an immediate, on-the-spot apprehension. Some of the procedures a company can follow in apprehending the discounting cashiers detailed earlier fall into this category.

Dishonest employees in other areas of the store may commit thefts during the course of their workday and so are accessible at any time. Thus a request to an employee to "see the manager in his office" is not necessarily perceived as a threat—even to the dishonest worker.

APPREHENSION IN CASES OF FRAUDULENT CHECKS

It is rare that bad check passers are apprehended on the spot. Suspicious checks without proper identification should be refused by the company. Bad checks that the company unwittingly accepts take several days to "bounce." However, if a company is presented with a check which it has good reason to believe is fraudulent, or is alerted to a "paperhanger" who is working the area and attempts to pass a check, it is recommended by most loss prevention experts that the police be notified while the suspect is still at the site.

Strong evidence that the check is stolen, forged or altered must be present via the check itself. Suspicion or belief is not alone sufficient to make an apprehension, and can result in difficulties for a company. As with shoplifting con games, professional thieves have developed routines involving checks as well. Cases of inviting a bad check accusation are admittedly extremely rare, but they do occur.

In most retail businesses, "insufficient funds" (or "NSF") checks make up the vast majority of bad check losses. It is important to note that insufficient funds by itself is not a crime. However, a record of chronic insufficient funds checks from the same customer may be construed as a crime if a specific case comes to court. As with shoplifting, the operating principle is intent to defraud or steal. In shoplifting, willful concealment, proven by an eyewitness, constitutes legal evidence of default in many states. With "NSF" checks, intent is much more difficult to establish.

INTERVIEWING APPREHENDED SUSPECTS

Procedures in business security remain quite different from those of police departments or law enforcement agencies. The basic difference is that corporations employing loss prevention departments generally strive for the lowest profile possible, so as not to create the impression of dealing with a "police state." Essentially, the policy is one of "walking softly but carrying a big stick." Gone from the loss prevention professional's vocabulary are such terms as "prisoner," "interrogation," "confessions," and so on. These very words, given the new concept of business security, can work against the company in creating an atmosphere not conducive to the apprehension of a dishonest employee or customer.

In interviewing a suspect who may not be quite sure of why he or she is being questioned, at least at the outset, it is likely that a security professional will be dealing with someone who is excited, strained, upset, stunned, bewildered. The basic idea is to maintain that very status of anxiety in the mind of the suspect, so that regardless of the questions asked, he or she does not really feel at ease. Under conditions of strain, it is much easier to exact the truth by discovering flaws in the facade of a covering story . . . and this discovery of truth can be obtained by either direct questioning or by elliptical questioning. The interviewer has the upper hand when the suspect constantly feels that the interviewer assumes wrongdoing. At the same time, a suspect should not be badgered or locked into a corner by an immediate demand for a yes or no answer.

Most security professionals follow a common sense approach in this too. Immediately showing strength by going for the yes or no answer can easily prolong the entire process. If a subject is asked outright, "Did you steal that money from the register?" he or she may very well answer, "No." To turn that subject's "no" into a "yes" now requires a three-hundred-sixty degree revolution—one which now includes some face-saving for having uttered a lie.

The positive action approach is generally agreed to be the best method. Such an interview, for example, could start with the loss prevention interviewer saying, "Let's discuss money missing from a cash register." At this point, the subject has not been backed into a corner, although the seeds of strain and anxiety have been firmly planted. The subject can be looked in the eye, and addressed in a positive, almost friendly manner that keeps the entire situation relatively calm and stress-free on the surface.

Positive questioning should be used whenever possible. For example, a suspect should not be asked, "Were you ever arrested?" Instead, this area may be approached by asking, "How many times were you arrested?" "When did you get out last?" This leaves no room for the suspect to mentally weigh whether the questioner is attempting to pinpoint the fact that he or she did or did not do something.

The idea of surface "friendliness" on the part of the interviewer relates to the importance of having witnesses on hand during a questioning period. When the suspect is female, female witnesses should definitely be present. What's more, the interview should always be away from the center stage of business—in the security office, or a manager's office, or a back room area free from interference by ringing telephones. Privacy and a number of friendly faces can be important because at this point, the suspect has no friends, and is searching desperately for someone or something to lessen the strain. This is the powerful advantage of the skilled security interviewer. It is a basic reason why the stern look, the conservative dress, the superior attitude, and the tone of outrage, should be set aside. Otherwise, the suspect may mentally revolt against letting the truth out.

There is nothing wrong with putting words in a suspect's mouth providing there is no demand for the yes or no answer. It is an accusation couched in the form of an understanding, reassuring pat on the back: "I realize you didn't really mean to steal . . ." is a good example. In essence, you are telling the suspect you know he or she did steal, but it also provides a comfortable, sympathetic tone to which the suspect might reply, unbottling the inner tension.

The suspect's reply could well be, "You're right, I really didn't mean to take it. I just thought I could use it. It was too expensive to buy and I was going to take it home with me." The suspect has omitted the word "stealing" as has the interviewer, but at the same time has readily, definitely admitted guilt, almost relieved to find someone who "understands."

Admission of Guilt

The admission of guilt following an apprehension is vital. Observation of the suspect stealing or even apprehension with the merchandise still can be reduced to the word of the company vs. the word of the suspect. An alert defense lawyer can win the case if there is no formal declaration. In apprehending criminals and arresting them for minor or major crimes, the statement or police confession plays the most vital role in the conviction of the suspect. In business security, the statement from the suspect may also be necessary in the event of involvement in union arbitration or negotiations, since union contracts may be highly specific on reasons for termination.

Identification of Evidence

At the point of gaining an admission, it is also important to make sure the suspect is aware of what has been illegally taken, whether it is merchandise or cash. Frequently, shoplifters or employees will grab something without fully looking at or realizing its value. Having the suspect observe the merchandise or cash in question, describing it to the suspect and having it described back is important if only to plant the particulars in the suspect's mind. When a case comes to trial, the suspect may be asked to admit to or describe exactly what was taken. A discussion of the evidence following the apprehension may well be the first and only time the suspect really gets a chance to evaluate what was stolen. For example, the suspect may be told, "Do you real-

Use of the lie detector or "Psychological Stress Evaluator" [shown here, and in detail] is subject to many varying state laws. Where allowed it can be an extremely valuable tool. Operators must be proficient.

ize that this ring is priced at $750 and has a main stone and two chips?"

If possible, the suspect should initial the evidence or the evidence tag. In addition, the arresting or apprehending security officer should initial the evidence and date it, along with any witnesses to the interview procedure.

The evidence should then be placed in a secure area. If the suspect is turned over to police, the evidence may also have to be turned over; in such cases, a receipt from the prosecutor's office is necessary.

In the event of cash thefts, if the money is recovered the serial numbers should be recorded and the money initialed by security and the suspect, if at all possible. Again, witnesses should also initial the evidence.

A final recommended step is the photographing of all evidence whether or not it is turned over to the police.

The primary evidence in instances of cashier discounting is the register tape. That is why, in apprehensions, it is important to wait until the transaction is completely finished. During the apprehension, the original register tape should be secured, and a second, correct register tape should be produced by a new ringup of the merchandise. On the back of the original tape, a complete listing of the items purchased and the comparative amount charged should be recorded. This tape should be initialed by security, any arresting officer, witnesses, and suspects—cashiers and customers involved—if possible.

STATEMENTS OF ADMISSION

Getting the suspect to personally prepare a statement is the culmination of a security interview, which, when correctly handled, can provide solid evidence in a court case.

In a shoplifting apprehension, for example, the suspect should be escorted to an office where there is a degree of privacy. In speaking to the suspect, he or she should be put somewhat at ease by the conciliatory tone of the interviewer, by the relative lack of authority or the making of undue threats. If appropriate, the evidence should be removed from the suspect. During the questioning, the interviewer should make it clear that there was an eyewitness observation of the theft and that evidence is present which shows the suspect has committed the crime. Arrest should not be threatened, but cooperation should be made mandatory to keep the situation calm. The conversation might proceed along these lines: ". . . you realize that you have taken merchandise that does not belong to you. You were observed and we know exactly what you were doing."

The interview has therefore been maintained on a positive level, never getting the suspect boxed into a corner where a yes or no question is forced. The conversation could continue as follows: ". . . we realize that, due to extenuating circumstances, you have become involved in a theft. We are not really interested in how you did it, but what we are interested in doing is preventing it from happening again. Do you know the value of the merchandise you have taken?"

At this point, the suspect has been offered sympathy and a ray of hope in that the company's goal is the prevention of further such occurrences. The interviewer has also obliquely evaded the yes or no question by asking the suspect to estimate the value of the merchandise stolen. The suspect might answer, "I don't know," or "I think it's valuable," or "It's about fifteen dollars," etc. The quick and proper follow-up question should be, "How many other times have you taken merchandise in our store?"

The interview, calm though it may be, has gone right into the actual instance that occurred. The manner of the interview tends to avoid any discussion of the suspect's problems at home, job situation, or other emotional situations. Until the admission is made, all other questioning should be set aside in favor of the primary goal. This is always: to get the suspect to admit to the crime. It is not the job of security departments in retail businesses to undertake the rehabilitation of habitual criminals or to analyze psychologically disturbed men and women. The job is to apprehend them, convict them in court if the offense is serious enough, and make sure they do not come lightly into the victimized company's places of business again.

Thus, by speaking in a positive manner, the questioner has put the suspect in a position where he or she believes the company has all the evidence it needs, while also having brought the suspect to the point of apologizing for what was done. This in itself comes close to serving as a legal admission of guilt. An interjection at this point by the questioner, such as, "I'm sure that if you had to go through this again, you wouldn't have taken anything in the first place," or "I'm sure that this was a spur of the moment thing on your part," may be all that is needed to get the suspect freely talking.

Even the most hardened, streetwise thief, if given the opportunity, will state, "It won't happen again," or that "this is the first time it ever happened." Giving the suspect an opportunity to relax by first

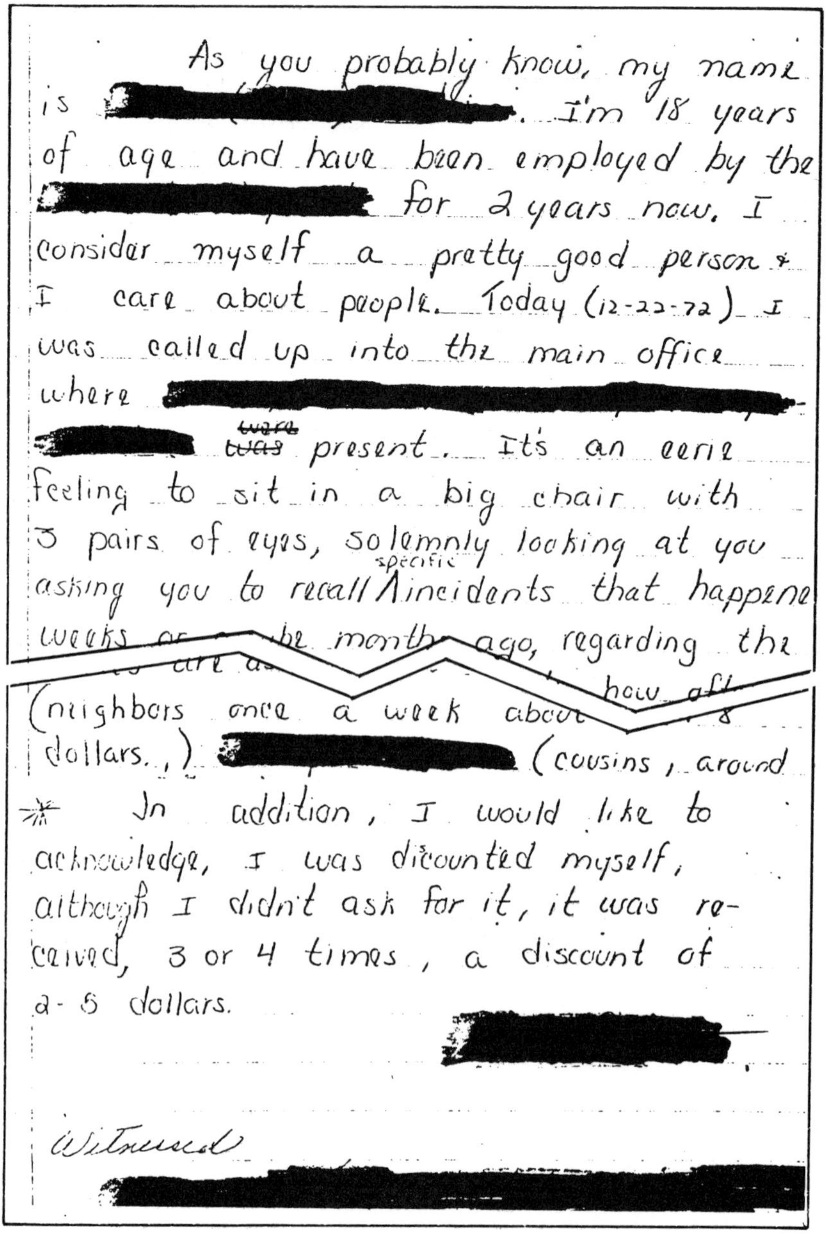

As you probably know, my name is . I'm 18 years of age and have been employed by the for 2 years now. I consider myself a pretty good person & I care about people. Today (12-22-72) I was called up into the main office where ~~was~~ were present. It's an eerie feeling to sit in a big chair with 3 pairs of eyes, solemnly looking at you asking you to recall specific incidents that happened weeks or maybe months ago, regarding the

(neighbors once a week about 8 dollars.,) (cousins, around

* In addition, I would like to acknowledge, I was dicounted myself, although I didn't ask for it, it was re-ceived, 3 or 4 times, a discount of 2-5 dollars.

Witnessed

Copy of an actual statement from an admitted dishonest cashier shows the statement to be in the employee's own writing [names have been blocked out]. Note the statement has been signed and witnessed by security personnel acting on behalf of management.

talking about family background and other non-related matters may postpone the admission of guilt indefinitely. This method of questioning has, in effect, subtly nudged the suspect into saying "yes." The immediate and vital next step is to get a statement of admission from the suspect. This may be broached in the following way: "I know you regret what you did, and I'm sure that once you get this off your chest, you will feel better and probably will never again be involved in a situation like this."

The Question of Preprinted Statements

Many security departments use preprinted statement forms that actually answer half the questions in any particular case and require the suspect to do little more than sign his or her name. The U.S. Supreme Court notes, however, that preprinted forms are often filled out under duress. In no major law enforcement agency in the country, including the FBI, are preprinted statement forms available for anyone to use or sign.

In a court case where a man had been apprehended while shoplifting in a department store, the suspect made a full confession, signing a preprinted form statement which had fill-in blanks for the date, time, suspect's name, what was stolen, the value of the merchandise and a space for the signature. The last line included a preprinted statement expressing the suspect's apology for having committed the crime. During the trial, the defendant's lawyer stated that his client had been under shock and duress, and didn't know what had been signed. After all, the lawyer said, it isn't every day that you get locked in jail. To prove his point about the preprinted admission form, he requested the court to ask the store's security department to produce the last 25 confession forms. When this was done, he pointed out that the only difference on the forms was the date, time, value of the merchandise and the signature. The lawyer pointed out that not everyone would make a similar statement, and not everyone feels regret for what they have done. The supposed hard evidence of a signed statement was thus called into serious question.

A statement should include certain key points, but it should also be written completely in the suspect's own words. It should not be dictated word for word to the suspect; difficult words should not be spelled out letter for letter. At the same time, someone should observe the suspect as the statement is being written to make sure that he or she is indeed admitting to what has already been stated orally.

What Statements Should Cover

Suggestions as to what points to cover in a statement can be made to the suspect, especially if, as they write, some of the answers are being skirted. The statement is basically a classic "who, what, when, where, why, how" document. As the suspect writes, a direct question, such as "When did this actually take place?" or "How did you do it?" can be asked. When the suspect replies orally, the questioner can state, "Why don't you put it into your statement."

A statement that contains the basic points listed above is among the most binding articles of evidence against an individual that the company can possess. Certain points of protocol should be followed. A suspect should be called a "subject." In writing a statement, the word "confession" should be assiduously avoided. Loss prevention departments should keep in mind the need to refrain from police language to help place the suspect in a cooperative mood.

Allowing the suspect to make the statement in his or her own words, spelling, and handwriting helps add to the relaxed mood. Official forms are far more terrifying to a suspect than an empty sheet of ruled legal-size paper.

The statement need not be lengthy. The shorter the better. But as a suspect writes a statement of admission, the door may be opened wider to provide evidence of motivation and other factors. This involves something more from the suspect in the area of why the crime was committed. But this addition at the same time can turn a relatively weak statement into a strong one. As a case in point, a weak statement would be, "I took a case of tuna." A much stronger version of the same admission would be, "This is the first time I ever took a case of tuna because my brother-in-law needed food for his family," or "I took the case of hams because we are expecting company over the weekend and my wife could not go shopping." The reasoning lends further credence to the statement and provides further evidence of the fact that the admission was not made under duress. It shows a court not only that the suspect did steal but also why he stole.

Gaining this input to a statement can be accomplished by observing the suspect as the statement is written or by asking, perhaps midway through the process, "Off the record, why did you take this particular pair of shoes instead of something else?" In the majority of cases an answer to a question put this way, following the informal conversation leading to the admission, will be forthcoming: "I took the shoes because I couldn't afford them, I had always liked this type of shoe, and I had no money."

At the close of the statement, the suspect should make some type of voluntary remark about his feelings in making the admission. In most instances, anyone who writes such a statement will close by expressing happiness in getting the truth out, that he or she was not forced to make the statement, and was admitting everything voluntarily. The questioning that produces these final statements should be varied so that suspects do not always close their written admissions in the same manner.

In gaining a statement from an apprehended shoplifter or vendor, a good practice is to follow up by asking if anyone else was involved in the thefts. This serves to convince these apprehended suspects that some consideration will be given to them if they assist the company. Often, shoplifters will inform on other professionals they know are hitting the company or store. Vendors may even mention company employees with whom they are working to defraud the firm.

Some Key Points Concerning Statements

1. Statements should be taken in more than outright instances of crime. Statements of a witness relating to a crime, statements of an unlawful act, or statements relating to accidents or unusual occurrences, should all be taken.
2. In the event of admitted crimes, statements should not be taken from a suspect if it is felt that he or she is not going to admit guilt. Some statements written by subjects under the eyes of young, nervous security workers could read, "I did not steal that merchandise . . . I am sorry that I am here and I will never do it again." Such a statement is completely useless and embarrassing to all concerned. Statements also should not be taken if the suspect is going to place all the blame on someone else.
3. Statements should be witnessed, preferably by two or more persons constantly in the room during the interview. Witnesses are to read the statement in front of the subject and sign their names in the suspect's presence.
4. Statements need not be notarized. Most retail stores do not have notaries on the scene, and a statement can be properly notarized only when the subject and all witnesses are present. Taking a statement to a notary without all parties present will not produce a notarized statement.

5. Statements do not always result in an arrest, or even termination. For example, loss prevention personnel observe a vendor apparently holding merchandise out of a shipment to a store. Upon apprehension and interview, the vendor admits to planning to steal the goods, but not going through with it. A statement can be taken from the vendor, and the vendor's own company may be notified, but there is no arrest.
6. Photocopies of statements should be made immediately, and then all copies should be placed under lock and key. The original statement should never be released except in court cases. Executives within the company seeking original statements should be referred to the security department, which can then issue a copy.
7. In dealing with labor unions, when an employee is apprehended and makes a statement, a full copy of the statement need not be issued to the relevant union unless there is continued action planned by the union on the matter. In many retail operations, the appropriate union will simply ask whether or not the company has a statement. If so, the union will often proceed no further. During arbitration, the security department can provide the union with a synopsis of the statement. If further action is taken, the union may then turn over a photocopy of the full statement.
8. While it is suggested that police be called and an arrest be made in most cases where there is a statement admitting to a crime, each individual case must be evaluated on its own merits, and the benefits or disadvantages to the company prior to making a formal charge and arrest must be weighed.

Example of a Typical Employee Statement

Following is a verbatim statement prepared by an apprehended cashier in a supermarket chain:

As you probably know, my name is ____________. I am 18 years of age, and have been employed by this company for a period of two years. I consider myself a good person, and I care about people. Today, when I was called into the main office, where representatives of security were present, it was an eerie feeling to sit in a big chair with three pairs of eyes solemnly looking at you and asking you to recall specific instances that may have happened weeks or months ago in the regarding of giving and receiving discounts, how often, how much and to whom.

I honestly don't recall some of the instances, but I will admit I have taken part in giving discounts to many of my neighbors and friends. I haven't done it often mainly because my face turns a tomato red, and I get a bad case of the shakes because I know I am doing something wrong. I consider myself a good cashier, hard working and reliable, and solemnly promise, as God is my witness, never to take advantage of this store in this manner again.

Now, as regards as to how much is taken off during the discount, I really can't say. Mainly, because it is one of those things that don't stick in your mind, but an approximation I would say in the area of 25% to 30% discount.

I have discounted some 10 different customers many times within the last 15 months. I am well aware of the fact that I am in a lot of trouble. I will accept any action that is taken against me, but I beg you to keep in mind that I love this store, I love the managers, and I love all the other employees, and you have my word this will never happen again if given another chance.

The above statement I have just finished writing was on a voluntary basis and the reason for it being written was to clear my guilty conscience held within me. My parents are fully aware of the discounts I have given out, and I can't tell you how many times I got yelled at for doing it, and that is one of the main reasons I was so scared when I got caught.

INTERVIEWING EMPLOYEES UNDER SUSPICION ONLY

Interviewing employees who are merely suspected of committing either a crime or a violation of the rules is a somewhat different ball game than interviewing employees caught in the act. Quite often, there is no positive proof other than the fact that store management or loss prevention was informed (often anonymously) that someone had been stealing in one way or another. There are several alternative directions in which to go at this point.

Armed with the fact that someone is a suspect, surveillance of the employee can be implemented to catch the crime as it happens. Or, the employee may be called into the office for an exploratory interview. Such a situation requires some care because a direct accusation of theft, no matter how the company may sugar-coat it, cannot be made. The subject has many recourses, such as complaining to the union, or directly to top management if there is a perceived harassment on the part of loss prevention with no clear evidence.

However, there is no reason why management or security cannot interview any employee at any time regarding possible "irregularities," and do this without pinpointing specific instances unless there is positive proof, or the subject becomes uncooperative during the course of the interview.

When a company receives information that a certain cashier is discounting, and a decision is made not to implement surveillance but to have the subject come in for an interview, the course of action may proceed in this fashion:

The subject is told that there is a "problem" within the confines of the company, and it seems to be in the area of "errors." The errors are essentially situations where cashiers find themselves overringing a penny or two, and sometimes underringing a penny or two during the course of business. The subject probably will agree with this because it is a common, everyday occurrence. Often, the subject may describe how customers immediately jump on cashiers when they overring, but never say a word when there is an underring. Again, understandable.

The subject is next told that there are many people working within the company who report to security, and that the loss prevention department has reports which show many gross errors occurring within the company. The subject may readily agree to this, too.

Then the skilled interviewer can zero in on the question at hand. According to security records, the suspect is told, it has been discovered that there are several people working in the subject's store who are making constant errors on the registers. At this point, the subject's composure may start to change. To break some of the tension, an obvious question, such as whether the subject takes lunch breaks or rest breaks with other cashiers in the store, may be asked. The answer will most likely be "Yes." The interviewer may then ask whether the subject has heard of these errors in conversations with other employees.

Then the interviewer attempts to solicit the help of the subject by asking whether he or she would be able to go back to work and send a message to all other employees notifying them that store security is aware of these errors, and it would be a very wise thing if the responsible employees made sure these errors stopped. Relieved, the subject will invariably say, "yes." The interviewer then thanks the employee, but as he or she proceeds to the door, the first in a series of anticlimactic questions may be fielded.

The subject is held at the door and is now told that security uses the word "errors" in the most general sense; that management is being very kind in that the policy in loss prevention is to correct problem conditions before any legal action need be taken. The subject may be asked directly if he or she understands what is meant by the term "errors." The answer could go either way. If the subject is not sure, the interviewer may discuss the amount of time the employee has spent with the company, that the employee surely is not naive, that the employee surely must know what the interviewer means by "errors," and that the company's policy could change at any moment, bringing about legal action. This usually improves the subject's memory.

It is important to note that nothing has been said about stealing. Everything has been classified under the heading of "errors." The subject has been told nothing that can be used against the company regarding either union or court action. However, if and when the subject states words to that effect that, "yes, I know what you mean about the errors, and it won't happen again," the interview can then go much further.

The "game" of almost letting the subject go and then holding the employee for "just one more question," alternately playing on fear and relief, can be continued until loss prevention has all the information it wants.

For example, the employee may now be asked if he or she recalls the last time merchandise was pushed through the register without charging. If the subject admits to this, the interviewer may ask the subject to define the relationship with the person or persons who were given discounts. If this information is volunteered, the interviewer can then tell the subject that in order to guarantee that this will not happen again, the company would like a verification as to how many times the discounting had occurred, with whom, etc.

At this point, the security interviewer may ask the subject whether he or she knows which other employees are involved. Often, by this device, additional names are revealed. Before the interview is completed, the subject is asked for a statement with complete admissions, following the guidelines set forth earlier in this chapter.

All of this does not provide sufficient evidence for a meaningful arrest, since there is no evidence of a specific instance. A statement admitting to illegal acts committed against the company, however, is more than enough evidence for problem-free termination of the employee. Without the hard evidence of comparative register tapes and eyewitness testimony described earlier, an arrest following this general type of admission would rarely produce a conviction.

The interview based on suspicion also allows loss prevention personnel to relent if the subject holds firm and no admission is forthcoming. In such cases, if the subject admits to no "errors" or "mistakes," the security interviewer can respond by saying this really can't be true because everyone makes mistakes. If the subject will then admit to only small errors, and that he or she will attempt to correct them when they are found, security can only thank the subject for his or her cooperation, again reminding the employee to pass the word that errors must be held to a minimum. Using this approach, there is little the subject can complain about to a union or to legal authorities under the heading of harassment. The company has maintained enough leeway to retreat without specific accusations.

One veteran security officer states that about 85% of interviews conducted along the lines of the case described above are successful in producing admissions. A reason for this is that admissions are made before the subjects even realize that they are in fact making an admission. The method does not allow sufficient time or sufficient maneuvering room to create a good lie. In the case of shoplifters or persons outside the company, however, this type of interview should be avoided. Positive evidence is a must. When there is such positive evidence, the extent of oblique, elliptical and hypothetical questioning described here is not fully warranted.

When employees do implicate other workers, the best advice is to follow up and question all personnel mentioned as soon as possible. Rapid action will prevent news from travelling through the grapevine, thereby giving other implicated employees advance warning that security is investigating their activities. This would allow such employees time to compose excuses or stories that could thwart loss prevention from gaining further admissions.

In formally announcing to employees at a location that security may be conducting interviews, the group may be told that Employee X has been interviewed and has been terminated or arrested, and that security is following up to make sure that everyone else who may be involved is interviewed. This is quite often all that is necessary to get voluntary statements that in turn require further decisions on arrests or termination.

A good deal of the foregoing descriptions of security interviews may represent an aspect of management activities that few retail personnel are called upon to engage in. Every company develops its own policies and operating styles in conformance with its particular philosophy and local, state and federal legal and civil liberties requirements. However, management personnel may be called on to act as witnesses, work closely with company loss prevention personnel or outside law enforcement authorities in apprehending and interviewing suspects, or appear in court cases as company representatives. A feeling for the differences between retail business procedures vs. police procedures, and the variety of approaches used in coaxing admissions from dishonest employees and apprehended shoplifters or outside vendors is important. Understanding the circumspection in which a company's loss prevention operation must operate generally provides a good deal of guidance in the relationships with employees and customers.

The laws pertaining to apprehensions of suspected shoplifters, vendors or others may vary from state to state. Most are quite similar in the critical aspects, but specific training as to the law in each state and municipality should be an important element of new employee and security personnel training. Some of the state laws covering shoplifting are capsulized in Appendix B at the end of this text. Most states hold that "a private individual has no authority to forcibly detain another individual short of arrest except as provided by law in the case of suspected shoplifters. A suspected individual may be questioned in an attempt to ascertain his/her business. However, unless there are reasonable grounds to justify an arrest, the individual may not be forcibly detained. It must be remembered that if an arrest is made by a private individual and it turns out that a crime has not been committed or that the person arrested is not guilty of the offense, there may be liability for false arrest/false imprisonment." (This is from the Illinois State Law.) Not all states authorize search of an arrested offender by a private citizen making an arrest. Such search may be conducted only when there is reason to believe the suspect is carrying a weapon, or has consented to the search.

Shoplifting is somewhat different, and most states specifically give a "merchant, his agents and his employees" the power to detain suspected shoplifters without incurring civil or criminal liability, providing they act within the law. The key in shoplifting is the determination of probable cause—a requirement satisfied by sufficient facts and evidence which lead to the belief that store merchandise has been taken by an individual who does not intend to pay for it. The permitted detention is conducted "in a reasonable manner and for a reasonable length of time for the purpose of investigating the ownership of such merchandise."

GUIDELINES FOR COURTROOM PROCEDURES

When a company establishes a loss prevention department, an important responsibility involves preparation for court cases. Often, corporation attorneys are not at ease with criminal law cases. Therefore it may be advisable for corporate attorneys to work with expert criminal lawyers in assisting the company in preparation of cases. In some retail organizations, the loss prevention department, working with the prosecutor's office, does its own preparations, presents its own evidence, and handles its own court procedures.

In general terms, the important points relating to courtroom appearances are these:

1. The company must be represented with dignity and accuracy.
2. Documentation of the entire facts of the case should be on hand in the form of security files or the employee's job folder. This is important in certifying that any question pertaining to the case can be answered with precision.
3. All pertinent evidence, including original copies of admission statements, should be available during the hearing or trial.
4. All testimony should be based on the evidence available. No hearsay evidence should be divulged.
5. An affidavit documenting the facts of the case and the evidence needed for a conviction should be drawn up and available in court.
6. On cross-examination, no information should be volunteered. Only direct questions asked should be answered.

The Question of Notoriety

Publicity concerning a certain case, a certain employee or an apprehended customer can be a valuable weapon for the company—or it could backfire. Some chains have gone on tough anti-crime crusades, sending stories to the local news media with names, addresses, even photos of apprehended shoplifters and employees. This may indeed have a deterrent effect. At the same time, a backlash can arise against a company in towns or neighborhoods where a young child or even a well-known adult residing in the community has been arrested by a relatively impersonal, anonymous corporation.

Obviously, if a case is serious enough, and results in a hearing or trial, publicity is almost impossible to avoid—especially in small cities and towns.

It is the smaller cases—where an employee may be fired for

discounting, or a customer nabbed for shoplifting—that require more careful handling. Each instance may have to be decided on its own merits regarding outside publicity, but to enhance the image of a retail loss prevention department, every apprehension and conviction should be communicated to the employees at large, if not by formal company communications, then by the efficient grapevine.

Many retail security professionals have become convinced that a more efficient security operation results from telling employees more, not less, about the functions of security and how it operates. Orientation and updating seminars have already been mentioned in this text. These are important tools because they demonstrate that the security department is knowledgeable and well-organized, while also serving as a deterrent to the potential thief. Security briefings involve each employee with the loss prevention function of the company. This added dimension can enhance the importance and responsibilities of employees, and make them feel their basic honesty and intelligence are valued.

SUMMARY

The apprehension, interviewing and disposition of suspected employees and customers of a retail business must be conducted with caution and adherence to the variety of laws operative in each state and municipality. False arrest can become a real problem for a company which is not careful to preserve the civil liberties of all individuals.

Despite the differences in legalities, a good deal of this "payoff" portion of loss prevention in the retail business is governed by common sense. Accusations cannot be made haphazardly; the existence of definite, factual evidence and eyewitness testimony is vital. Company legal personnel, abiding by the applicable state laws, should set guidelines for apprehensions.

Frequently, in retail business, security interviews are necessary to uncover instances of employee theft and determine severity of individual instances of shoplifting. The objectives of security interviews may be set forth in this rank-ordered list, starting with the most important objective, and proceeding to the least important from the retail business' standpoint:

1. The guilt or innocence of the individual, with a written admission statement.
2. The method of theft.

3. The timespan during which the thefts occurred.
4. The amount of cash or merchandise involved.
5. Why the crimes were committed.
6. The disposition of the stolen cash or merchandise.
7. Implication of other individuals or employees involved in such thefts.
8. Extent to which any stolen cash or merchandise may be recovered.
9. Details on the suspect's background, mental condition and prior criminal involvement as relative to questions of prosecution and restitution.

In cases which result in court hearings or trials, the retail company representatives should be prepared with the entire facts of the case in fully documented folders, to answer any and all questions with precision. Court cases may preclude the possibility of quiet handling and disposition of retail apprehensions, with each company having to weigh the pros and cons of a general policy of notoriety in all cases. In terms of communicating information about successful apprehensions of customers and employees to the company's employees at large, it may be necessary to develop some kind of information flow, since the company "grapevine" will take over this role if management does not fill it.

NOTES

[1] **Crime in Retailing,** U.S. Department of Commerce, U.S. Government Printing Office, Washington, D.C. 20402, August 1975, p. 13.

5 CHECK CASHING AND CREDIT SYSTEMS

This chapter will describe:

- **Size of check cashing's impact on retail**
- **The seriousness of the bad check and credit card fraud problem**
- **Who is involved in the problem, and how they strike**
- **How store policies can help control the problem**
- **Training for proper check and credit card approval**
- **Monitoring services and equipment; home-grown retail systems**

THE MONUMENTAL SIZE OF CHECK CASHING

The check has become the *sine qua non* of the modern capitalistic society. In 1974, it was estimated that more than 90% of all business transactions in the U.S. were by check . . . that half of all adults had checking accounts . . . and that by 1980, there could be as many as 39 billion checks used. Also in 1974, the American Bankers Association estimated that 75% of all checks were cashed in retail stores, the majority of these in supermarkets. The retail grocery industry, in fact, is the biggest source of check cashing in the country. The scope of supermarket check cashing has been directly responsible for the growth of in-store bank branches as well as electronic funds transfer. The development of in-store bank branches has appeal because it can obviate the need for the store to utilize armored car services and reduce certain crime insurance premiums while providing a financial resource for handling the on-site check cashing volume.

In electronic funds transfer (EFT), workers can have deposits made automatically to a participating bank. In some retail businesses wired into EFT programs, customers with their own identification cards can transfer funds from one account to another—or get cash—by inserting the card in special machines and "programming" instructions to the terminal or automatic teller machine. In retail stores, special point-of-sale systems wired into registers may have an EFT capability in addition to pricing information and scanning capabilities. EFT systems can also allow customers to have their checks verified and guaranteed at the checkout, with the point-of-sale system "communicating" with the customer's bank via computer.

The desirability or efficacy of either in-store branch or electronic funds transfer is not really an issue. What is critical is the cost justification to go with either alternative, and also consumer acceptance or rejection, especially regarding electronic funds transfer. Then, too, there is the privacy issue. Government regulations and state banking laws are certain to play a vital role at least in the planning stages of electronic funds transfer. In 1974, a National Commission on EFT was established to investigate the entire topic and recommend appropriate action and legislation regarding competition and discrimination among financial institutions and businesses involved. The commission was also established to investigate individual rights as related to EFT.

It is far too early at this point in time to predict the phaseout of check cashing in favor of electronic funds transfer, the so-called "Checkless-Cashless" society trumpeted by futurists in the mid-1960's. Right now, retailers use check-cashing privileges in part as a merchandising tool and some will probably admit that they accept the risk of getting stung with some bad checks rather than lose sales. There is also the "float" value of checks that would be lost to customers via EFT. Many customers will pay for groceries by check after banking hours, intending to deposit money to cover the check the next day. With EFT, this would be impossible.

Today, check-cashing privileges are a must in the modern high-volume retail store. The annual Burgoyne Survey (National Study of Supermarket Shoppers), which includes questions on check cashing, finds that more than 41% of shoppers surveyed feel that check cashing is a valuable service which would definitely influence their choice of where to shop.[1]

The extent of check cashing in supermarkets was revealed by a *Progressive Grocer* study.[2] In the study, it was estimated that supermarkets were cashing a total of more than $1.1 billion in checks every week and that the average store cashed checks amounting to 127% of total sales. In other words, a store was extending collective short-term loans beyond its earning capacity, at the same time it was suffering an average of 10½ checks returned from the bank each week. Of these returned checks, stores in the survey were able to ultimately collect 65% of the funds, leaving 35% of the checks, plus all handling, processing and collection costs, as a source of profit loss. A recent estimate put the supermarket loss due to bad checks at $650 million, with *total* business loss due to bad checks at $1.72 billion. The fact that supermarkets are in an extended position in terms of the size of their receipts vs. the total face value of checks cashed is not surprising: There is reportedly nine times as much buying power in checking accounts than there is in the amount of cash in circulation. To readily appreciate the problem from the standpoint of the individual retail company or store, almost all operations cashing checks allow for some overage beyond the size of the purchase. How big the allowance will be is a critical policy decision for each chain.

With the Food Marketing Institute[3] reporting that retailers handle about 1,700 checks per store in an average week, with 7%-11% of those checks bouncing back for one reason or another, the problem is even more dramatic. And, as with anything handled in a business enterprise, there is a cost factor involved even for legitimate checks.

The same FMI study indicated that retailers pay nearly 26¢ for every check handled per week, or nearly $23,000 per year at the 1,700-checks-per-week level. This handling figure includes a 3.4¢ charge for bad checks ultimately written off, 1.8¢ for check collection fees, 5.2¢ cost for collectible bad checks, and store labor and other internal charges of 12.8¢ per check. According to the study, courtesy card and check authorization control systems represent 6% of the cost of check acceptance. Check handling costs account for 68% of the total—with in-store labor/approval representing 29% of handling costs, in-store labor for check payment representing 20%, and processing and deposit adding another 19% to the total. The cost of bad checks represents 32% of total check handling costs—11% for value of checks written off, 13% for collection costs of bad checks recouped, 2% for bank fees and 6% for float.

Additional studies indicate that bad checks are showing increases of 40% in areas across the country. This increase is partly due to the credit-card crunch that was part of the Federal Reserve's mid-1980 anti-inflation strategy. One check verification service reported that calls from merchants served increased 15% in one month alone, with overall check volume up 20% during the same period. If increases like this are sustained, it would indicate a reduction in the use of credit cards and a switch to cash and checks.

What's the Answer to the Problem?

A simplistic answer to the problem of check cashing is to eliminate all check cashing privileges. However, this would punish a vast majority of good customers for the sins of a relative few; it could cost each store untold dollars of lost sales from good customers who expect their supermarkets and other frequently-shopped retail businesses to grant them the courtesy of trust. The pat answer also runs up against a series of factors relating to bad checks that simply do not apply to other forms of crime. These factors may add a dimension of understanding as to why the problem of check handling in general is so immense. Consider these points:

1. When a check is returned to a store by a bank, does it indicate a crime on the part of the maker, or mere forgetfulness? Many returned checks for insufficient funds cannot be immediately tagged as deliberate bad checks vs. innocent mistakes.
2. A check cashed in a retail business like a supermarket normally includes payment for merchandise—often a large order.
3. In many cases, check cashing policies set by the store are either themselves lax, or if strict, not strictly enforced. The majority of check cashing customers who offer the retailer perfectly valid, negotiable instruments, will lull any store into a false sense of confidence.
4. State regulations concerning bad checks frequently favor the maker of the check. Even if convicted, a bad check passer's sentence is often suspended, and the problem of collecting the value of the check, depending on the individual State's law, may ride on the shoulders of the store operator. The problems involved in bad check regulation and prosecution will be treated in more detail later in this chapter.
5. A bad check is not revealed for several days, giving the passer precious time to either repeat the crime or leave the area. The store operator does not know a crime is taking place when a bad check is approved in the store.
6. Time works against the retail operation in another way: The normal and understandable reaction of a cashier, manager or anyone responsible for approving checks in a crowded store with long lines is reduced vigilance. Unlike the robber, burglar or shoplifter who may crave privacy, the bad check passer likes nothing better than a jammed, busy Saturday morning in a supermarket when everyone is in a hurry.

Can Blame Be Placed for the Bad Check Problem?

Retailers for years have argued that banks are in part responsible for the size of the bad check problem, by allowing people to easily open accounts with a minimum cash deposit. Banks in turn argue that a portion of bad checks have nothing to do with the banks themselves since they are forgeries, stolen checks or drawn on accounts long since closed. The nub of the problem is put quite nicely in a film produced by the Highway Safety Foundation entitled "The Paper Hangers": Before the customer arrives at the checkout, he or she is the buyer, the proverbial boss, and the store must serve the customer's wishes. But if the customer presents a check to the cashier, the store now becomes the customer, and must consider whether or not to "buy" the check. Banks could weed out chronic "insufficient funds" check writers, or impose higher limits on checking account balances but at the point of decision, it is up to the store manager or delegated cashier to accept or reject the check. An unwarranted rejection may lose the sale, or worse, the customer.

Loophole-Filled Bad Check Laws

As noted above, the bad check laws on the books are a state-by-state proposition, with many laws apparently short-sighted in terms of protecting merchants against bad check passers. That is why any retailer's program regarding the handling, acceptance and processing of checks should be written with an understanding of the appropriate state's law regarding bad checks.

Most states agree that one of two principles, and most often both, are required to prove that a bad check violation has been committed on a premeditated basis. One is an *intent to defraud* the merchant on the part of the maker or passer of the check. The second is *knowledge* of insufficient funds, of a closed account, etc., on the part of the check maker or check passer. These principles are designed to protect a customer who has made an honest mistake and overdrawn his/her account or unknowingly used a bad check.

Most states determine premeditation by waiting. That is, to ascertain intent to defraud or knowledge of insufficient funds, no fewer than 26 states have required the merchant and bank to wait a stated length of time following the return of the check from the maker's bank before formally initiating a check violation complaint. During this period, which ranges from two to ten days, the victim is supposed to contact the maker and attempt to have the check made good. If the check passer then promptly pays the check, the matter is legally ended, although a retailer should check this customer very carefully before accepting another check.

If the check passer does not pay or cannot be contacted during the waiting period, the merchant now has *prima facie* evidence of intent to defraud with knowledge of insufficient funds.

States which do not have a waiting period treat the notice from the bank itself as *prima facie* evidence of intent to defraud with knowledge of insufficient funds. This provision has the advantage of speeding the prosecution procedure, thus curtailing the activities of the professional bad check passer.

Regardless of the speed with which bad check passers may be prosecuted, the penalties dispensed in instances of bad check convictions vary widely. Many states use the dollar value of the check as a determinant for the class and severity of the penalty, e.g., misdemeanor or felony/larceny conviction. Knowledgeable bad check passers can choose their states very carefully based upon their awareness of the penalties of being caught in one particular state vs. another.

Finally, convictions for bad check passing do not normally result in collection for the merchant; this must be collected in a separate civil suit. Even worse, some bad check trials result in dismissals, often upon a hurried payment of the check. In some states, the defendant now has the right to sue the store or its agent for false arrest, defamation of character and a long list of personal recriminations. In some states, the retailer is protected from this by a stipulation that no damages/liability can be imposed upon a store providing it notifies the check maker by registered mail that the check has been refused by a bank, and a specified number of days have elapsed without payment being made.

A number of states may hold a retailer liable for accrued court costs if a case is dismissed at the retailer's request; this provision often deters merchants from prosecuting.

THE BASIC TYPES OF BAD CHECKS

There are seven major types of bad checks:

1. Non-sufficient funds or insufficient funds (NSF) checks are those cashed by a customer with proper identification, but later returned by the bank without payment because there are insufficient funds in the account on which the checks are drawn. This is the most common reason for checks being returned by a bank, as mentioned by 75% of

respondents to a *Progressive Grocer*[4] retailer survey on check cashing. Often, such checks are simply a matter of poor customer bookkeeping or confusion over the assumed balance. This especially happens when the checking account is a joint account and two parties might be writing checks simultaneously. In many other cases, customers overplay the "float" value of writing checks—utilizing the clearing and processing time for checks to invest or use that money in other ways.

2. No-such-account (NSA) checks are those drawn upon accounts which either never existed, or have been closed. Such checks are usually written with outright fraud in mind, although many states include NSA with NSF checks under a more general "Deceptive Practices Act" umbrella. Fifteen percent of the *Progressive Grocer* survey respondents mention NSA checks as a serious problem. Both NSA and NSF checks are the hardest to detect and prevent initially because in both instances, the checks appear good and are backed by proper identification.
3. Incorrectly written checks, containing one or more errors or mistakes: A "stale" date (more than six months old), or postdate (dated after actual time of writing, and, if accepted, tantamount to a short-term loan), an amount in figures that does not agree with the amount in writing, etc. Such incorrectly written checks are mentioned by 25% of retailers responding to the *Progressive Grocer* survey.
4. Deliberately altered third party checks—generally payroll, social security or cashier's checks with either the amount payable altered to make a higher sum, or the payee's name altered to match the check passer.
5. Stolen checks with forged endorsements on otherwise valid documents—are mentioned by 10% of retailers in the survey.
6. Fictitious checks—forgeries or phony checks drawn on fictitious banks, fictitious companies, etc. Twenty-four percent of the retailers cite this as a key bad check problem. Most states provide for forgeries under a different law than is applicable to NSF and NSA checks. A typical law may define the offense of forgery as having been committed when an individual acting with intent to defraud knowingly "makes or alters any document apparently capable of defrauding another in such manner that it purports to have been made by another or at another time, or with different provision, or by authority of one who did not give such authority," etc.
7. Counterfeit checks, which resemble real checks but are not issued by the bank so named—a form of forgery.

Many state laws hold that if a person merely has possession of a forged check that is "capable of defrauding," then that person could be convicted of forgery. Government checks are most often forged or counterfeited because they have been relatively easy to steal and retailers may cash them without much questioning. In 1974 alone, according to one report, some $7.1 million worth of government checks were stolen and cashed.

Who are the Bad Check Passers?

Including all NSF bad checks in the total makes pinpointing the *typical* bad check passer an impossibility, since the majority of these bad checks will be redeemed, and were not deliberately passed with intent to defraud. All other instances, from no-such-account through forged and counterfeit checks, apply more narrowly to the professional bad check passer. According to one check verification service, the typical bad check "pro" is between the ages of 28 and 35, with the number of women involved increasing twice as fast as men. Amazingly, according to this firm, "about 8% of the people write about 80% of the bad checks."[5] The assumption is that professional "paperhangers" are a small, identifiable group. This, naturally, is a necessary working assumption for the check verification services.

Looking at it in another way, NSA, forged, altered or counterfeit checks are the bad checks seen least frequently, but they entail the most money. Since bad check passers have to prove themselves worthy credit candidates whenever they appear in a retail business and present a check for approval, they are accomplished, consummate showmen. They will observe the premises, the check cashing system, the people responsible for approval—"casing" the store just as a professional robber or burglar would. Accomplished professionals can rarely be spotted by appearance, mannerisms or looks. Amateurs, however, may show signs of nervousness or unusual actions, such as a shopping cart with a strange combination of products just thrown in as a cover. Most loss prevention experts advise being wary, if not downright suspicious, of *anyone* seeking approval of a check in a store.

Basic Policies on Returned Checks

To recap, checks will be returned by a bank with the reason for the rejection clearly stamped or indicated, although the majority of checks are returned for insufficient funds. Many security experts recommend immediately contacting the maker of an insufficient funds check by telephone, informing the party about the returned check, and requesting that they appear at the store to redeem the check on site. Most security people advise not to redeposit such checks although this is standard policy in many businesses.

Redeposits are a courtesy to a presumably honest customer who has made an innocent error, which, in fact, is the case with most NSF checks. The problem with automatic redeposits is that many customers will exploit this policy and gain additional time to float a check on which a retailer could have collected much sooner. Security people may advise that customers with checks coming back NSF be advised that their credit rating could be in jeopardy if restitution is not made promptly and the bad check picked up.

Every retailer must develop a policy and a philosophy for this extension of credit that is comfortable for the company, provides good results in terms of NSF check collection, and does not overly penalize the customer who has made an honest mistake. Each company must decide, as a matter of policy, whether returned checks should be automatically redeposited.

If a check is returned marked "Forged," "No Such Account," "Stolen Check," "Check Altered," "Signature Incorrect," "Forged Signature," etc., police and/or loss prevention departments should be contacted immediately. If photos were taken of the subject cashing the check, these should be developed and forwarded to police. Since such checks have most frequently been passed by professionals, police departments may have records in bunco or confidence squads to match any photos taken on store equipment of known professionals with prior convictions. In any event, regardless of how small the forged or altered check might be, it is good policy to forward complete details to the police so that this method of operation can be incorporated into police files, where the information can be passed to other business people in surrounding areas or adjoining cities and towns. A more thorough examination of special services and retailer cooperative systems will be discussed later in this chapter.

STORE POLICIES TO CONTROL THE BAD CHECK PROBLEM

The retailer has a number of options available to help put a lid on bad checks. A prime technique is a limitation on the value of checks cashed. The majority of stores limit personal checks, some going as far as allowing checks only for the exact amount of the purchase or the next even dollar amount. The majority, however, allow personal checks to be written $20-$50 above the amount of the purchase. Far fewer stores put any limitations on payroll checks, according to the *Progressive Grocer* survey. Only 17% of the retailers who responded limited the size of payroll checks at all, dramatically indicating why so many supermarkets cash checks far in excess of their sales receipts.

Why do supermarkets have the somewhat dubious honor of being "paymaster to the nation"? The reasons are many. First, it is easier to cash a payroll check in a supermarket—often easier than at a bank. Second, in many areas, grocery stores are more convenient to reach than banks, not to mention other possible check cashing sources. There are more grocery stores, many are open late at night, on weekends (a boon to factory workers on late night shifts), and on many holidays. Third, in many cases, food is the first purchase out of a paycheck. Why go through two steps of cashing the check in the bank and then heading for the supermarket when the supermarket will give the service with a smile? Payroll check cashing is the reason why many supermarkets require such a high amount of cash on hand at any given moment. From *Progressive Grocer*'s survey, the average store had about 37% of weekly store sales on hand in the form of cash and 29% of weekly sales in check dollar volume. Daily amounts probably fluctuate and peak only on traditional paydays and heavy sales periods. This also helps make supermarkets juicy plums for more serious forms of crime.

Another form of control available to the retailer is the location within the store for check cashing and approval. In the *Progressive Grocer* survey, 54% of the respondents mentioned the checkouts as the most favored area, with the store office noted by 24%. Next in popularity is the courtesy booth, listed by 10% of the stores, although such booths in many cases are adjuncts to the store office.

Using checkouts as the check cashing area is certainly logical, but it has disadvantages. Check transactions take longer than straight cash exchanges and will hold up a checkout line. Crowded conditions can unconsciously force the cashiers to hurry check transactions, resulting in some checks being passed through without adequate inspection. Finally, some checks will be turned over to the manager from this location, tying up at least a portion of the manager's time with this task.

The split between stores who favor locating check cashing and/or approval areas in one centralized location vs. using each checkout as a mini-approval area is reflected in the mechanical tools and machines

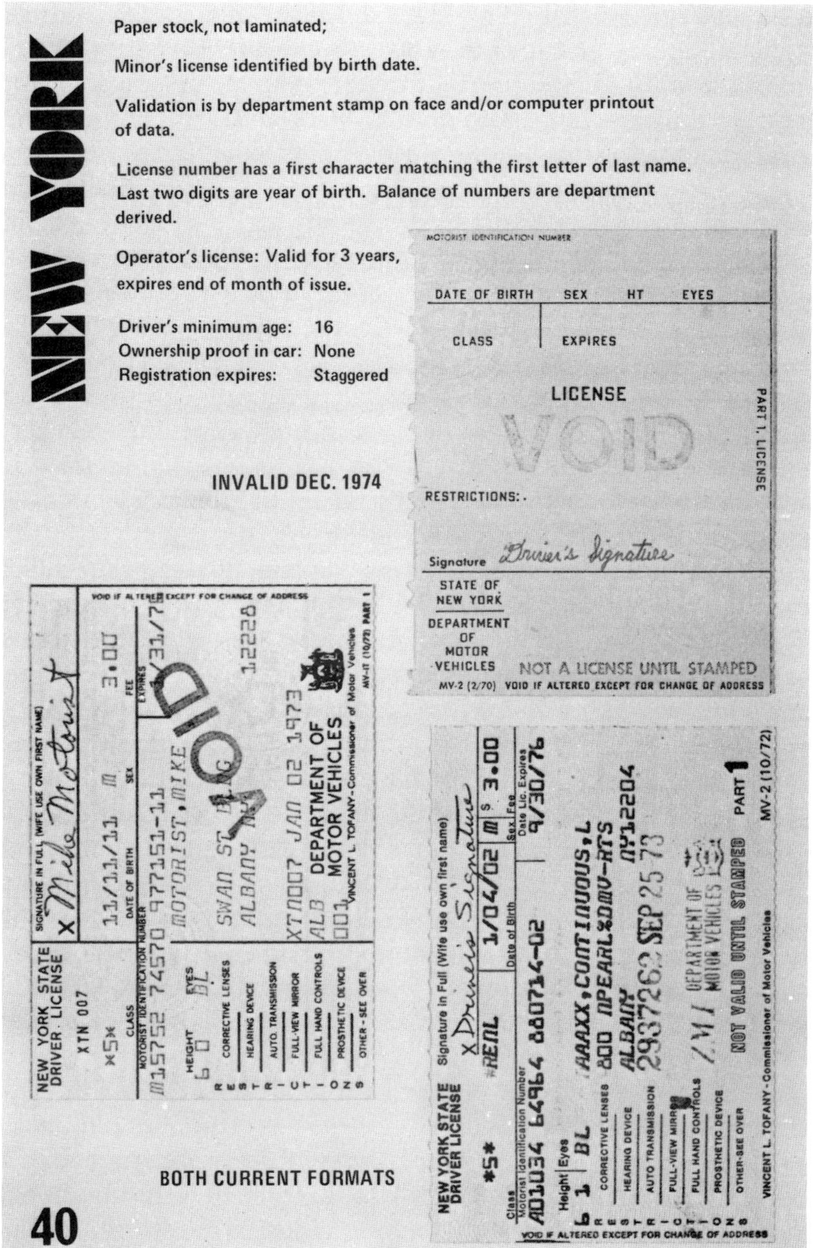

NEW YORK

Paper stock, not laminated;

Minor's license identified by birth date.

Validation is by department stamp on face and/or computer printout of data.

License number has a first character matching the first letter of last name. Last two digits are year of birth. Balance of numbers are department derived.

Operator's license: Valid for 3 years, expires end of month of issue.

Driver's minimum age: 16
Ownership proof in car: None
Registration expires: Staggered

INVALID DEC. 1974

BOTH CURRENT FORMATS

40

Contents of the Drivers License Guide *depict front and rear views of drivers' licenses in all states and Canadian provinces. License plates from each state are also pictured in a separate section. The guide is a valuable reference for ascertaining the validity of the form of identification requested most often in check cashing.*

on the market to assist stores in establishing valid checks. Aids such as photographing machines are too unwieldy and expensive to be located at seven or eight points in the store, and too cumbersome to be employed in conjunction with normal checkout transactions. Computerized credit-checking devices, on the other hand, are geared for use at individual checkstands since they stress, and even invite, check cashing in great volume, along with speedy approval and rejection.

Probably the most effective single policy a retailer can employ to control bad check passing is strict adherence to approved forms of customer identification. Most supermarkets will issue check cashing courtesy cards to customers on request. The application form is usually quite comprehensive, enabling the firm to withhold cards from those with a poor credit rating or history of writing bad checks. In the absence of such a system, the retailer may minimize a bad check problem by controls on acceptable consumer identification. Generally acceptable as proof of identity is the driver's license. In some states, licenses bear photographs, and in all cases, they indicate physical characteristics such as sex, height, and color of hair and eyes on which proper identification can be based. A California-based company, in fact, issues an annual driver's license reference manual, depicting a sample of the driver's license for every state in the U.S. plus all the Canadian provinces, in full color. The guide also includes a similar depiction of the license plates for these states and provinces.

The driver's license is by far the major source of identification of check cashing customers for stores in the *Progressive Grocer* survey, with 89% including the license as the key piece of identification needed. While the license is valuable for all the reasons above and also because it includes the signature of the holder, these documents are easily forged or obtainable from pickpockets who steal wallets, keep the money, and sell the identification and credit cards inside.

Some veteran loss prevention experts insist that the best policy is to require more than one form of identification, but the very best single piece of identification is an electric, gas or utilities bill made to the customer's name and address. A vehicle registration with the license plate number is also excellent identification. In questionable cases, a retailer may discreetly follow a customer presenting a vehicle registration as identification to his or her car, checking to see that the license plate of the car matches that on the registration; the assumption here being that few people, if any, would steal a car to cash a check.

Charge plate and credit cards of local stores—not national bank

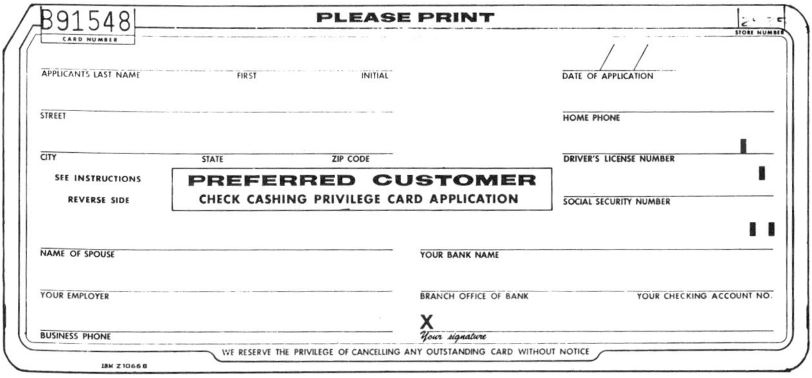

B91548
CARD NUMBER

PLEASE PRINT

STORE NUMBER

APPLICANT'S LAST NAME — FIRST — INITIAL — DATE OF APPLICATION

STREET — HOME PHONE

CITY — STATE — ZIP CODE — DRIVER'S LICENSE NUMBER

SEE INSTRUCTIONS REVERSE SIDE

PREFERRED CUSTOMER
CHECK CASHING PRIVILEGE CARD APPLICATION

SOCIAL SECURITY NUMBER

NAME OF SPOUSE — YOUR BANK NAME

YOUR EMPLOYER — BRANCH OFFICE OF BANK — YOUR CHECKING ACCOUNT NO.

BUSINESS PHONE — X Your signature

WE RESERVE THE PRIVILEGE OF CANCELLING ANY OUTSTANDING CARD WITHOUT NOTICE

IBM Z10668

Prior to issuing check cashing courtesy cards, proper identification is vital. Best is not a driver's license, but a paid bill—preferably a utilities bill.

CONFIDENTIAL

FILMDEX ALERT

SUSPECTED FRAUDULENT CHECK PASSER — NO. 453 — DATE 7-22-74

BE ALERT TO RECOGNIZE THE PERSON IN THIS FILMDEX PHOTOGRAPH

The above Filmdex photograph was taken at a West Hempstead, New York Department Store. Suspect is using fradulent I.D. to pass stolen checks throughout the New York metropolitan area, usually for large amounts.

DESCRIPTION OF THE ABOVE CHECK

DATE: April 17, 1974 AMOUNT: $86.58
MAKER:
BANK: Franklin National Bank

Filmdex represents only that the information stored by it herein is accurate to the best of its knowledge and belief. Filmdex assumes no liability or responsibility for use of this bulletin beyond that authorized by Filmdex. This bulletin is intended for use by Filmdex customers and government authorities only, and should not be reproduced without written permission from the Filmdex Corporation.

PLEASE NOTIFY THE FILMDEX CORPORATION WHEN THIS PERSON IS APPREHENDED.

P.O. BOX 490, CENTREVILLE, VA. 22020, PHONE 631-0600, AREA CODE 703

THE FILMDEX CORP.

P.O. BOX 156, COLLINGSWOOD, N.J. 08108, PHONE 854-6553, AREA CODE 609

SUSPECTED FRAUDULENT CHECK PASSER — NO. 453 — DATE 7-22-74

Special services circulate "alert" sheets to assist retailers in spotting known professional bad check passers.

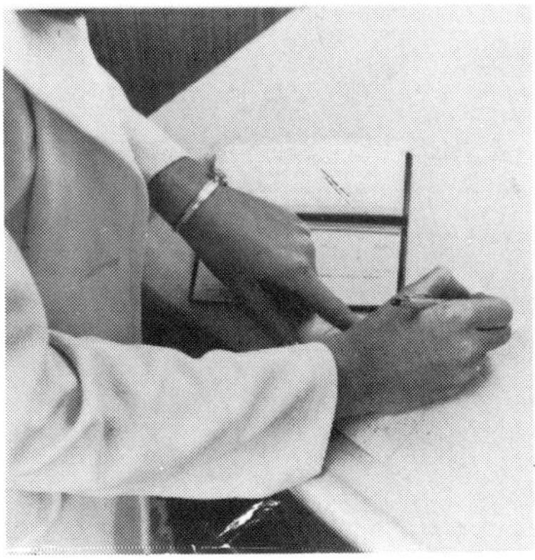

Checks made out to "cash" must be endorsed in the presence of store management.

In-store teletype machines perform many functions—an important one can be alerting all stores to bad check passers known to be operating in the area.

credit cards—can also be used to identify check cashers if the cards have been signed by the bearer. Such credit cards, too, have been issued only after investigation of the applicant. Employee identification cards or building passes with the owner's photograph may also be acceptable identification.

Business cards, bank books, social security cards, library cards, club membership cards or commercially printed "I.D." cards such as those found in new wallets are not reliable indicators of identity. Social security cards in particular are very poor identifiers since they carry no address, date, description of the holder or photos. Yet, because these are issued by the government, no fewer than 31% of the stores in the *Progressive Grocer* survey report accepting social security cards among the roster of valid identifiers.

The mix of acceptable check cashing identification is variable and under the control of each retail company. The guidelines above suggest that two forms of identification be required even when the store issues its own courtesy cards (these, too, can be forged and do not address the problem of transient customers or first-time check cashers in the store). Regardless of what suitable identification is presented, the cashier or person authorizing or approving the check should compare the photograph and/or signature and physical characteristics with those of the customer—an obvious requirement, but one that is often overlooked. In addition, the name, address and phone number on the check should match that on the I.D.

WHAT CHECK APPROVERS SHOULD LOOK FOR

The following list of procedures can be used by employees involved in check approval and authorization when presented with checks by customers:

1. Identify the Customer.

- Do not accept the following forms of identification:
  - Social security cards
  - Library cards
  - Tax receipts
  - Union membership cards
  - Voter registration
  - Army discharge papers
  - Bankbooks
  - Deposit slips

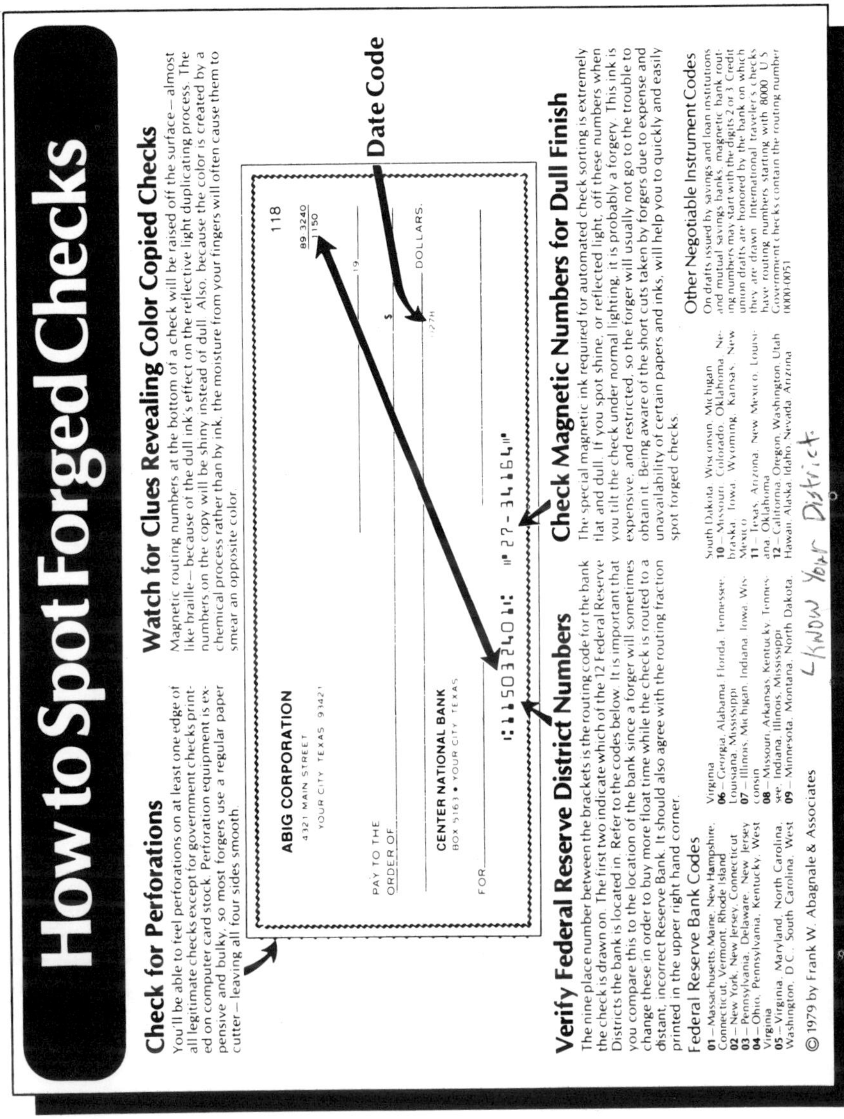

How to Spot Forged Checks

Check for Perforations

You'll be able to feel perforations on at least one edge of all legitimate checks except for government checks printed on computer card stock. Perforation equipment is expensive and bulky, so most forgers use a regular paper cutter—leaving all four sides smooth.

Watch for Clues Revealing Color Copied Checks

Magnetic routing numbers at the bottom of a check will be raised off the surface—almost like braille—because of the dull ink's effect on the reflective light duplicating process. The numbers on the copy will be shiny instead of dull. Also, because the color is created by a chemical process rather than by ink, the moisture from your fingers will often cause them to smear an opposite color.

Verify Federal Reserve District Numbers

The nine place number between the brackets is the routing code for the bank the check is drawn on. The first two indicate which of the 12 Federal Reserve Districts the bank is located in. Refer to the codes below. It is important that you compare this to the location of the bank since a forger will sometimes change these in order to buy more float time while the check is routed to a distant, incorrect Reserve Bank. It should also agree with the routing fraction printed in the upper right hand corner.

Federal Reserve Bank Codes

01—Massachusetts, Maine, New Hampshire, Connecticut, Vermont, Rhode Island
02—New York, New Jersey, Connecticut
03—Pennsylvania, Delaware, New Jersey
04—Ohio, Pennsylvania, Kentucky, West Virginia
05—Virginia, Maryland, North Carolina, Washington, D.C., South Carolina, West Virginia
06—Georgia, Alabama, Florida, Tennessee, Louisiana, Mississippi
07—Illinois, Michigan, Indiana, Iowa, Wisconsin
08—Missouri, Arkansas, Kentucky, Tennessee, Indiana, Illinois, Mississippi
09—Minnesota, Montana, North Dakota, South Dakota, Wisconsin, Michigan
10—Missouri, Colorado, Oklahoma, Nebraska, Iowa, Wyoming, Kansas, New Mexico
11—Texas, Arizona, New Mexico, Louisiana, Oklahoma
12—California, Oregon, Washington, Utah, Hawaii, Alaska, Idaho, Nevada, Arizona

Check Magnetic Numbers for Dull Finish

The special magnetic ink required for automated check sorting is extremely flat and dull. If you spot shine, or reflected light, off these numbers when you tilt the check under normal lighting, it is probably a forgery. This ink is expensive, and restricted, so the forger will usually not go to the trouble to obtain it. Being aware of the short cuts taken by forgers due to expense and unavailability of certain papers and inks, will help you to quickly and easily spot forged checks.

Other Negotiable Instrument Codes

On drafts issued by savings and loan institutions and mutual savings banks, magnetic bank routing numbers may start with the digits 2 or 3. Credit union drafts are honored by the bank on which they are drawn. International traveler's checks have routing numbers starting with 8000. U.S. Government checks contain the routing number 0000-0051.

Special employee/store training materials, such as this "How to Spot Forged Checks" card issued by Frank W. Abagnale & Associates of Houston, TX are valuable in maintaining a strong defense against bad check "paperhangers." This aid concentrates on assuring the genuine nature of magnetic numbers, as well as recognizing the source of Federal Reserve District numbers and spotting bad checks mass-produced on four-color copiers.

Employee I.D. badges without photos
Hunting or fishing licenses
Lodge or fraternity memberships

- Acceptable identification may include:
  Utilities bills
  Driver's license and registration
  Unexpired credit cards of known companies
  Store's own courtesy card
  Employee badges with photos
  Government or active Army I.D. cards
  Bank-issued I.D. cards
- Beware of customers whose identification leaps too quickly to their fingertips when asked for it.
- Beware of cashing a check for reasons of sympathy or in response to hardluck stories.
- Beware of cashing a check for juveniles; they may not be legally responsible.

2. Inspect the Check.

- Inspect the paper: Check the edge of the check for perforation marks; be suspicious if they are not there. Check the back of the check for impression indentations. If the back is smooth, the check may have been counterfeited by photo-offset printing.
- Check magnetic numbers for a dull finish. The special ink required for automated check sorting equipment is flat and dull. If, while inspecting the check, any shine or reflected light is apparent, it is a good possibility that the check is a forgery.
- Verify Federal Reserve district numbers, which appear as the first number of the "denominator" of the bank transit number found in the upper right hand corner of each check. There are 12 Federal Reserve districts, with low number districts (1-6) on the East Coast, numbers 7-11 in the Midwest and Southwest, and District No. 12, in San Francisco, covering the West Coast. Phony checks will be printed so that the bad check passer will negotiate the checks at the furthest point from the Federal Reserve district to which they will be sent, thus gaining maximum time for the professional to move on.
- Inspect the writing: Do not cash checks written in two different inks. Do not cash checks written in pencil. Do not cash checks that show signs of possible erasure or alteration.
- Inspect the address: The address or location of the bank must be

shown on the check. The check must be drawn on a bank, not an individual or a company. Inspect the dating: Checks must always bear a date, but avoid checks more than 15 days old, and do not cash postdated checks, which are, in effect, short-term loans or promissory notes. Do not cash checks that have the legend "Hold" or "To Hold" written on them anywhere.

- Inspect the endorsement or signature: Make sure the check is endorsed or signed. Attempt to have the check endorsed in the presence of the approver. Make sure the check is endorsed exactly as made out in the case of two-party checks. If the signature is illegible and the name is not printed elsewhere on the check, put the name and address of the maker clearly on the check before cashing. Avoid third party checks from customers not frequently seen in the store. Inspect the handwriting to see if the writing and maker's signature are comparable. Use caution in accepting checks if the customer lives far from the store. Use caution in accepting checks much higher than the amount of the purchase.

3. Be Wary of Payroll Checks.

- No check with a company name that is handwritten, rubber-stamped or typed should be cashed. In addition, use caution if payroll checks are made out in even-dollar amounts.
- Do not cash a payroll check if the company is unknown, or the name looks wrong, is misspelled, etc.

4. Be Wary of "Special Types."

- Beware of blank checks. Make sure of the identity of the maker.
- Be cautious of government checks; they are most prone to theft. Know the endorser.
- Do not accept "bank counter" checks; they are not negotiable outside the bank.
- Do not accept insurance or collection drafts.
- Before accepting traveler's checks, compare the signature to the signature on the identification tendered.
- Do not cash checks drawn on foreign banks, and avoid if possible out-of-state and even out-of-town checks, unless the customer is known personally to store management. Clearance takes too long in checks drawn on out-of-town and foreign banks.
- Be wary of "certified" checks or "cashier's checks." Anyone can buy a rubber stamp with the word "certified."

5. Watch the Timing.

- Use caution in accepting checks during non-banking hours, especially before weekends and bank holidays.
- Do not allow personnel who can approve checks to be rushed, despite store traffic or long checkout lines.
- Never hesitate to ask questions.

6. Follow Through.

- Stamp the backs of all checks "for deposit only."
- On a daily basis review check warning lists or blacklists of known or suspected bad check passers.
- Do not hesitate to call on superiors in questionable cases.
- Have the check cashing approver initial the backs of the checks.
- Attempt to separate the food purchase and check cashing into two individual transactions.

Types of Checks

In addition to procedural training, personnel in a retail operation who are responsible for check approvals or cashing should be able to recognize and distinguish between various types of checks. Good loss prevention departments often provide retail locations with "exemplars"—sample checks and credit cards and various types of identifications for use in this training. The first step is a grounding in the basic types of checks that are commonly seen in retail business:

1. **A Personal Check,** written and signed by the individual offering it. This person makes out the check to the company, store name, etc.
2. **A Two-Party or Third-Party Check,** issued by one person to a second person who endorses it so that it may be cashed by a third party. Into this category fall special types such as payroll checks, government checks, etc.
3. **A Payroll Check** is issued to an employee for services performed. Usually the name of the employer is printed on it, it has a number and is signed. In most instances, "payroll" is also printed on the check. The employee's name is printed by a check writing machine, or is typed. Thus purported payroll checks need not be accepted if they are handprinted, rubber stamped, etc.
4. **A Government Check** can be issued by the Federal Government, a State, a county or a local government. Such checks cover salaries, tax refunds, pensions, welfare payments, veterans benefits and

many other payments. As noted earlier in this chapter, government checks, automatically deposited into accounts notwithstanding, represent a major bad check problem since they are often stolen and endorsements forged. In fact, according to the Small Business Administration, in some areas, thievery is so great that some banks refuse to cash Social Security, welfare relief or income tax checks unless they know the customer, or the customer has an account with the bank.

5. **A Blank Check**, sometimes called a "universal check," is no longer acceptable by most banks because of Federal Reserve Board regulations prohibiting standard processing without the encoded characters. These characters, optically readable and printed in magnetic ink, allow machine sorting of checks at the rate of 2,500 per minute, making it easier for banks to handle the 30 billion-plus checks written in the United States each year. Blank checks may still be used, but they require a special collection process on the part of the bank, and therefore may incur a special cost.
6. **A Counter Check** is still used by a few banks and is issued to depositors when they are withdrawing funds from their accounts. Sometimes a store has its own counter checks for the convenience of its customers. A counter check is not negotiable and should be so marked. Local bank practices should be part of employee training regarding check approval, since conditions may vary somewhat from area to area. For example, in some areas, personal printed checks may have the individual's bank account number, together with the identifying numbers of the bank and its Federal Reserve area, all in "MICR" (Magnetic Ink Character Recognition) numbers.
7. **A Traveler's Check** is a check sold with a preprinted amount (usually in round figures) to people who do not want to carry large amounts of cash. The traveler signs the checks at the time of purchase, and should countersign them only in the presence of the person who cashes them.
8. **A Money Order** can be passed as a check. Money orders, however, are normally purchased to send through the mail. Stores should be wary of accepting money orders in face-to-face transactions.

The most important governing principle concerning a check presented is: "If there is the slightest doubt about its validity, don't cash it." No store is under obligation to take anyone's check. Even when an individual presents satisfactory identification, the check need not be accepted. The professional bad check passer, by virtue of his or her "professional" status, is an accomplished salesperson. Professionals usually strike at the end of the business day after the banks have closed, when it is impossible to verify whether or not a check is drawn on a good account. They may also seek a time when employees are busiest. Professionals tend to seek out the least experienced cashier or sales clerk and seem to have an almost uncanny accuracy in picking on the "greenest" member of the staff.

The professional bad check passer, or "paperhanger" in police jargon, often uses checks which are either forged or stolen from large companies. When a burglary occurs in an office of a large company, often blank checks with the company name and account number are also stolen. Frequently, these checks are sold to paperhangers. A book of stolen checks from a large company may be worth many thousands of dollars on the street. This makes payroll check cashing something that requires great caution, since a stolen company check can be forged as an authentic payroll check and can be used to defraud a store of a large sum of money.

In addition to blank checks, professionals obtain forged identification papers, develop a smooth, time-tested cover story, and use all the modern technical devices, such as check money amount writers, to make the checks appear authentic. The sad fact is that retail stores like supermarkets are a key target of the professional, with 30% of all forged checks cashed in these locations.

THE HIGH COST OF COLLECTING ON BAD CHECKS

The contortions a retail store must go through to collect on a bad check are symptomatic of the shaky nature of check cashing. The cost of collecting the average bad check is high, with some sources estimating the cost at about 50¢ for every dollar of bogus check. A Detroit trade group views this number as conservative, reporting that for every $4 of a bad check, it costs $3 to collect. Since an estimated 35% of bad checks prove to be ultimately uncollectible, this procedure approaches the prohibitive cost mark.

Collection costs are high for several reasons. The collection procedure must isolate from the store's body of check cashing customers those who are regular customers but pass insufficient funds checks, and the minute group who entered the store to pass a single bad check, never to return. This isolation procedure must be handled with tact since the vast majority of bad checks are in the insufficient funds category. For this reason, notification by letter has been the favored technique for collection, mentioned by 37% of the respondents to the *Progressive Grocer* survey. Telephone calls often act as supplements or substitutes for the letter. Many retailers today, however, are much more apt to get right on the phone when a check is returned. In such calls (or letters) a time by which repayment must be made should be set. In addition, a written record of the time and date of any phone conversation should be kept. If payment is not made by the agreed date, then the maker may be informed that criminal prosecution is being initiated and proper law enforcement authorities should be contacted. This procedure alone may make the check writer realize the seriousness of the situation, with repayment far more preferable to criminal prosecution.

Redepositing—pushing through an NSF check a second time on the assumption that cash to cover the check will be deposited—is often an automatic procedure on the part of the bank, as noted earlier in this chapter. When the procedure is automatic, the bank will notify the store that the check is being redeposited, allowing the store manager to initiate a letter or phone call to the maker. Letters may also include an official-looking form listing the reasons for the check return, plus extracts from appropriate state laws.

Closed account, stolen and forged checks present less of a problem in terms of office procedures, since there is little chance here of "mistakes" on the part of the makers. Such checks often are turned over immediately to police or collection agencies.

All of these procedures entail costs: office costs of processing within the store itself, charges from the bank and collection agency fees, not to mention the face value of the uncollected check itself. For these reasons, it is not hard to understand why many retailers chalk a stubborn bad check up to an inevitable profit shrinkage.

With bad check losses mounting, it is not hard to understand why a growing number of retailers tack returned check fees right onto the amount of the check. An alternative to returned check charges is an across-the-board fee on any check transaction at the time of acceptance by the store. This is generally considered risky from the standpoint of customer relations. A point in its favor, however, is that unlike returned check charges, which could not cover all the handling costs of the store's bad checks, a fee on every check cashed might allow the store to approach the breakeven point on this facet of loss control. In any event, fees of any type will still have little or no effect on reducing the *incidence* of returned checks.

Because of countless returned checks, many retailers have adopted ever-tightening check acceptance policies. Here are the requirements and caveats one Midwest chain operation put into effect:

1. Only personal checks for the amount of purchase, not to exceed $10.00 over the amount of purchase.
2. Check cashing card must be approved and on file.
3. No payroll checks accepted.
4. No government checks accepted.
5. No two-party checks accepted.
6. No out-of-area checks accepted.
7. No counter checks accepted.
8. No predated or postdated checks accepted.
9. No checks payable to cash accepted.
10. No traveler's checks or money orders cashed.
11. No bonds cashed.
12. $3.00 service charge on checks returned for any reason.
13. 10¢ charge for cashing checks except for employees and for checks in the exact amount of the purchase.

Although normal costs for collecting bad checks range from 40%-50%, as indicated above, charges may be higher when a professional collection agency retained also prosecutes on the company's behalf. This can bring charges up to 60% or more of the face value of the check. These organizations will send dunning letters, will physically go to a residence, and actually make an apprehension of a professional bad check passer when necessary. In collection of insufficient funds checks, these companies generally have a good track record, but the procedure is quite costly. For this reason, most retail companies make an effort, on their own initially, to collect a bad check, by working through the loss prevention department in conjunction with store management. Any checks turned over to a collection agency for further handling should be considered in the uncollectible category, so any recovery the collection agency can effect is tantamount to "found money."

In smaller retail operations, retail personnel should become accustomed to contacting customers on a personal basis regarding returned checks. Trained security personnel at retail chains estimate that about 50% of returned checks can be collected by a single direct phone call, using the tone and weight of the "Loss Prevention Division of XYZ Company" in making the call. Unless full restitution is made immediately, this subtle message tells the customer that police or legal action may subsequently be taken.

EQUIPMENT AND SYSTEMS TO MINIMIZE BAD CHECK LOSSES

Mechanical devices available to supermarket operators and other retailers fall into three general groups:

- **Camera and Fingerprint Systems** Several "countertop" systems are on the market, and all are nearly identical in operation. Essentially, the camera systems utilize dual cameras mounted on stands which can photograph the customer, the check and pertinent identification simultaneously. A number is imprinted on each photographed transaction for filing and retrieval purposes. Film itself is normally supplied by the manufacturer or lessor of the camera system, with each loading, depending on the machine used, yielding between 1,800 and 3,000 transaction photographs. As a result, most stores would require more than one reloading per month. Film used during any given time period is not developed unless a check is returned. At this point, the manufacturer will process the film to identify the check and the maker.

  Deterrence is the major value of these cameras in terms of dealing with the professional paperhanger. The photos can provide all the evidence needed for a bad check conviction. For this reason, many professional bad check passers will avoid stores with this device. The good customer may be offended by what he or she considers a "police-type mug shot" taken in the store, but resistance can be overcome if it is explained that this, like any other verification system, protects the customer as well as the store. Customer protection is realized when a check payable to the individual is stolen, and an attempt is made to cash it through stores using photographic systems. It must be recognized, however, that these systems only work after the fact; they cannot stop the bad check from being passed.

  Another system currently available uses fingerprints—a potential public relations headache for the store.
- **Computer Linkups** These systems, with several available across the country, function as instant credit bureaus for the store, with some installing small memory banks right in the retail location. Retail costs average 2%-4% of the face value of verified checks. Programmed into this electronic card file is the store's complete check-cashing history, customer by customer. Tapes in the computer are updated as necessary by trained store personnel. Each check

cashing customer is issued a card with an identifying number corresponding to a file number in the computer. The final element is a series of data input and output keyboards located at each checkout and wired into the memory bank. The check is presented to the cashier, the cashier pecks out the card number on the keyboard, and one of three lights will flash on the keyboard. A green light indicates immediate approval, a yellow light means a limited amount check is acceptable, and a red light indicates approval is needed by the manager, or no approval. Some programs work directly through sophisticated point-of-sale entry systems at checkouts. Other types of computer systems are based on driver's license numbers, with a centrally-based computer for all subscribers. A check cashing customer presents his/her driver's license at a courtesy booth or to a cashier and a toll-free call is then placed to the computer center. With this system, an attendant feeds the license number into the computer, and a rating of "good," "questionable" or "bad" is reported. The rating call will also indicate a number of critical factors about the license number: whether or not the number is valid, if the license has been reported lost or stolen, if previous checks passed through the computer on the same number, and so on.

- **Check Guarantee System** A check guarantee company becomes the co-maker of the check along with the customer when the check is accepted. Customers are issued identification cards by the company, which could be a bank affiliate or a separate division of the retail operation. When a check is accepted, the information from the card is imprinted on the back of the check. If the bank refuses to pay the check, the check guarantee firm will assume payment for the amount of the check up to a specified limit. Thus, with guaranteed checks, any follow-up to collect on returned checks is the problem of the check guarantee company. Such a system is geared mainly for personal checks, since it imposes a check limit too low for many payroll checks. It also does not encompass all the check cashing customers of a store. New customers, transients or infrequent check cashing customers must be handled separately.

"Homemade" Systems in Stores

Retail stores can gain additional protection from their own file systems on regular check cashing customers, including a running account of each customer's credit status, and by participating in associations that offer police-type services to identify known bad check passers. A mail or telephone advance alert system to warn subscribing members when bad checks surface at any member's store is one such example. Such systems generally work best in areas with a population under 150,000. Independent warning services can be developed, offering subscribers a package program including photos, descriptions, tactics and past records—including signatures—of known bad check passers operating in an area.

Within individual retail locations, enforcement of check cashing rules, periodic retraining of employees, signs posted prominently, and awards for cashiers or check approval personnel for "100%" records are all important in keeping bad check losses to a minimum.

CREDIT CARD FRAUD

A growing number of supermarket chains have extended customers the courtesy of credit card purchases utilizing bank credit card plans. With this courtesy supermarkets join department stores, discount stores and drug chains, most of whom have always offered credit card purchase convenience to customers. Banks operating these plans have reduced their losses by more carefully screening applicants, a procedure also used by large retail firms operating their own plans.

Credit card fraud can result from the following illegal uses:

1. Use of a credit card without the cardholder's consent.
2. Use of a revoked or cancelled credit card.
3. Knowing use of a counterfeit or altered card.
4. Use of an expired credit card.
5. Use of an illegally-obtained card to negotiate a check.
6. Theft of a card from a cardholder with intent to defraud.
7. Sale of an illegally obtained credit card.

Whether the fraud is perpetrated by casual amateurs or hardened criminals, credit card misuse involves fraudulent use in purchasing retail goods, leaving the retailer and credit card company holding the bill. Retail merchants can prevent many credit card losses by checking "stolen or revoked" card lists each time a credit purchase is made, or using electronic point-of-sale terminals similar to those used in approving checks. The printed lists are sent out weekly by each of the major credit card issuers; point-of-sale terminals are always on-line, and reflect changes in terms of entry of new, stolen and revoked cards immediately.

One of the best ways to minimize loss from fraudulent credit card transactions is to require a second form of identification to be shown. Another good policy is to refuse to honor altered or mutilated credit cards.

Credit cards of retail stores are less desirable to pickpockets who steal to resell credit cards and other identification illegally. Multiple-use credit cards, such as those issued by American Express, Diner's Club, Carte Blanche, and bank cards are those most in demand. A retailer's own credit cards require preliminary questionnaires to ascertain for all applicants where they live and for what length of time, whether the residence is a private home, apartment, condominium, with whom they live, employment data, bank and bank account data, and salary or family income information.

In checks and credit cards, "training" is the magic word. Training must come from loss prevention people or management personnel who can impart both knowledge of proper techniques in handling checks and credit cards, while supervising employees until these techniques become an ingrained part of their work habits. Since the acceptance of a check or credit card is purely voluntary on the part of the retail operation, the extent of that company's bad check loss is ultimately a mirror-reflection of the strength of training and enforcement of proper company procedures.

SUMMARY

With more than 90% of all business transactions in the U.S. made by check and with 75% of all checks cashed in retail stores, the conditions for a major cause of retail loss are clear. The growth of in-store branch banking and electronic funds transfer, while perhaps the harbingers of a new form of cashless/checkless business transaction, are both still limited in scope. Bad checks and professional forgeries remain a critical retail security problem. In fact, some studies indicate bad checks are increasing as much as 40% in some areas.

A key to the bad check problem is the lack of enforcement of tough in-store procedures. States with weak laws regarding bad checks and the time needed to reveal a bad check represent a few additional factors. Unlike other forms of retail crime, bad checks occur through the voluntary acceptance of a worthless instrument by the retailer; it is a crime of delay rather than stealing or subterfuge.

Most bad checks are of the insufficient funds variety, including deliberate bad checks passed in the store, and honest mistakes by customers.

Stores have a number of options to help control the problem of bad checks. One way is to limit the value of checks cashed. Another form of control is specified locations for check cashing, with only specific personnel authorized to accept checks. Better yet is a dual-identification policy.

People who approve checks should methodically study every check presented for approval. The customer must be identified, the entire check should be inspected from perforations to on-site endorsements. Policies prohibiting acceptance of certain checks should be enforced. Stores may have "exemplars" of various types of checks handy to compare against checks presented by customers.

A tough set of policies will help minimize the cost of bad checks, of which a good portion involves the collection of bad checks. Professional collection agencies may be employed, but on insufficient funds checks, the store should consider a preliminary effort by its own loss prevention division as a first step.

The growth of check cashing has brought with it a number of mechanical systems to help verify or authenticate checks and check passers. Dual-photography setups, computer linkups and check guarantee firms are a few examples. Most stores also develop their own systems, including card files and special telephone or mail alert systems for stores in smaller trading areas.

In supermarkets, credit cards have not gained the prominence they enjoy in other classes of trade, but their use is growing, and with that growth, the expected forms of credit card fraud will appear. Here again, proper identification of customers and tough overall policies on what will be accepted and refused must be maintained. Thus the magic word in bad check and fraudulent credit card control is really "training."

NOTES

[1] **The National Study of Supermarket Shoppers,** 1977 (City Profile), Burgoyne, Inc., p. 28.

[2] "How to Wage War on Bad Checks," **Progressive Grocer,** March 1968, p. 51.

[3] Cited in "FMI Study Estimates Stores Pay 25.9¢ for Every Check Cashed," **Supermarket News,** February 6, 1978, p. 35.

[4] "How to Wage War on Bad Checks," **op. cit.,** p. 51.

[5] "Check Verifying Companies Grow," **The Christian Science Monitor,** February 5, 1976, p. 38.

6 ROBBERY AND BURGLARY

This chapter will describe:

- **The size of the robbery and burglary problem in retail operations**
- **Some of the "why's" of the problem and who is involved**
- **Methods of operation in robbery and burglary**
- **Prevention and detection: procedures, alarm systems, safes**
- **A code of conduct during robberies**
- **Procedures following robberies and burglaries**

HOW BIG IS THE PROBLEM?

So far in this text, the criminal acts described are comparatively small on an individual basis, regardless of the cumulative impact on the financial health of the retail operation. In addition, employee theft and pilferage, shoplifting and passing of bad checks involve no threat of physical harm against store employees and innocent bystanders. Robbery and burglary, in sharp contrast, represent major external crimes against the retail business and may involve bodily endangerment of workers and shoppers in the store environment. Add to this the fact that both robbery and burglary have been growing at astounding rates, and the seriousness of the problem from a retail loss prevention standpoint should be clear.

A person commits a robbery when property is taken from the person or presence of another by the use of force or by threatening the imminent use of force. The offense is armed robbery when it is committed by a person armed with a dangerous weapon—a gun, knife, razor, broken bottle or other hazardous instrument—and is more severely penalized. A person commits a burglary when, without authority, the person enters or remains within a building with intent to commit a felony or theft. Forcible entry may not be a necessary element of burglary in every state: burglary may be established where entry is by use of an unauthorized key, an unlocked window, by stealing or any other unauthorized means.

Robbery is generally considered the fastest growing form of crime in the United States. In 1979, armed robbery was increasing on a par with the inflation rate—about 13%. In the period 1960-1974, according to U.S. Department of Commerce statistics,[1] while robbery increased 207% nationally (an average annual increase was about 15%), in chain stores the increase during the same period was 427%, or a 31% average increase per year. During the same 1960-1974 period, burglary increased 183%, or on the average 13.1% a year. In the retail community, burglary accounts for more than 10,000 instances per week.

Robbery is largely a crime of big cities. These major metropolitan areas have 30 times more robberies than small communities. According to an "Armed Robberies Profile," robbery is a crime of youth—76% are under 25 years of age, and 56% are under 21. Robbery is committed overwhelmingly by men—93% vs. 7% female, and it is skewed heavily to minorities—35% of apprehended robbers are white, 63% are black, 2% other minorities. Consequently, the robber is young, often already has a prison record, may be a resident of the store's trading area, may be allied with a gang, and is generally familiar with lethal weapons.[2]

Robbery is also a crime of speed and ease, and for this reason, small convenience stores and gas stations are heavily victimized. One recent Southland (7-Eleven) survey indicates that the average convenience store chain suffers 25 robberies a year, costing nearly $7,000 in total. Robbers barely need to enter the convenience store or gas station premises to demand all available cash and dart back into a car.

Burglary is less confined to big cities; it occurs anywhere and everywhere with equal probability. As with robbery, burglary is a crime of the young. In a study of those apprehended, 85% were under the age of 25, and 53% were under 18. Burglars tend to work with others, plan their crimes and will almost always follow the same method once it proves successful.

With all of the published statistics from the Department of Commerce and the Federal Bureau of Investigation, the true picture may be even worse. A Presidential Crime Commission report implied that FBI figures on crime may reflect only one-third to one-half of the total. For retail store operators, perhaps the most tangible proof that robbery and burglary continues to rise is the fact that crime insurance is growing more costly and harder to obtain. In some inner city areas, in fact, crime insurance is not much more than a fond memory.

Despite all the increases in robbery and burglary, a disturbingly large percentage of retail operations take only minimum precautions. A *Progressive Grocer* study[3] of supermarket chains determined that:

- 70% of responding companies had burglaries and/or robberies committed within a timespan ranging from 6 months to 5 years.
- 33% reported the crime rate in their companies rising by an average of 124% over a 6-year period, or better than 20% a year.
- Virtually all responding companies were unable to recover lost cash or merchandise except through insurance claims.

The same study also revealed that:

- Only 36% of companies surveyed use alarm systems or other anti-theft devices.
- 13% have an alarm system linked to local police.
- 40% give employees special instruction or training regarding robbery and burglary.

Determining Each Store's Particular Needs

Retail stores may be preoccupied with the steadier but smaller individual loss of profits through employee theft, shoplifting and check and credit card loss. From a cost-efficiency standpoint, there is an issue of relative costs of sophisticated alarm systems vs. typical robbery and burglary losses to resolve. It is, therefore, a management decision as to the degree of protection a given store receives. One security director notes, "A program to reduce losses from burglary and robbery requires analysis from a security point of view as to market locations, layouts, hours of operation, operating procedures (cash handling-banking-receiving, and so on), history of criminal attacks, frequency of patrol by police and adequacy of criminal prosecutions in each jurisdiction." Another loss prevention director adds, "A retail outlet's location and general area will, in most instances, dictate what additional security procedures should be utilized. Such services as shopping center patrols are available in large center locations. Freestanding stores in inner-city districts would normally require additional security. Stores with easy getaway routes for robberies should be considered in a different light. Stores that have had repeated burglaries and robberies should be given serious study for more sophisticated physical security.

There are several additional factors that come into play when a store's security needs are assessed:

1. The store's past record of crime. The crime rate in the surrounding area is no indication of what can happen in the future. The crime

rate, even in once relatively "clean" metropolitan areas, continues to shift and move. In addition, a store, once successfully robbed or burglarized, becomes a well-known target among professional thieves. A study conducted by the Southland Corporation found that 72% of the robberies occurred in 27% of the stores.

2. In a robbery, especially, lives may be at stake.
3. A well thought-out anti-crime system, no matter how costly, is a budgeted expense that can pay real dividends. An uninsured holdup or burglary loss, on the other hand, skims off unreturnable profit dollars. Referring back to the "Theft Make-Up Grid" in Chapter 2, if a store is robbed of $6,000, and operates on a 1% net profit, that store will have to sell an additional $600,000 worth of merchandise to make up the lost profits on the robbery.
4. The intangible benefits of improved security. These include the well-being that employees will feel in a better protected store, and the overall image and reputation of the store at large. A store well guarded against burglary and robbery tends to maintain more of a deterrent posture against any form of crime.

A sound philosophy regarding robbery and burglary could be summarized this way: Even if maximum protection is used, crimes will still take place. A retail business cannot prevent the thief with a gun from entering the store to commit a robbery, nor can the company prevent the burglar from attempting to obtain the store's money or merchandise. The approach should be one of creating conditions which will discourage the robber and burglar from doing so.

Characteristics of Robberies And Burglaries

Like shoplifting, robberies are committed by both amateurs and professionals. Amateurs rob most often on a spur-of-the-moment basis. The amateur does not plan his or her thefts, usually works alone, may well have no police record, is generally successful in committing the robberies, and probably steals to fill a personal need, often to obtain money to buy drugs. The professional carefully plans jobs, often works in a gang, will cautiously use stolen cars or plates, and almost always carries a weapon. Professional robbers find a method successful for them and generally stick with it.

Burglaries by amateurs vs. professionals may be impossible to distinguish. This is what makes burglary a difficult crime to solve. Burglars attempt to work under the cover of darkness, and try to defeat or take advantage of weaknesses in protective devices. Finally, police are generally up against a situation where they have more cases than they can handle, and to investigate each one with the same degree of thoroughness is difficult.

PROTECTION AND DETECTION IN ROBBERIES AND BURGLARIES

While well thought-out security procedures to be followed by store employees are critically important and are covered in detail later in this chapter, an in-store protective network starts with a reliable nighttime and daytime alarm system. The purpose of an alarm system for the store operator is not primarily to catch a thief. In facing reality, any store operator would have to admit to being more interested in protecting his livelihood and securing his property than with criminal justice. An effective alarm system, therefore, first minimizes a loss or deters a criminal attempt. Leading to the arrest of the thief is only secondary.

An alarm system should cover the possible points of entry into a store, including doors, windows, skylights, ceilings, and—especially if the store is of cinderblock construction or adjoins other buildings—the walls. The store safe may need separate, additional protection.

Many advances have occurred in the past two decades resulting in more sophisticated alarm systems, but basically, there are only four types of alarms. To qualify for insurance discounts, any of these alarms must be approved and wired according to the Underwriters' Laboratories manual specifications, and local or municipal requirements.

1. **Bell, Gong or Siren System** This is a simple electric circuit drawing power from a transformer which can be wired to cover one opening or 100 openings. It provides a local noise alarm only. The wires themselves are encased in thin silver and tinfoil stripping, and hook up to the actual alarm-sounding device, housed in a tamper-resistant box. When the circuit is broken, the alarm goes off. Skylights are brought into the system by the use of special screens containing fine wire. Walls and ceilings can be included with the addition of vibration or other sensors that, set for a predetermined amount of tolerance, will open the circuit and trigger the alarm.
2. **Direct Line System** This system starts with the basic bell, gong or siren alarms, and can include an on-the-spot noise alarm, but primarily is connected silently to either a police station or the alarm maintenance company. In large cities, police cannot handle the hundreds of such lines that would require monitoring, but in rural areas, police or sheriff's offices will permit these lines to

terminate at their headquarters. When an entry is made, the broken contact or sensing device in the store triggers a buzzer at the alarm monitoring station, and the store name and location is identified, frequently by coded tapes. If the line does not go directly to police, the alarm maintenance company will notify police through direct lines. This system can be supplemented with extras like telephone dialers that can automatically dial an unlisted number (the store owner or store manager's home, for example) instead of, or in addition to, the alarm to police or maintenance companies.

3. **Central Station Alarm** This alarm is essentially identical to the direct line system with the exception that instead of sounding an alarm at a police location or maintenance company, the alarm is sent to a central station which immediately dispatches an armed guard, who may also have a key, to the premises.
4. **Holdup Alarms** All of the above systems are designed primarily to thwart burglaries, and are in full operation when the store is closed. The systems, however, can be adapted for partial operation during open hours by removing common entry points from the circuit. A holdup alarm cannot stop a robbery attempt but it can summon help. The wiring can be done in conjunction with a nighttime burglary alarm through a control box in the store with night and daytime settings, or it can be wired independently of the night system.

   Unlike burglar alarms, the holdup system does not cover points of entry, but is a direct line to police, alarm companies or central stations. The major difference is that in most cases, the holdup alarm is triggered manually and sends a silent signal to the monitoring station. It is not advisable for a holdup alarm to sound a bell or siren in the store. The armed robber may not bolt and run at the sudden noise; instead, the robber may panic and start shooting.

   The manual triggering devices for holdup alarms range from simple pushbuttons to footrails to pressure-sensitive tapes. They also include remote control units similar to those used on TV sets. These triggering devices can be installed out of sight at checkouts, manager's offices or in stockrooms.

"New Generation" Alarms Offer Better Detection

The current crop of alarm systems will be treated in more detail in a later chapter. It is important to realize that such systems cannot really increase the speed or efficiency of any of the basic alarm systems outlined above. As improvements on burglary alarms, their value is in enhancing the detection of a thief who may elude a simpler system. Collectively termed "space alarms," all must be connected ultimately to one of the basic systems. For supermarkets, the most valuable space alarm is a capacitor unit for safes, but storewide protective space alarms are also available. These systems include:

- **Capacitor Units** Specifically designed to protect safes and vaults, these units create an electrical field around the entire safe (including the sides, rear, top and bottom) that will trigger the alarm when the field is penetrated. The field can be varied to open the circuit when something penetrates it two inches or more from the actual surface of the safe at night, or it can be "tuned down" to trigger the alarm only if the safe itself is actually touched.
- **Ultrasonic and Sonic Detectors** These are radio transmitters that can send radio waves throughout the entire store, or channel the waves to protect a specific area. The devices use high-frequency waves and trigger the alarm when the waves are interrupted by a preset amount of air turbulence, created by movement within the store. The sonic detectors use low-frequency waves which trigger the alarm when an actual noise bounces off the radio waves. The system is preset to avoid chance small noises in the store. An additional application of this system is a set of sensitive microphones in the store that can hook the building up to a monitoring station once the sonic detector sets off an alarm. Monitors can then actually listen to what has caused the alarm to sound.
- **Electric Eye** This device throws an invisible infrared beam which, if broken, can trigger any of the basic alarm systems. Since it acts like a trip wire, the electric eye is limited to open "line of sight" areas such as store fronts. Additions include photoelectric cells wired to cameras that can snap a photo as the beam is broken.
- **Stress Alarms and Radar** Stress alarms are triggered by shifting weights on metal surfaces or floors. Radar units offer a complete circle of protection that can be varied within a radius. An alarm is sounded when anything moves within the area covered.

The costs of even the most modest alarm system is fairly high in today's inflationary economy. The larger the store, the greater the expense. Many national companies, however, will lease equipment and maintain it on a per-store basis for attractive rates. Some even offer a lease arrangement leading to ownership after several years. The much lower per-unit cost of leasing, which still brings the same insurance discounts, merits consideration in security planning.

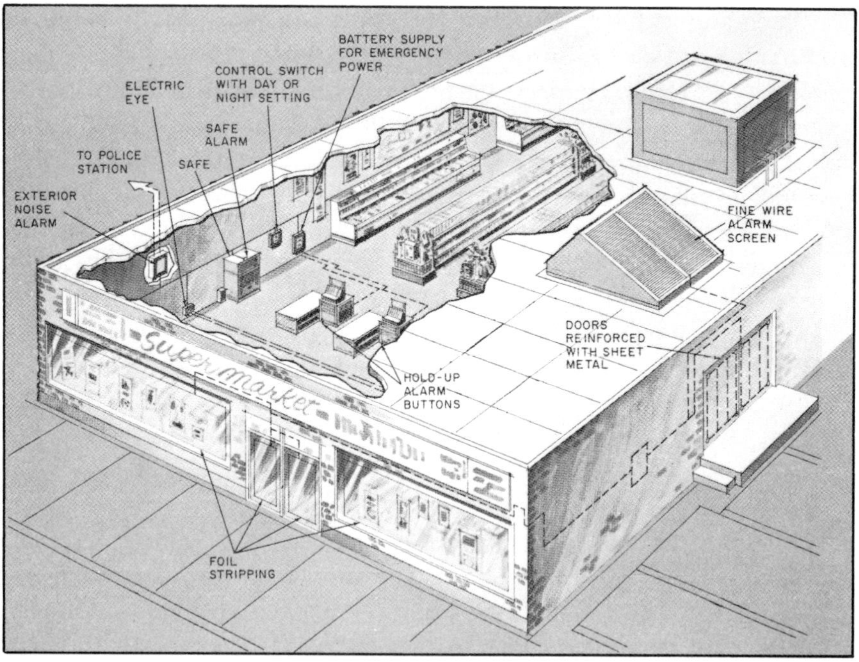

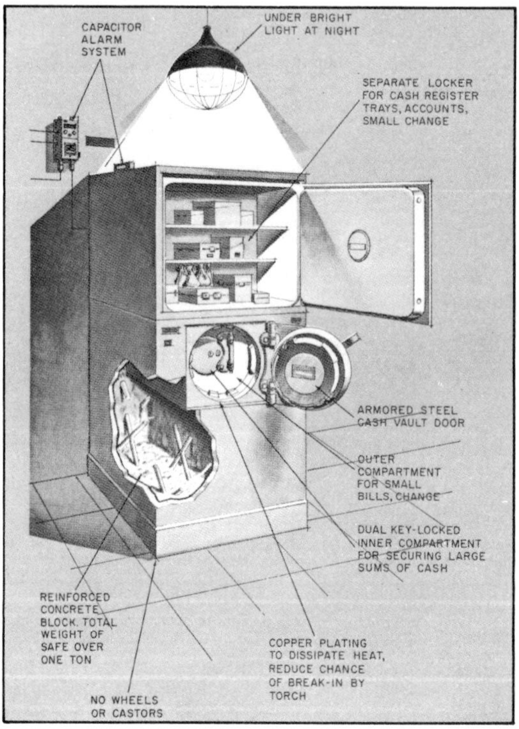

The well-protected supermarket (above) uses a combination of silent and sound alarms equipped with backup battery power for use in the event of power failures. Special alarm systems are employed to protect the store safe. A good safe (left) for retail locations is a dual unit featuring a locker for easier access to cash register drawers and an armored vault for bulk cash storage. Stores should keep safes brightly lit at night and locate them where they are visible from front windows—all to help discourage safecrackers, who crave privacy.

In addition, burglary and holdup alarm systems can often be wired in conjunction with fire alarms, to get the most mileage from the lowest expense. Other integrations of alarm systems include heat sensors in freezer units which will trigger an alarm when the temperature rises by a predetermined amount. Such a system hooked up with a crime alarm could protect a store from spoilage of perishables in the event of a compressor breakdown during the night.

In-store TV cameras, normally proposed for retail stores primarily as a shoplifting deterrent, are finding new applications in deterring and thwarting armed robberies and even burglaries. The cameras, which can optionally be monitored live, run for 24-hours a day, take periodic photos or record on videotape, may use flashing lights and make enough noise while oscillating to focus attention on them.

How Safe is the Safe?

The store safe is the prime target of the burglar and in some cases the armed robber. Yet according to an FBI report, "75% of the presently-owned safes in the U.S. are obsolete. They belong to the horse and buggy era. Built primarily for fire protection, their locks are not made to resist the present-day burglar."

A supermarket doing substantial dollar volume can ill-afford not to invest in a good safe. Of the available safes on the market today, the most secure and most advantageous is a dual safe which weighs at least one ton, includes a separate locker for storage of cash register trays and small change, plus has a bulk-cash armored steel money safe. In fact, the quality of the store safe is often *the* major determinant of the cost of a store's broadform crime insurance coverage. Some safes include bonded copper plates around the money vault opening that will dissipate the heat of an acetylene torch, thereby increasing the time necessary for cutting through the metal.

Some modern safes also offer the double-door money vault as an additional security precaution. With these, the outer door is opened by a combination, allowing access to an outer chamber for storage of change. At the rear of this chamber is a second door secured by two key locks that work in tandem to open the inner vault door, the system used in all bank safe deposit box locks. The manager of the store retains one of the two keys, while the bank messenger or armored car service keeps the second key. This allows access to bulk cash only when both keys are present, and when armed protection is at its maximum in the supermarket.

Modern safes generally have no wheels or castors because their weight obviates the need to have them bolted to the floor. The best safe is not worthwhile if it is not protected by an alarm system, nor installed in plain sight, preferably in view of the front window. Burglars crave privacy, and a money vault hidden in a backroom or manager's office gives them ideal working conditions. The employees of a Texas supermarket some years back reported a safe burglary where the thieves entered the store through the roof, found the safe in a secluded spot, and went to work on it. Shielded from view, the burglars had the entire night to crack the safe. After drilling a hole through the vault and obtaining all the cash they could easily reach, they next poured water into the hole to float any remaining bills up to the level of the hole and into arm's reach.

Armored Car Service Can Pay Off

A high-volume store, especially one in a high crime rate area, should consider the use of armored cars for delivery of cash to the bank. In making pickups, three armed guards are normally used, two of whom enter the store to pick up the cash, while one remains in the truck. The rate charged by the service firm can vary according to several factors: distance from the bank, store location along a normal pickup route, fixed pickup time or fluctuating system, need for return trip from the bank with change, and so on.

A key benefit of armored cars is the reduced possibility of "parking lot" holdups of store personnel detailed to carry cash to the bank. The use of the service is both a psychological relief to store management and employees, while at the same time a deterrent to the armed robber. As with many other security systems, use of armored car services can earn a store an additional insurance premium discount.

Door Locks Shouldn't Be Taken For Granted

Modern supermarkets and other high-volume retail stores, with their aluminum frame/narrow-stile doors, can be broken into without leaving a single visible sign of damage. Locks in themselves cannot qualify for an insurance discount. Without visible damage to a store from a break-in, or a triggered alarm to provide recorded evidence of a break-in, an insurance claim may not be collected.

No door lock is pick-proof or absolutely unopenable. For a high-volume retail store, the door locks should be resistant enough to force a burglar to abandon the job or find a different means of entry. If a lock does not have a deadlatch bolt that projects at least 1″ into the strike hole, it can easily be sprung open without leaving so much as a scratch. This is especially true of aluminum doors, where the metal is flexible enough to give ¾″ with nothing more than two screwdrivers used for leverage.

In addition to a long deadlatch bolt, the cylinder face of the lock may be protected by a bevelled steel guard that prevents a gripping tool from gaining a purchase on the key cylinder and simply unscrewing the entire assembly. The bolt itself is most secure when it has two roll pins—one near the top, one near the bottom—encased within. The pins prevent a hacksaw from cutting completely through the bolt, causing the saw blade to let the roll pins merely roll back and forth under the pressure of the saw rather than get cut through.

Additional security may be gained from a three-point locking system that can operate at the turn of a single key. This setup includes a long-bolt latch plus two rods, one projecting up into the door header, the other down into the threshold. The rods move into place with the turn of the key.

Retail store door locks should require key openings from within *and* without the store, to stall the exit of a burglar who may have hidden in the store until closing.

While time recording locks are aimed at reducing employee theft, they do have a preventive application to burglary, since they force the store manager to lock all the doors at closing and avoid a chance omission. Since such locks work in sequence through overlapping double key arrangements, the front door cannot be locked until every other door has also been secured.

Other protective measures can also be taken by store operators. A night watchman service may be one answer to a store repeatedly victimized. Such guards normally operate with special keyclocks placed in various positions around a store and its backrooms, or at a warehouse location. At a set hour, a special key must be inserted into a keyclock, automatically recording the time. The guard has to make a complete round of inspection in order to hit all the clocks. Such a system may also be wired silently to a central alarm office. Each time the guard inserts a key, the system sends a signal to the central station. If a signal is not made within a certain prearranged time, a different signal is sent, automatically alerting the central station that the night guard could be having a problem.

Retailers may also install bars on side windows, or reinforce infrequently used doors with sheet metal or bars. But it takes people to make the various protective devices jell to form a solid anti-robbery and burglary system. Untrained employees can lead to increased crime losses as surely as a back door carelessly left open at night.

PROCEDURES AND TRAINING TO MINIMIZE ROBBERY AND BURGLARY

Training to minimize robbery and burglary parallels that of employee detection of shoplifting: trained employees learn what to look for and how to be aware. In the case of robbery, employees should notice loiterers, persons parked in a nearby car for long periods of time, vehicles at the premises early in the morning or late in the evening that appear suspicious and have not been seen before.

In order to achieve this level of awareness, the physical condition of the store interior or exterior should be as shipshape as possible, offering robbers, and burglars as well, fewer places to lurk and hide. Constant activity in the store is important since a lack of activity may invite robbers and burglars to strike. Coffee breaks or rest breaks should be carefully scheduled to allow enough employees on the selling floor to maintain the deterrent value of a busy, lively retail environment.

25 Anti-Robbery and Burglary Procedures

Procedures and policies should be set by store management and followed scrupulously since these are both sound business practice and the best way to maintain the integrity of a store's security. Here are a number of such policies, culled from the operating manuals of a number of major food chains:

1. Make sure all employees know the location and operation of burglary alarm settings and holdup alarms.
2. Keep one or more posted lists of several alternative police telephone numbers, central stations, etc. in the store.
3. Establish and rehearse set opening and closing routines. Commit such routines to "countdown" style checklists.
4. Do not leave the task of opening and closing to one person. One major chain's loss prevention director notes: "It is our policy that a manager must never open or close the store alone, and that an employee be posted a safe distance from the store to observe the

opening and closing. Further, this employee should have a dime handy to phone the police in the event our people are accosted."

5. Coordinate store opening and closing with passing police patrols as much as is practicable. Notify police also when bank drops may be made to obtain additional protection via police patrolling the route during these times. Make bank trips as often as necessary to keep excess money out of the store.
6. Make a search of each store when opening and closing to assure that no one is hiding on the premises.
7. Keep all doors except main entrances locked whenever they are not in use.
8. Record some cash serial numbers when making deposits.
9. Keep the store well-lit at all times, even after closing. Consider leaving some lights on in the parking lot, energy crisis notwithstanding, along with lights over loading docks and platforms. Store safes should be situated under a good night light as well.
10. Test alarm systems several hours before closing by using a prearranged signal with the police or alarm maintenance service. This verifies that the store alarm system is in good working order.
11. Do not leave alarm-wired doors open in wet weather; this can give foil contacts the opportunity to corrode. Similarly, do not allow stiff brushes to be used in washing down wired windows or doors. The brushes can peel away the contacts and render the alarm system useless.
12. Keep empty safes and cash registers obviously open and/or unlocked overnight.
13. Limit knowledge of the safe combination to no more than two people, and change the combination often, perhaps even monthly. Never write down the combination to a safe anywhere in the store.
14. Never allow safe doors to be kicked closed or slammed shut; if bolts are in open or locked positions, they may be damaged.
15. Secure excess stock of vulnerables such as tobacco and liquor products in locked storage rooms overnight.
16. Do not admit customers into the store after closing hours. Talk to them only through the door.
17. Use the store's public address system and a code to alert other employees when late-hour loiterers or other suspicious persons are spotted.
18. Keep store cash at the minimum necessary for conducting business, and do not let cash accumulate in register trays over a given

amount. Set a cutoff figure and make sure that all cash over this is deposited in the safe.

19. Consider the use of small strongboxes or "drop boxes" located under each checkout to temporarily store money not needed for register transactions.
20. Lock all registers when not in use.
21. Instruct checkers never to turn their backs on an open register.
22. Never count cash register tallies in front of customers or discuss store money procedures in front of customers.
23. Time trips to a bank randomly so that a pattern cannot be established.
24. Consider a split deposit system for bank trips. A large northwestern food chain handles it this way: All checks are placed in clear plastic bags, while cash and coins are placed in a regular deposit bag. A robber could then have the option of taking the checks. Many will not, fearing they may be caught with the checks in their possession.
25. Move signs and displays as necessary to allow a clear view inside the store.

What Can Preventive Measures Do?

Can these procedures have an effect? The answer would seem to be that following proper procedures a company selects as the right "mix" in terms of its particular locations, type of operation, and so on can be effective.

In 1974, the Southland Corporation, operator of the 7-Eleven convenience store chain, cooperated with the Western Behavioral Sciences Institute in performing an experiment to test robbery deterrence techniques in convenience stores.

The premise behind the study was that robbers are very selective in choosing their targets, something that Southland had already concluded, as mentioned earlier in this chapter. Drawing on the experience of reformed robbers, behavioral scientists drew up a list of simple measures that would increase the risk and decrease potential profits for a robber choosing a target store. The gist of the program comprised these steps:

- **Keeping minimum cash on hand,** using a conspicuous drop safe, depositing large bills immediately, making bank deposits as frequently as needed.
- **Maximizing visibility,** leaving windows clear to give passing patrol

cars a good view of events inside the store, and allowing store employees to spot anything suspicious outside.

- **Keeping employees on guard,** reporting suspicious activity prior to trouble developing, welcoming each customer with a smile and a face-to-face greeting, maintaining good working relationships with local law enforcement officers, keeping stores clean, uncluttered and well-stocked.

In addition to these three basic areas, individual Southland stores complemented the training necessary to achieve the basics with such commercially available systems and devices as drop safes, delayed action time locks, silent holdup alarms, and special money clips in registers which set off alarms and start cameras operating.

Two groups of 60 stores were selected as typical of other stores in the 7-Eleven operation. One group implemented the WBSI robbery prevention techniques while the other group maintained normal Southland security programs, and was thus used for control purposes. During the seven month test, the two groups of stores were robbed a total of 97 times. While the control stores were robbed 57 times, the experimental stores had only 40 robberies, a 30% difference which implies the merits of strong anti-robbery measures. Southland is also well-known for its policy of hiring former convicted felons as advisors in the design and direction of the company's security programs. In fact, former prisoners were instrumental in the creation of the WBSI program detailed above.

In a *Wall Street Journal*[4] article, Southland executives said, "We've hired psychiatrists and psychologists in the past to tell us how to cut crime at our stores, but nothing seemed to work. These ex-robbers have given us a new insight into the problem. . . . they've given the company 'credibility' in efforts to persuade store operators to make changes to reduce robberies." The former prisoners assessed 7-Eleven stores as if they were going to rob them, rating the stores as attractive or unattractive to potential robbers.

Despite the insights gained in hiring ex-cons, such a program can produce a number of problems. As the *Wall Street Journal* article concludes, "Companies need professional guidance in selecting ex-cons. And it takes a great deal of sensitivity to work with them. They are generally loners who don't trust people."

Special measures taken by the Safeway Stores Division in the District of Columbia resulted in a reduction of robberies of stores and bank messengers by a reported 53% over a one-year period. The reduction drive, involving both Safeway management and the Retail

Clerks International Association, involved the use of two-key drop safes, armored car services, installation of holdup alarms and television cameras. Safeway also showed special anti-crime films to all employees.

A CODE OF CONDUCT DURING ROBBERIES

Despite all of the precautions taken by a store, robberies and burglaries will occur. There is no way to absolutely prevent these crimes from being attempted in public places, especially in self-service types of operations or retail businesses with a large cash turnover.

The single most important rule to follow in the event a store is held up by an armed robber is: *cooperate with the robber.* Do not try to become a hero. Use a manual holdup alarm, activated by a silent button or foot pedal only if it will not be obvious, nor endanger any customers or employees.

Most loss prevention experts advise "taking the part of the robber . . . instructing employees and customers to follow the robber and any accomplices, doing exactly what they ask anyone in the store to do." The most important fact to keep in mind is that the person committing the crime may be under the influence of a narcotic or alcohol, and that the least bit of panic may trigger a violent action.

At the same time, employees should attempt to observe the criminals carefully, making mental notes of the number of thieves, their appearance, clothing, voice, nicknames used, personal items, identifying marks, peculiarities and weapons.

Employees who are out of sight when a stickup takes place may have access to a telephone. In such cases, care should be taken to secure the area where the phone is located prior to making a call to the police. In other instances, some employees may notice a holdup in progress from a backroom or a concealed area from which they are able to leave the premises. Judgment must be used as to whether or not the thieves may detect someone leaving the store from the rear to summon help. If there is any doubt, it is preferable to stay put and offer no resistance.

If, during a robbery, employees are ushered into back rooms and warned not to leave the premises for a certain period, they should continue to follow the robbers' demands. At the end of the period, slowly open a rear door or side door in the event that the criminals may be observed in the process of leaving the scene in a vehicle. In this instance, the make and model of the car, color and type, and license plate number should be recorded if possible.

It is standard operating policy for stickup teams to have lookouts or getaway drivers. Police officers are generally taught not to rush into a premises, announce themselves as police officers and tell the robbers to drop their weapons if a holdup is taking place. The first action is to observe the entire scene to see if there is a getaway car or anyone acting as a lookout for the holdup men. Police officers have been shot in the back by these lookouts as they bolted into a store after seeing a robbery in progress. This same element of caution should operate for employees and customers under the gun.

How to Observe Robbers for Later Identification

To help apprehend and successfully prosecute a robber, victims and other witnesses must be able to identify an offender and link him to a criminal act. Remembering the personal characteristics of the robber will aid in later apprehension, identification and conviction. A good checklist would include:

1. Body build (thin, medium or stocky); height and weight.
2. Any readily distinguishable marks, scars, tattoos or deformities.
3. The color and style of the robber's hair, facial characteristics and complexion, presence of a beard or mustache, color of eyes.
4. Type of clothes the robber was wearing.
5. Peculiarities—distinguishable mannerisms, accent, limp or other characteristic.
6. Type, color, size and shape of weapon.
7. Mode and direction of escape—if by car, get a description of the car, its license number, and, when possible, a description of the driver.
8. Type of receptacle the money or goods were placed in, e.g., paper bag, cloth bag.

AFTER-ACTION IN BURGLARIES AND ROBBERIES

Successful prosecution and apprehension in burglary and robbery cases is often the result of proper follow-up procedures when burglaries are discovered or when robberies occur. Training employees to observe sound after-discovery or after-crime procedures is therefore vital.

In the Event of a Burglary

Most burglaries are committed during evening hours or hours when a retail business is closed, and therefore are generally discovered when the store is opened or premises entered at the beginning of the next business day. A good practice to follow is to not touch or disturb anything on the scene when an apparent burglary is revealed, but to call police or local law enforcement agencies. Following these notifications, store or company management and insurance carriers should also be notified. A company's loss prevention department should also be called. It is important that no employees or customers who arrive on the scene disturb anything, especially in an area where fingerprints could be taken.

Stock and inventory should be checked when a burglary is discovered to approach as accurately as possible the total loss. Coupons, food stamps, any checks received but not recorded should all be checked. This may affect the insurance claim, the recovery of the property and the apprehension of the criminals.

A final step for store employees or management to take is to determine how the entry into the store was made. This should be recorded as part of the investigation procedure.

Final reports on missing cash or merchandise should be forwarded to the police department and to the insurance company. Information that may be important in insurance company adjudication or for income tax purposes would include the following items:

1. Date and time of the crime; time police were notified.
2. Name of police or sheriff's officer notified.
3. Police or sheriff's officer investigating the case or on the scene.
4. Apprehending officer, if an apprehension is made.
5. Name of the suspect apprehended and date of apprehension.

In the Event of a Robbery

After a robbery it is important to keep everyone—customers, employees, vendors—at the scene of the crime. At the same time it is also good policy to see that these witnesses do not discuss the crime even though it is normal for people to immediately come together after a traumatic event like a robbery and discuss it at length. The reason for this prohibition is to keep each witness' individual impressions of what happened and who committed the crime as separate as possible, so no one is overridden by a more domineering personality who can force his or her interpretation of the events on the rest of the witnesses.

In addition to the need to keep the witnesses present, the following is a list of proven after-robbery procedures, culled from top retail chains:

1. Close the store or cordon off areas the robber(s) may have touched so police can take fingerprints.
2. Have every witness write down everything that can be remembered about the robbers. Stores should have criminal description sheets available; sample forms are available from police.
3. Ascertain and record exactly what was stolen, while prudently keeping this information confidential from the news media.
4. Refer all questions to police; do not discuss the crime with outsiders until police give permission to do so.
5. Encourage any victimized employees or customers to testify against suspects. Along with the police, store management, loss prevention personnel, and insurance carriers should be notified. Calls to report robberies to the police are an excellent time to provide as many details about the robbers, their procedures, and getaway, as possible. A call to police from a store employee might include this detailed description:

"My store was held up several minutes ago. There were three black men and two white men. One man was carrying a sawed-off shotgun, another had a pistol. I didn't see any weapon in the other men's pockets. They emptied all the registers. They got away with a large sum of money, which they carried in a paper bag. One white male wore a beret, one black male had a beard. They wore dark clothes except for one fellow who had a very loud sports jacket. They got away in a yellow convertible, but I did not see the license plate."

There should be no question of the need for prompt arrest and prosecution where suspects are apprehended following burglaries and robberies. These are major criminal acts, regardless of the emotional, social and economic problems that may have driven the perpetrators to commit the crime. Retail businesses should establish and maintain a good level of rapport with local law enforcement agencies. This policy always pays dividends, of course, and none more so than in the speed and promptness with which a police department handles a major crime against such a business.

Retailers must also take into consideration the effect on public image and customer feelings of risk in stores that have been recently or repeatedly victimized by either robbers and/or burglars. In many

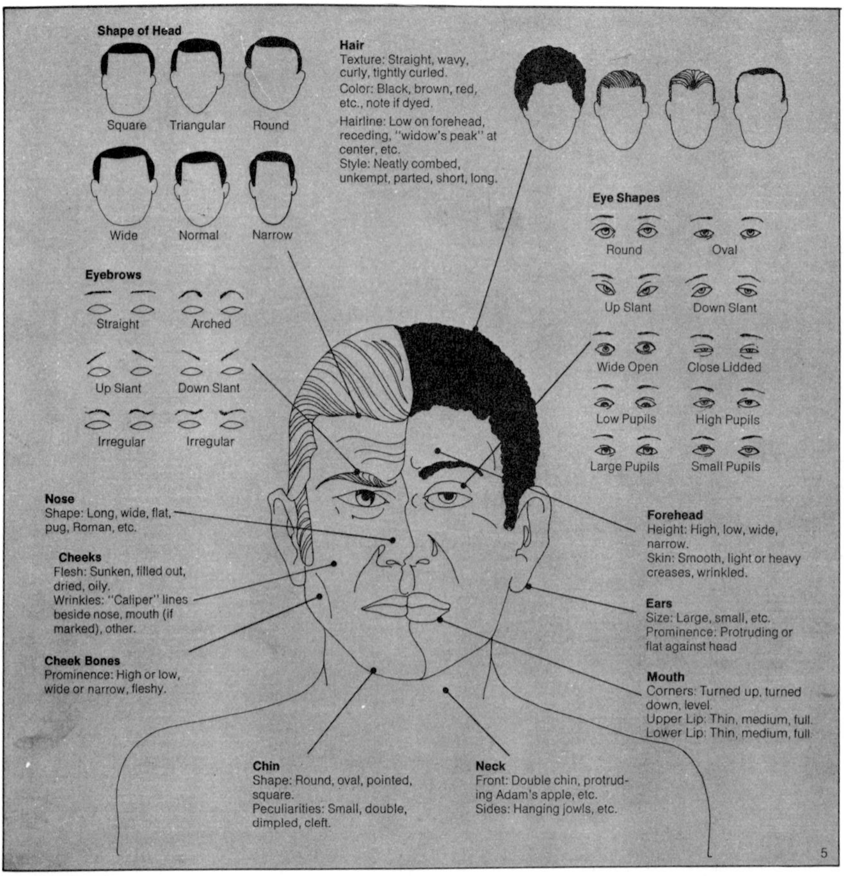

Special description-assistance materials made available to each store can help witnesses to a robbery better identify a suspect. Such materials are also valuable in store or headquarters training sessions designed to teach store employees what to look for and how to observe robbers holding up a store, burglars who may be caught in the act, and even shoplifters pilfering merchandise.

cases, badly-hit stores may not be suffering their high crime rates accidentally. In addition to poor security measures being utilized by the company, current or former employees may be implicated. In fact, one loss prevention director notes, "Our experiences have revealed that many burglaries were performed by employees of the company. . . . Investigations have even shown that owners and managers participated in burglaries."

This security man cites this example: "In investigating a burglary which took place and involved the theft of some $150,000 worth of fur coats, the complainant was so upset and made such a fuss about getting results that half of the local police detective division was placed on this case. During the investigation some evidence was found which linked a former employee to the burglary. After intensive investigation the former worker broke down and gave a complete confession. He was involved with the owner in burglarizing the owner's own store. His job was to take the merchandise and dispose of it, sharing in the proceeds with the owner, who was making an insurance claim at the same time. The case resulted in two former employees, a current employee, and the owner all going to jail."

For reasons such as this, many retailers find it good practice to limit the people who know the money-handling procedures in the store. Further, another good practice is to periodically make changes in the method in which the monies are being handled, or in how a safe is being opened or locked. Combinations of safes should be changed periodically as a routine matter. Should a business lose a manager or assistant manager, all locks should be changed.

SUMMARY

Robbery has been the fastest growing crime in the United States for many years. In 1979, the increase is reported to have matched the inflation rate for that year—13%. Retail burglaries reportedly total more than 10,000 instances per week. Robbery is more a crime of big cities, caused by many of the urban problems. Burglary occurs with equal possibility anywhere and everywhere. Yet the disturbing fact is that many retail companies take little or no measures to protect their stores against robbery and burglary.

Each store's basic needs are different. These needs are determined by local crime rates, the location of the store and past history of all types of crime in the area. Regardless of the sophistication of an anti-robbery and burglary system installed, attempts against the store may still occur. The approach should be one of creating the maximum possible deterrence.

The heart of a store's anti-robbery and burglary program, aside from the proper training of employees, is the daytime and nighttime alarm system, which should cover all possible points of entry into a store. Store safes should have separate alarm systems. Other services, such as armored car pickup of cash, or uniformed security guards and night watchmen, may also be required in high crime areas or badly hit stores.

Training of employees consists of observing proper money handling and store opening-closing procedures, of observing suspicious people in and around the store at any time, and not hesitating to call police or store security when there is any question of possible criminal intent. The other side of employee training involves proper procedures following the discovery of a burglary or the commission of a robbery. If one single rule were to be carved in granite, it would be the preservation of life. Robbers, or burglars surprised in the act, are desperate people. If armed, they may not hesitate to use their weapons. This is no time to gamble with the lives of anyone that may be threatened: Cooperate totally with the criminal's demands; then call police promptly when criminals leave the scene.

NOTES

[1] **Crime in Retailing,** U.S. Department of Commerce, U.S. Government Printing Office, August 1975, pp. 2-3.

[2] "Armed Robberies Profile," **Convenience Store Merchandiser,** December 1975, p. 34.

[3] "How to Protect Your Store Against Robberies and Burglaries," **Progressive Grocer,** January 1968, p. 42.

[4] "Warning: Premises Protected by Cons Who Know the Score," **The Wall Street Journal,** March 9, 1976, p.1.

7 WAREHOUSES AND SHIPPING

This chapter will describe:

- **Dimensions of the warehouse security problem**
- **Types and sources of loss**
- **Security measures for existing installations**
- **Preplanning for security at new installations**
- **"Weak-link" nature of shipping or "transit" theft**
- **Types of "transit" theft**
- **Preventive maintenance to minimize trucking theft**
- **Trucking security procedures—incoming and dispatching**

While virtually everything produced for sale will eventually arrive or depart from a distribution center, most of these facilities are very much the same regardless of type of business. Naturally, warehouses do vary according to the specialized merchandise they are constructed to handle. A frozen foods warehouse, with enormous refrigeration requirements, has different equipment than a warehouse used solely for furs, where perishability is not a factor, but security on this valuable merchandise is extremely critical.

In the sense that warehouses are collection points and switching stations whereby merchandise from several supply/manufacture sources is combined and subsequently sent out to clients of the warehouse, every such operation is fundamentally similar.

HOW SERIOUS IS WAREHOUSE SHRINKAGE?

Losses from warehouses and distribution centers proper are rarely as serious on a *percentage* basis as those from a retail location itself. First, warehouses are not generally open to the public (a trend which the development of "warehouse outlet" stores may reverse) and as a result are spared losses due to customer pilferage, payment by bad checks or stolen credit cards. Additionally, because warehouses with their concentrations of merchandise are far more security conscious than retail locations, robberies and burglaries are probably less frequent, even on a percentage basis. Where the distribution center remains completely vulnerable is in the area of employee theft and collusion between employees, vendors, drivers, salespeople and other outside personnel who deal with the distribution center on a regular basis.

Security experts estimate that overall loss in warehouses ranges from ¾% at a minimum up to 1½% of the gross cost of merchandise handled, although some firms have admitted losses of 3% in warehouse shrinkage. This average band of loss is somewhat lower than for retail stores in general, but when the total value of merchandise that can be stored at any given moment in a 150,000 sq. ft. warehouse is considered, the dollar loss based on ¾-1½% shrinkage can be staggering. The actual extent of distribution center shrinkage is often directly dependent on the caliber and type of security.

In warehouses and distribution centers, the layout and makeup of the physical premises and size of the plant relative to the number of employees, actually enhances the possibility of employee theft. It gives workers the feeling—if not the actuality—of being left totally alone and unsupervised. There are many areas where employees can operate without being watched, where employees have access to more merchandise and more types of merchandise, boxed and packed in regular containers, to a far greater extent than employees in any retail location. It is hard to imagine any employee who can look at 50 or 100 cases of wristwatches and not consider the possibility that the company might not miss one small carton. And it is carton loss, not piece loss, that can make warehouse shrink particularly costly.

TYPES AND SOURCES OF WAREHOUSE LOSS

The major source of warehouse loss is the secreting and removal of merchandise from the premises on a regular basis:

When Employees Leave the Premises This can happen during coffee breaks, lunch hours, leaving work, changing shifts, or other times. Every opportunity an employee has to leave the confines of the warehouse or distribution center provides an opportunity to steal merchandise. Therefore, every employee should pass through an area that is controlled either by security or management of the company at every entrance/exit.

Some of this merchandise loss involves taping small valuables such as jewelry, cosmetics, and drugs to the body, although dresses, furs and even canned goods have been stolen in this way. Often, it is almost impossible to detect merchandise taken in this way unless a complete search is made, and a complete search is generally in violation of civil rights and union regulations. Normally a search cannot take place unless there is positive knowledge that the merchandise is on the person.

Here are just a few of the many other ways employees can remove merchandise:

1. **Thermos jugs** Innocuous and unnoticed, thermos jugs are part of the everyday scene. They can easily go unsuspected; just as easily, they are perfect hiding places for small, expensive items.

2. **Pocketbooks** Handbags should never be allowed in warehouse work areas. Most companies require all handbags to be left in employee locker rooms without exception.

3. **Removal of workclothes** Carrying out bundles of workclothes is also part of the everyday warehouse scene, but this can be a simple way for employees to remove quantities of merchandise concealed in the soft, loose bundles.

4. **Pallets** Merchandise in cases on pallets are like toy building blocks because other cases of merchandise can be slid in between or behind the palletized merchandise. Then, employees can remove the contents of the pilfered cases piecemeal.

5. **Railroad sidings** Growing more common is the use of railroad cars as "mute carriers." Employees will strap or nail cases of merchandise to the underside of railroad cars making shipments to the warehouse. When the cars are moved back on the siding and out of the distribution center premises, employees can follow the car until it is moved into a railroad "drop" area and then recover the stolen merchandise.

6. **Eating of grocery merchandise** This is a form of theft which can grow quite costly, especially when workers develop gourmet tastes and casually consume all sorts of expensive, exotic imported foods. Discovering empty packages in a warehouse is a big red flag that this may be occurring, and the inescapable conclusion is that if employ-

ees are eating some of the food moving through a warehouse, they could also be stealing some of it.

7. **Throwing merchandise over a fence** or perimeter wall around a warehouse is simple and an easily accomplished form of theft unless the layout of the distribution center area makes such theft prohibitive or at least difficult.

Separation Between Shipping and Receiving Areas This shipping/receiving area problem is also found in microcosm in retail store backrooms, and the result can be identical. One loss prevention director describes an example where a vendor shipment of cartons of cigarettes was being made to a warehouse. As soon as the driver backed his truck up to the platform for unloading, he opened the doors of the truck, and took his papers to be processed by receivers. Some warehouse employees immediately went into the truck, removed some cigarettes, and left the truck prior to the driver returning with the signed papers. The warehouse employees immediately started selling the cigarettes to other employees. All of this took place in the space of a minute or so.

What made it so easy was the fact that other merchandise already offloaded from other trucks was also on the loading dock, providing concealment, cover and confusion for employees stealing merchandise from the truck. Naturally, such a setup could and often does work the other way, with the driver quickly grabbing a case of merchandise sitting on the loading dock, and putting it into his truck. This is a prime example of why the distribution center operation must be set up to keep merchandise flowing and moving in one direction all the time.

Collusion Between Warehouse Employees and Drivers and Other Outside Personnel The fact that either a trucker or warehouseman can easily steal merchandise from a warehouse makes the "double hit" of collusion another major cause of distribution center shrinkage. Collusion can exist between guards and warehousemen, guards and vendors, vendors and warehouse workers—any combination of internal and external people. Losses from collusion occur as a result of merchandise that was signed for but never received, merchandise taken from incoming trucks, or merchandise stolen after having been delivered to the warehouse. Outright vendor theft can occur in the absence of collusion with warehouse employees. In one instance, a vendor made a delivery that coincided with a coffee break at the warehouse. The warehouse employees left their posts while on break, and during that time, several pallets of merchandise on the loading dock were placed in the vendor's truck and the truck door closed. When the warehouse employees returned from break, the stolen merchandise was removed from the truck and recounted as newly delivered goods. Since the vendor/driver's delivery tally was accurate, the receivers signed his pass and permitted him to leave the premises. Fortunately, the firm had a policy of searching every trailer or truck leaving the premises, and in searching this trailer, the undelivered or stolen pallet loads of merchandise, amounting to about $12,000, were revealed and recovered. The vendor was arrested, since there was no paperwork to account for the merchandise.

PREVENTIVE MEASURES TO IMPROVE WAREHOUSE SECURITY

The same pre-employment screening many companies use for retail employees can be applied to warehouse employees, drivers, and all of the people in the retail chain or wholesaler's work force. According to the National American Wholesale Grocer's Association, 10% of a company's work force will attempt to steal regardless of the risk, while another 10% will remain honest despite any lack of precautions taken by a company. The remaining 80% will stay honest as long as they are not tempted too much.[1]

The chapter in this text dealing with internal theft discussed at length the systems and professional apparatus retail companies may use in screening and testing employee candidates. In addition to background checks, many companies now utilize a "personnel security inventory" test to try to understand the applicant's basic notions of honesty and responsibility. Background checks may help bring to light instances of a candidate's former chronic absenteeism or lateness on prior jobs, problems with former fellow workers or managers, police records, severe emotional and financial problems, and so on. Many companies continue to help verify information obtained from background checks via use of the polygraph and voice stress analyzers in states where use is permitted. A recent *Time Magazine* article[2] indicated that there are currently about 3,500 polygraph examiners in the country, claiming an accuracy rate of 90% in polygraph examinations. However the article also indicated that the "uneven quality of the (polygraph) operators is an admitted industry problem."

Whatever the battery of testing and screening methods used, all of the money and time spent in the process can be considered an investment in improving the future performance of the organization. As is true in so many areas of life, an up-front investment to help assure the best qualified and best suited personnel for the jobs available is far less costly in the long run than the discovery, dismissal or prosecution of a dishonest employee.

Use of Guard Services

Most retail companies retain uniformed guard services to provide a visible and in-depth ring of security around an entire warehouse or distribution center. The best guard services attempt to instill a real sense of pride and dedication in their own uniformed employees assigned to any location. Here, for example, are the "General Orders" of one West Coast uniformed guard operation:

1. My first responsibility is the protection of life and property surrounding the post or patrol to which I am assigned.
2. I will maintain a neat appearance at all times in keeping with my position of responsibility.
3. I will maintain a military bearing and a courteous attitude at all times while on duty.
4. I recognize that I may be the first person with whom a visitor comes in contact at my client's organization. I will strive to make that first contact pleasant and to be as helpful as possible in line with my assigned duties.
5. I will follow all written and verbal orders given by my supervising officers. I will, daily, review all such orders to prevent misunderstanding.
6. I will pass on to my relief any and all orders pertaining to my post. I will not permit anyone to relieve me who is not "fit for duty." I will notify my immediate supervisor and remain on duty until properly relieved.
7. I will not leave my post without authorized relief under penalty of immediate dismissal and may not perform or engage in personal work or activities while on duty without specific permission of my supervisor.
8. I will not use foul, abusive or blasphemous language at any time regardless of provocation.
9. I will not wear or carry any firearm or other weapon except with special permission of my Area Manager. In addition to my Area Manager's permission, I will comply with all state laws and requirements before wearing any firearm. I will, when required to wear

such a weapon, maintain it in serviceable condition at all times and maintain proficiency in its use.

10. I will report any and all unusual incidents occurring while on duty to my immediate supervisor and make a written report of such incidents no later than the end of my current watch (shift).
11. I may not, under penalty of immediate dismissal, sleep, drink intoxicating beverages, engage in horseplay or fight while on duty or while in uniform.
12. Familiarity or unnecessary conversation with employees or other persons on the premises is prohibited.
13. I will familiarize myself with the functions and operations of any emergency communication system, police and fire hydrants, first-aid facilities and use of fire-fighting equipment. I will know how to reach the police and fire departments.
14. Smoking on duty is prohibited except within the confines of the guardhouse or station when not on fixed post, and then only when not engaged in business. This also applies to eating of lunches or snacks.
15. I will avoid being known as easygoing or careless.
16. I will refrain from conversation, on or off duty, concerning any official or company problem with anyone not authorized to receive the information.
17. I will never issue a statement to a newspaper reporter or any member of the press, radio or television relative to any activities of the company. Such inquiries will be referred to the public relations department or security manager.
18. I will not permit vending, soliciting, collecting contributions for any purpose whatsoever or distribution of handbills on the premises of a client's facility without authority of management.

Such stringent requirements can help produce the best qualified personnel for guard services or plant protection agents. Use of careful screening and testing can yield an outstanding group of store and warehouse employees. Even with the best hiring practices and selection of uniformed services, a retail organization can still face serious theft problems, since it is a combination of people and systems that increase or decrease the security problems of any company.

Certain standard procedures should be followed when, in a review of security, a company's warehouse or distribution center comes up for consideration. There is very little physical change possible in a distribution center short of a major remodel once the facility is in operation.

A security review should encompass the physical layout of the premises, parking, entrances, exits, location of valuable merchandise, receiving dock facilities and procedures, specially protected areas for such items as narcotics or dangerous drugs, firearms, jewelry, furs, tobacco or other valuables.

Access and Pass Systems

A simple security gap occurs when there is the opportunity for visitors to the company to leave in private cars without passing at least a routine security check. This can be remedied by the erection of a fence separating entrances and exits to visitor parking areas. Posting a uniformed guard at the exit to the lot and funneling all traffic past the guard would at least deter some amount of shrinkage loss. If surveillance in such an area cannot be conducted, the feasibility of closed-circuit television should be considered.

If anyone can leave a company without some kind of challenge, it is well worth investigating the desirability of a *pass system* with identification pictures. Passes may be color coded, with each department having its own separate color. Duplicate copies of these badges, filed with loss prevention departments, can be used for checking purposes when necessary. Employees who have resigned or have been terminated should turn in their badges prior to receiving final salary checks. Use of temporary passes or badges extends to drivers and visitors to a corporate location.

Locking systems within a distribution center should be the type where a control key can remove cores of locks on a moment's notice, permitting replacement with new cores. This is a relatively inexpensive way to control keys and locks and also to rotate them periodically according to plan, or have them changed at once should an emergency arise.

Locks should be changed routinely when a member of middle or upper management leaves the company. In sensitive areas where expensive, valuable or dangerous items are warehoused, locks should be rotated when anyone who has access to the keys in that area leaves the company.

In warehouses stocking valuable items, *motion detection devices* and *alarm systems* may be used to minimize the need to separately protect roofs, walls, ceilings or floors. Door contact alarms should be used in conjunction with such systems. This adds a double layer of protection to the highly sophisticated motion alarm system.

Offices in which highly confidential records are maintained should be off-limits to all personnel and protected with alarms during closed hours.

Railroad sidings adjacent to distribution center property should be gated, with keys given to railroad employees when making a "drill," or upon arrival of a car. Railroad engines should get the same checkout as truck cabs each time the vehicle leaves the company premises.

PREPLANNING FOR SECURITY AT NEW INSTALLATIONS

It may be doing a company a disservice to make security considerations paramount in the development of a new warehouse or distribution center. But no opportunity to bring security personnel directly into the planning stage in any new construction should be passed up. A basic recommendation in developing distribution centers from the ground up is for space to be set aside for security department operations at the distribution center site.

Perimeter protection around the distribution center or warehouse should consist of a minimum 10 ft. high fence topped with three strands of barbed wire. The wire on top can be angled facing in toward the complex or out, away from the center. The nature of the business can help determine how the wire faces. Bent in, facing toward the warehouse, the wire will help prevent or deter merchandise from being removed from the warehouse and thrown over the fence. In warehouses stocking grocery products, housewares, and other household goods, the barbed wire is usually turned inward. However, in firms dealing with medicines, narcotics, or expensive jewelry, where a threat from the outside equally as strong as internal theft exists, the barbed wire may be turned out, away from the premises, to deter would-be thieves from climbing over the fence to gain access to the warehouse premises.

A minimum number of openings in the perimeter fence should be allowed. The fewer the gates, the fewer the manhours or number of guards needed to protect those gates. For every gate opening a company has, on a full seven day basis, a total of 168 manhours is needed to provide round-the-clock protection. Limiting the number of gates is critical from a security cost standpoint and also from a relative safety basis.

At each gate, a *guardhouse* should be positioned either in the center or on one side, with a pedestrian walk feature to provide full entry and exit to all trucks and company personnel vehicles, as well as to visitors who may park their cars in a special visitors' parking lot.

Semaphore arms that can be opened with a pushbutton operation

TRAILER - TRACTOR RELEASE

G - 40300

ENTER ABOVE #	GATE NO.
DATE	DESTINATION
TRACTOR	TRAILER
DRIVER NAME	DRIVER NO.
DIVISION	NO. PALLETS
DISPATCHER SIGNATURE	TIME DISPATCHED
SEAL NO'S	
GUARD SIGNATURE	TIME
SPECIAL INFORMATION	

FORM #30-059

Special release form should be used for all vehicles leaving the distribution center.

should be installed to control vehicles going in as well as out. Painted arrows showing entering and exiting directions for trucks should be prominently visible. All personnel vehicles and trucks must go past the guards on duty.

The *parking area* or docks for trucks should be distanced away from the perimeter gate; some veteran security experts insist that 40 ft. is the minimum distance. This provides a kind of "no man's land" sandwiched between parking areas and perimeter fencing to allow visual inspection of the perimeter. Visitor and executive parking should be either off the premises or also at a minimum distance from perimeter fences. A fixed path should be available for visitors and employees to use between the parking lot and the building. Some companies also require employees to sign forms authorizing inspection of their cars while they are located in the company parking lot or within the distribution center enclosure.

All outside areas should be well-lit, both to deter burglaries and minimize employee theft attempts. Lighted areas should include all parking lots, loading and unloading docks, entrances, active storage yards, building exteriors and materials handling areas. Automatic controls should turn lights on according to specified times, or be preset to go on at certain lighting levels.

Closed circuit TV cameras (CCTV) can be installed to cover the entire fenced area, bringing maximum security into play: Guards at the gates, a proper fence, an open area between fences and cars so that unusual occurrences near the fences cannot be concealed, and TV equipment for continuous monitoring of the area. Labor unions have in the past challenged the use of CCTV cameras for these purposes, but National Labor Relations Board arbitrators have constantly ruled that this type of protection does not represent an invasion of privacy or a menace to any unions except in such specific areas as lockers, bathrooms and dressing areas.

In such areas, distribution centers may have to separate the dressing room and locker facilities to improve security control. This can deter some internal theft since employees will be forced to physically carry stolen merchandise with them, rather than conveniently drop merchandise off in their lockers during the day, especially on breaks when they can use the dressing room/locker room facilities.

High-ticket merchandise should be separately caged and wired with alarms in separate fenced areas. Closed circuit TV can be used here to provide continuous monitoring, and consequently act as a deterrent to theft in the protection of such merchandise. This area can include such items as watches, transistor radios, electric shavers and other personal care appliances, tobacco products, drugs and health and beauty aids. In addition to the physical protection, procedures should be arranged so that doors to these areas are kept locked at all times, with logs and records maintained of the authorized personnel entering and leaving the area.

Alarm systems were discussed briefly earlier in this chapter and also in the chapter on robberies and burglaries. A review of current systems now on the market will be presented in a subsequent chapter, but it is important to emphasize their importance in the protection of the warehouse or distribution center, especially those which do not operate around-the-clock. Modern alarm systems give almost immediate notice of an attempted burglary or a robbery in progress when alert employees manually trigger holdup alarms. The new breed of space alarms can also detect fire, smoke or dangerously high or low temperatures anywhere within the premises. These space alarms include ultrasonic transmitters, radio-frequency microwave transmitters, infrared systems and photoelectric beams, vibration sensors and stress sensors.

Each installation needs to be evaluated individually as to the need for and type of alarm systems to be used. The locations to be covered when selecting types of alarms should be considered. Guardhouses, for example, would require more manually triggered devices; remote areas need more automatic equipment.

Additional procedures can also be built into a new distribution center when the facility is still in the planning stage. For example, an operation with many company-owned vehicles might consider special entrances and exits for its own trucks. This reduces waiting time when incoming and outgoing traffic of all types is at a peak. Downtime on company-owned vehicles costs a good deal in time and money, and special entrances/exits, even taking into account the cost of extra guard protection, may be cheaper in the long run. Such decisions are custom-tailored to the company, and are based on the number of vehicles operated by the company and the physical capabilities of the distribution center.

When a company employs its own drivers, color-coded special identification passes or badges should be issued to them as noted earlier in this chapter. Such identification should be produced when they drive into the premises, and even more critically, when they leave the distribution center site. This will minimize the possibility of any unauthorized people leaving the compound without proper identification.

Security personnel or guards should be trained in first aid and emergency fire procedures (see the list of uniformed guard duties earlier in this chapter). Guard houses should not only have direct lines to fire, police and emergency services; they should also be equipped with an adequate supply of fire fighting and first aid equipment.

While every warehouse will differ significantly in its security needs because of size, location, merchandise specialties and volume of business, many of the points covered here are general in nature and apply to virtually any warehouse operation.

TYPICAL DISTRIBUTION CENTER SECURITY PROCEDURES

The processes involved in step-by-step receiving and handling of merchandise in distribution centers varies only slightly according to type of goods flowing in and out of the facility. What follows is how one major grocery chain keeps goods moving through the system with maximum security control:

1. At the gated perimeter the driver is stopped by a guard. The driver then signs a form allowing the truck to enter the premises, and also allowing the truck to be searched before and after making the delivery.
2. The truck is then directed to a waiting strip for the delivery "appointment."
3. When the receiving dock is ready for unloading the truck, the driver is called by a guard and directed to proceed to the appropriate bay.
4. The unloading team then unloads the truck, counting each individual carton on board and finally signs a bill of lading.
5. The receiver then signs a vehicle pass allowing the truck to leave the premises. The pass should be documented as to those items or delivery equipment remaining on the truck. If a shipment into the warehouse is a part-shipment, delivery papers for the balance of the shipment should be attached to the pass so that the guard at the gate can check to validate the fact that the truck is making a further delivery at another location.
6. Grocery merchandise received at the warehouse is then placed into stock, normally by an identifying numeric slot code, where it remains until orders are received to pick the merchandise and ship it out to one or more stores.

Clear "viewing space" should be left between parked vehicles and the distribution center gate. In an operation warehousing high-volume, low-cost merchandise, fence should be angled in, as shown here, to prevent potential burglars from exiting by climbing over the gate. Operations warehousing expensive merchandise would be better served by fence angled out, to prevent burglars from entering the compound over the gate.

"Telautograph" machine transmits vehicle information from dispatcher's office to gate house guard station.

7. Merchandise picked for a particular order is funneled to a shipping dock, joining other merchandise being gathered for shipment to one or more stores.
8. The merchandise is checked by recounting on the shipping dock, and then loaded onto the truck. When the load is complete, according to the picking orders, the truck is then sealed.
9. If more than one stop is to be made, the delivery papers will contain additional seals for each stop.
10. At the exit gate, the same procedure is followed by the guard in checking the seal number on the shipping papers with the seal itself, and reviewing other seals which may be attached to their appropriate delivery papers carried by the driver. The guard will also check the driver's own identification card or papers.
11. At the delivery truck's destination store, or first stop, the store's security receiver will accept the delivery papers and check the papers against the seal number on the truck. If the receiver is satisfied that the numbers match and the seal is intact, the receiver *only* will break the seal and have the truck unloaded.
12. In off-loading grocery merchandise, a count is normally made simultaneously by the driver and receiver of the merchandise, but each maintains separate written counts of the goods.
13. If merchandise is coming in by pallet, each pallet load is separately checked. The count should be stopped periodically at agreed intervals, such as 25's, at which point the receiver and driver will both confirm the identity of their counts.
14. If the twin counts do not tally, both driver and receiver should recheck that portion of the count immediately. Since each off-loading is checked by 25's, 50's, or any other subtotal, the entire load need not be recounted.
15. If the truck is making a partial shipment, and has other stops to make (this is often true in delivery of perishable goods such as meat, fish, dairy or delicatessen items), each stop has its own shipping papers and a new seal, as indicated above.
16. At a delivery truck's last stop, the receiver for that store should carefully check the truck, look beneath pallets and around load lockers to make sure there is no merchandise of any type still on board.
17. Once this is verified, the receiver places a final seal on the vehicle so that the truck can return sealed to the warehouse. This strategy prevents drivers from returning to the warehouse with merchandise concealed in the truck, or from picking up merchandise

along the return route to the warehouse and then dropping off this merchandise into a private car along the route, without breaking the seal.

18. If a truck arrives at a store with the seal already broken, the standard operating procedure is for the receiver to immediately call security personnel at the warehouse and report the broken seal. The driver may then explain the reason for the break. This can happen for many reasons beside that of dishonesty or theft: the sealed door may not be properly set on its hinges, and the constant jarring may have broken the seal; the truck may have stopped short at a red light causing the seal to break; or youngsters may have jumped on the truck, breaking the seal in the process. In any event, when this occurs, a record of the broken seal is made by the security department, and a personal interview is conducted with the driver upon his return to the warehouse or office.

    In such interviews, a notation is made in the driver's personnel record. If such records reveal that this occurrence has happened quite frequently with this particular driver, an investigation may be necessary which can involve tailing the driver, maintaining close surveillance on his whereabouts, and making an apprehension when necessary.

19. If a truck leaving the warehouse is checked at the gate and is found to have a seal not properly secured, a new seal should be affixed and recorded on a "seal change form" which documents this on paper. These forms are prepared by exit gate guards and attached to the delivery papers so that receivers at the stores will recognize it as an authorized change of seal.

    The importance of seals is obvious, especially when many part-deliveries of merchandise are made. Many companies use color-coded seals sold by vendor companies. Veteran loss prevention experts are doubtful about the use of color-coded seals since these can denote the type of merchandise on board. Professional hijackers may gather enough information about a company to know what merchandise the color-coded seals signify as being on the truck. They may then "cherry-pick" their thefts, selecting those vehicles carrying valuable merchandise only—meats, TV sets, drugs, cosmetics. A distinctively colored seal may be used to denote an empty truck; this can conceivably forestall hijacking attempts from professionals who have detailed information about company procedures.

VEHICLE CONTROL PASS

S067501

ALL VEHICLES ARE SUBJECT TO INSPECTION – SURRENDER THIS PASS TO GUARD AT EXIT GATE

GUARD COMPLETES THIS SECTION WHEN VEHICLE ENTERING

DATE	TIME IN ☐ AM ☐ PM	GUARD'S SIGNATURE	
☐ TRUCK ☐ TRACTOR ONLY	☐ TRACTOR AND TRAILER	☐ PASSENGER CAR	DOOR #
☐ CAFETERIA ☐ REPAIR ☐ MAINT. ☐ SALVAGE	☐ OFFICE ☐ PICKUP ☐ PALLETS ☐ VEND MACH. ☐ OTHER		
NAME OF TRUCKING COMPANY:		VENDOR:	

DRIVER COMPLETES THIS SECTION BEFORE ENTERING COMPOUND

TRACTOR LICENSE #	TRAILER NUMBER	DRIVER'S SIGNATURE
PASSENGER CAR LICENSE PLATE #		HELPER #1
		HELPER #2
NUMBER OF PASSENGERS		–HELPERS MUST LEAVE WITH TRUCK–

RECEIVING DEPARTMENT COMPLETES THIS SECTION

PRO #

☐ MAKING PICKUP OF ______ PIECES ☐ REJECTED (NO DELIVERY)

☐ FULL COUNT RECEIVED (VEHICLE DEPARTING EMPTY) ☐ FULL COUNT RECEIVED (VEHICLE DEPARTING PARTLY LOADED)

☐ FULL COUNT RECEIVED (VEHICLE DEPARTING EMPTY, BUT HAS __ PALLETS) ☐ DRIVER RECEIVED PAPERS–SIGNATURE RECEIVING CLERK

☐ OTHER ______

______ SIGNATURE OF RECEIVING CHECKER ______ CLERK ______

☐ ______ CASE OVERAGE, MERCHANDISE LEFT ON TRAILER	SIGNATURE OF RECEIVING SUPERVISOR

	ITEM OR ITEMS:		
☐ PICK–UP	QUANTITY:	DEBIT #:	INVOICE #:
	REASON:		
	SIGNATURE:		

☐ NO PALLET EXCHANGE	☐ NO PALLETS ON TRAILER	☐ PALLETS REJECTED ______	
☐ NO PALLET EXCHANGE	☐ DRIVER HAS OWN PALLETS ______		
☐ PALLET EXCHANGE	48 X 40 GMA	RECEIVED ______	RETURNED ______
☐ PALLET EXCHANGE	36 X 40 SM WING	RECEIVED ______	RETURNED ______
☐ DRIVER BREAKDOWN	RECEIVED ______ OF ______ 48 X 40 GMA PALLETS		

DATE	TIME OUT ☐ AM ☐ PM	GUARD'S SIGNATURE

GUARD MUST CHECK ENTIRE PASS AND VEHICLE BEFORE RELEASING VEHICLE. F 78–501 5 72

Vehicle control pass requires entries to be made by driver entering the compound, the guard at the gate and the receiving department. The pass is surrendered when the truck leaves the compound. Spot inspections of vehicles are routinely carried out.

SHIPPING: WEAK LINK IN THE DISTRIBUTION CHAIN

One of the weakest links in the distribution chain in terms of security is transshipment of goods. It is a weak link because, on a relative basis, it is the most unprotected part of the system, with no fences, gates, solid buildings, armed guards, closed circuit TV monitoring or any other formal systems to minimize theft.

Theft during shipping is of three major types: *hijacking*, or the taking of merchandise and vehicle enroute by force; *drop-box or truck trailer theft*, or the theft of merchandise enroute not by force but by concealment—a form of rolling burglary; and *driver theft* either alone or in collusion with other employees and/or criminals.

Hijacking

Hijacking most often is the result of positive information filtered to the perpetrators. This information is provided by either the shipper, employees at the distribution center or the trucker. The best sources are those at final destination locations who are aware of all the merchandise to be delivered to the location, at what times, in what amounts, and by what form of transportation.

Many police departments assume that hijacking is *always* committed with inside information of a highly detailed nature, but apparently this is not always so. One security director recalls a situation where a grocery truck was hijacked, and the criminals discovered the contents amounted to a total value of $6,500. The thieves then "dropped" the load at once; the labor of getting rid of that quantity of merchandise was not worth its street value. While some items may be relatively expensive, the "outlet market" for this merchandise may be almost nonexistent. In another instance, a load of eggs was hijacked from a grocery chain, but the criminals, in attempting to remove the load, found that they were breaking so many eggs that the entire load was abandoned.

In other instances, cases have been documented where a load of meat was hijacked, but the refrigerated trailer's cooling system was malfunctioning to the point where the inside heat in the trailer rose to 78 degrees, ruining the meat. The hijackers were traced and arrested following the identification of a store selling bad meat.

A truly professional group of hijackers will, prior to the theft itself, have a drop schedule, a drop meeting point, and a drop meeting setup where they can unload the merchandise and deal with receivers who will immediately buy the merchandise. Hijacked goods generally will be sold for about one-quarter of their retail value.

Drop-box Theft

Larceny of trailers containing merchandise differs from hijacking because the trailer is taken without the use of force. It could, for example, be parked alongside the road while the driver is having lunch or dinner. Sometimes drop-boxes are unhooked and dropped during certain hours of the day, held at a store or location until the load can be removed at leisure or when store personnel have more time. Theft can easily take place by backing up a tractor to the drop-box, hooking up and pulling the trailer away.

One food chain concluded an investigation that spanned a full year, during which time 22 trailer loads of merchandise were stolen. Since all were stolen when fully loaded with merchandise, the pattern and "method of operation" indicated that the same person or group was responsible. The crime was always committed in a similar manner; what was sought was an unattended drop-box parked in an out-of-the-way location where the hookup and drive-away would not be readily noticed.

The company's investigation also showed that the thefts took place within a 30-mile radius of the firm's distribution center, and always between 10 p.m. and 2 a.m. The chain's location vs. the areas where the stolen drop-boxes were eventually recovered showed that most of the stolen merchandise was going across state lines. The chain's loss prevention department therefore contacted local police, state officials and the FBI.

The chain also informed other grocery companies that, should a product with their private label turn up in any store other than theirs, a notification should be sent to the chain's loss prevention department at once. Some time after this, a customer called to complain about rancid merchandise purchased in a store. The item in question was a private label product from the victimized chain, but sold in a grocery store operated by a different company. The date code on the can also indicated a very old item, further arousing suspicions.

Law enforcement officers were asked to investigate since the store was in another state. During the course of this investigation, a carton of brand-name aluminum foil turned up, with crayoned numbers on the side that matched the numbering system the chain used to break down loads of merchandise by store. Such numbers are written on the cases before they are placed in trailers and sent out to the stores. In this case, the written store number turned out to be the same as a store which had suffered the loss of one of the drop-boxes earlier in the year. When this information was reported back to the chain's loss prevention department, a request for round-the-clock surveillance on the store selling the stolen merchandise was made. Ten days later, a truck was observed pulling up to the store with the victimized chain's name on the trailer. Local police were notified and an arrest for grand larceny was made. A further investigation revealed that a group of several people working together had actually stolen 24 trailer loads of merchandise from the chain, and were regularly selling the goods to five other supermarkets.

THE IMPORTANCE OF DRIVER SCREENING

One of the underlying causes of increased hijacking and larceny of trucks is the failure to make proper background checks of drivers by companies hiring them. The fact that a man has been a truck driver entrusted with many thousands of dollars should not mislead companies into thinking that just because of this past experience the driver is a responsible worker. Personnel departments should treat all potential employees as if they were going to be entrusted with cash outright, and run background checks accordingly. As a group, drivers are hardworking individuals, and like the majority of employees, are basically honest. But some of them will steal if given the opportunity. A record of this may surface when proper checking takes place.

Some security directors note that more in-depth information about the past record of an applicant may be obtained by contacting the loss prevention department, rather than the personnel department, of the previous employer. In specially sensitive positions like shipping, when a good deal of property is at stake, cross checking with loss prevention departments may be a valuable move.

Many companies also exhibit a somewhat lax attitude toward merchandise shipping. The chronic problem of thieves preying on valuable merchandise, such as the well-headlined airline cargo thefts of gold and diamonds, should be a red flag to all companies with extensive transshipping operations. Ships are famous places for thefts of imported electrical items, televisions, radios, toasters, etc. Truck hijacking lately has centered on perishables such as meats, and higher-ticket merchandise such as cosmetics and small appliances. The garment industry and fur trade have also been hard hit. It is no longer a matter of hijacking or grand larceny of vehicles, but also small thefts—grabbing a carton and fleeing down the street while a delivery is in progress.

In cases of collusion, drivers often attempt to befriend loaders of merchandise on one end, and store receivers at the other end. A case in point involves a bread truck driver who worked out a deal with a loader at the bakery resulting in an excess amount of bread being loaded into the driver's truck. While the route consisted of about 40 stores, the driver was now able to sell a lot of excess bread en route and pocket the money, with a cut for the loader. Management suspicions were aroused when it was noted that this driver was flashing a lot of money around town. A subsequent surveillance revealed that he was making 20 stops a day compared with his normal 14. The extra stops were "his own" stops.

Regardless of how many people are involved in internal transit loss, the driver is almost always the common denominator. Loaders and receivers may plan the crimes, but they cannot function without the driver. A smart driver, however, can work alone, and if dishonest, can be one of the biggest sources of shrinkage to a company.

Because of this, security departments may solicit the aid of loaders and receivers to provide information concerning over-friendly drivers who, for example, will bring gifts to receivers at holiday times. This will indicate that a driver is attempting to win over a receiver so that a theft can occur either with or without the knowledge and cooperation of the receiver.

If a company is suspicious of a particular receiver, a good policy is to observe the receiver's car from time to time. This surveillance could be rewarded by noting that drivers delivering merchandise to a store may also be delivering merchandise to the receiver's car. Similar situations can arise between drivers and loaders in shipping departments. Management should see to it that limited "fraternization" goes on between drivers and shipping department personnel. Large scale collusion rings often involve shipping departments and one or many drivers.

Electronic Homing Devices

When investigations zero in on a driver, tailing the driver's vehicle is often the only way to bring about an apprehension. Direct tailing with a vehicle is extremely difficult, especially when a knowledgeable dishonest driver is involved. Drivers are also expert in concealing merchandise in areas of the vehicle, like tool boxes, sleeper compartments, or cavities under the driver's seat. Electronic homing devices, however, can be attached to vehicles to allow another vehicle to follow at a distance. This helps eliminate the possibility of the driver becoming suspicious.

One security director reported tailing a company trailer in this manner. No more than 10 minutes after the vehicle left the warehouse, it stopped, whereupon a small delivery van appeared and 15 cases of merchandise were transferred from the trailer to the van. The trailer then continued on its route.

One of the chain's security cars continued to follow the trailer while two other cars were assigned to follow the small delivery van. The van was observed pulling up to a non-company store and unloading the 15 cases of merchandise. At this point, police were called in. The owner of the store and the driver of the delivery van were arrested. A call was made to the trailer driver's next stop, where he was also arrested.

After extensive interrogation, the three admitted that this type of theft had been going on for quite some time, that other drop points were used and many other types of merchandise were being stolen from the company.

What helped make this initial apprehension successful was the use of electronic devices to tail the truck without the driver's knowledge. Another factor was the availability of sufficient security personnel and cars to completely follow the entire sequence of events, which resulted in receivers of stolen goods being apprehended along with the thieves themselves. This type of total follow-through, when word is allowed to spread through a company, becomes a strong deterrent and warning to others contemplating something similar.

Use of Numbers and Seal Colors

A good strategy for company-owned vehicles is to place large numbers on the roofs of trailers which correspond to identifying numbers on the sides and front of the trailers. These numbers should be in red on a black background—the color combination police department helicopter units suggest for easy spotting from the air.

Colors should not be used on door seals, as discussed earlier in this chapter. If a distribution center ships out fur coats with a red seal and dresses with a green seal, it doesn't take much imagination to guess that knowledgeable hijackers will wait for a red-sealed truck to pass their way. Grocery chains should consider using different seal colors only to denote loaded or empty trucks for convenient surveillance by distribution center guards and dispatchers.

For companies in food distribution particularly, road supervision should be instituted. Indeed, it would be difficult for any company operating 50 or more trailers to operate without road supervision. These supervisors are not totally involved with security per se, but the functions are closely related. They should have their vehicles equipped with radios or mobile telephones, and should report their locations periodically. Security department personnel should be cross-trained in road supervision to properly coordinate security in transit and manage large fleets of vehicles making deliveries and pickups over a radius that may extend 300 miles from a distribution center.

SECURITY CONTROLS IN TRUCK DISPATCHING

Along with proper pre-employment screening of potential company drivers, sound truck dispatching procedures should be adopted to exercise maximum security control. The following is the system used by one of the top food chains in the country:

1. Truckdrivers entering the distribution center premises report to the dispatcher, where they receive their shipping orders, bills of lading and routes.
2. Trucks are loaded from 2 p.m. to 1 a.m. and then parked on strips, according to merchandise. This chain utilizes separate trucks for health and beauty aids, meats, groceries, produce, dairy/delicatessen, and frozen foods.
3. At no time does any driver know in advance which truck he will be assigned to or which route he will follow. The assignment varies from week to week and even day to day. Drivers ordered in to work at earlier hours may only be aware that the route they will be running that day will involve more stops than is normal.
4. After a driver receives his papers from the dispatcher, he proceeds to his assigned trailer, hooks his tractor onto the trailer and then checks to see if the hookup, load balance, etc., is secure. The papers are cross-checked against the seal for matchup.
5. When the driver is ready to roll, he proceeds to the gate, where the guard is presented with the driver's I.D., including his photograph, and all the shipping paperwork. The guard also verifies that the seal number on the papers corresponds to the seal

TRACTOR/TRAILER MISSING FORM

PART 1

REPORTED BY:
DATE ______ TIME ______
NAME ______
TITLE ______ PHONE # ______
STORE # ______
STORE ADDRESS ______
STORE PHONE # ______

TRAILER:
TRAILER # ______ MARKED ______ UNMARKED ______
COLOR ______ SIZE ______ FEET
SERIAL # ______ MAKE ______
REG # ______ VALUE ______
VALUE OF CARGO ______ CARGO ______
INVOICE # ______

TRACTOR:
TRACTOR # ______ SERIAL # ______
COLOR ______ TMT PLATE # ______
REG # ______ YEAR ______
VALUE ______

LAST SEEN BY:
NAME ______ TITLE ______
PHONE # ______

DISCOVERED BY:
NAME ______ TITLE ______
PHONE # ______
REMARKS:
______

TRACTOR/TRAILER MISSING FORM 3-14-72

PART II

VERIFICATION INFORMATION

DRIVER:
NAME ______
ADDRESS ______
PHONE # ______

FOOD HAULERS: (CHECK TO SEE IF VEHICLE ACTUALLY LEFT THE COMPOUND)
NAME ______ TITLE ______
TELAUTOGRAPH PASS # ______

NOTIFICATIONS

LOCAL POLICE:
NAME ______ RANK ______

STATE POLICE:
NAME ______ RANK ______

F.B.I.: 622-5613
NAME ______

NEW JERSEY HIJACKING SQUAD: 256-0646 (DAY)
NAME ______ PHONE # ______

ALARM:
ALARM # ______ DATE ______ TIME ______
NAME HOME PHONE # OFFICE #

[illegible] NOTIFIED FOR RE-SELECTION OF ORDER (IF [illegible], HE WILL BE THE ONE TO SELECT THE ORDER) HAS BEEN
[illegible] ______

MISSING TRACTOR/TRAILER REPORT

IS THE TRACTOR/TRAILER

☐ STOLEN

☐ MISSING

DATE OF CALL ______
TIME OF CALL ______
RECEIVED BY (CCTV OPERATOR) ______
TITLE AND OR POSITION OF CALLER ______
______
TIME NOTIFICATION WAS MADE TO SUPERVISOR ______
REMARKS: ______
______
______
______

CCTV OPERATOR'S SIGNATURE ______

Various missing or stolen tractor trailer reports require completion by warehouse, driver and security personnel.

actually on the door, and that the seal is intact. He then takes one copy of the bill of lading, the dispatcher's assignment and the driver's signature, and the truck is allowed to roll out. An entry is made in a log noting the exact time the particular trailer left the compound, with what type of load and the bill of lading number.

6. Simultaneously, a duplicate pass system verification is in effect. This involves a TelAutograph machine that mechanically transmits a document being prepared in one office—in this case the dispatcher's office—instantly to another office at the receiving end of the machine—the guard house at the gate. The dispatcher transmits the bill of lading number, tractor number, trailer number, driver's name and routing information to the guard house via the TelAutograph. This is a redundant but important cross-check to the guard that the proper tractor and trailer is leaving the compound with the proper merchandise going to the proper location with the proper driver. If nothing else, this system prevents a trailer from proceeding to the wrong store, or carrying the wrong merchandise to the right store. This benefit alone can save the company thousands of dollars a year.
7. Once a truck leaves the warehouse or distribution center, its routing instructions are very firm and have been worked out very carefully. The exact mileage for that route has also been prepared by the chain's transportation department. If a driver has several stops to make en route, the system holds firm: the route has been outlined and the driver cannot deviate from its instructions. This deters the driver from taking his truck off route, getting lost or stalling while rolling toward stores. The time element is also checked very carefully because in a high volume operation, all deliveries to stores and warehouses should, of necessity, be made by appointment.
8. When the truck arrives at a store, because of the chain's controls and the appointment system that is in effect, the receiver at the store knows what to expect and when. Most trucks arrive within no more than half an hour of their appointment time.
9. The truck is then backed into the unloading dock, and systems outlined earlier in the chapter take hold.
10. After unloading the merchandise for this destination, the driver then gives the receiver the bill of lading for the next stop, which has a new seal attached. The receiver acts as another dispatcher in this case, verifying the seal number with the bill of lading

number. The receiver then personally reseals the vehicle and the driver leaves, again following the designated route prepared by the transportation department.

11. At the next stop, the driver goes through a similar procedure.
12. If "backhaul" stops are scheduled prior to an empty trailer returning to the warehouse (these are stops where a retail or distributing operation truck passing by a manufacturer's distribution center can pick up merchandise directly and thus gain some freight charge savings from these manufacturers), seals are issued to the driver, who must present them to the loader of the backhaul merchandise at the manufacturer's loading facility. The loader will seal the trailer and sign papers to that effect. When such trucks return to the chain warehouse, the guard will check to see if the seals are intact. Entries on the log are made to this effect.

THE ELEMENT OF SURPRISE

Spotchecking of loads should be conducted by retail loss prevention departments on a periodic basis, with no forewarning. This can take place at a loading dock prior to loading merchandise into a truck. As a final check, security personnel can be dispatched to the store destination of that truck to see if the original count made on the loading dock has been confirmed.

Checking mileage or routing can be very helpful in instances of suspected collusion where a truck has been met en route and some merchandise off-loaded. A group of road supervisors should be employed to work closely with a security department and constantly check that vehicles are maintaining proper routes, thereby insuring that company vehicles are not stopped in unusual places at unusual times.

SUMMARY

Security experts estimate that warehouse shrinkage ranges from ¾% to 1½% of the gross cost of merchandise handled, with individual companies noting far higher amounts. Because of the volume of goods moving through a warehouse, minimizing this source of loss is vital to retail operations working on low gross margins.

Warehouse theft can occur when employees leave the premises with merchandise secreted on their person or in lockers during their work shift, by throwing merchandise over a fence to waiting accomplices, and by collusion between warehouse employees and drivers and other outside personnel. Burglary is another major source of warehouse loss, and while such theft can be completely external in terms of perpetrators, most often there is some inside involvement or information passed to the burglars.

Preventive measures to improve warehouse security involve employee screening tests and other interviewing techniques discussed at length earlier in this text. The use of armed guard services can be crucial to a well-run distribution center. Good access and pass systems for all employees, easily changed locking systems and the entire panoply of modern alarm systems may all be brought into play. Perimeter protection in the form of high fencing, with viewing space along the length of the fence, and the use of guardhouses at each gate is important. Closed circuit TV cameras and alarm systems add an additional dimension of security control.

The shipping process itself is probably the weakest link in a retail operation's distribution chain since it is the portion of the system with the least protection. Thefts during shipping occur as a result of hijacking, larceny or theft of trucks or trailers, and through driver theft, either alone or in collusion with others. This makes driver screening of paramount importance in reducing loss of goods during shipping. Chains may also utilize electronic homing devices to track suspected drivers in their trucks, large numbers painted on truck roofs for police identification, and ironclad dispatching, receiving and truck sealing systems.

NOTES

[1] **Warehouse Security Manual,** National American Wholesale Grocers Association, New York, 1974, p. 7.

[2] "Blood, Sweat and Fears," **Time Magazine,** September 8, 1980, p. 44.

8 SECURITY HARDWARE: STATE-OF-THE-ART

This chapter will describe:

- **Basic categories of security hardware and systems**
- **New developments in security hardware and systems**

Throughout this text the use of alarm systems, check verification/photographing devices, polygraphs and voice stress analyzers, and other types of security equipment or services have been alluded to or described. While some equipment is specialized and should be operated or handled only by specially trained or licensed loss prevention personnel, many pieces of security hardware are used daily by store and warehouse employees. Check verification equipment, store safes and drop-boxes, alarm control boxes, and special door locking systems are part of the everyday scene, with many retail workers having access to these fixtures and systems.

The rapid development of miniaturized electronic circuitry and the growth of new technologies involving microwaves, lasers and sensing equipment has brought with it a new generation of security hardware that retail employees should be aware of, since this equipment will be the accepted standard in retail stores of the future— or even major remodels and re-fittings.

Understanding the capabilities of security hardware can help bring about a better appreciation of the benefits of equipment and systems a retail operation chooses to employ in its business. Better understanding is always the key to better follow-through in the proper application and use of equipment. This spirit should inform not only retail or distribution center employees, but also those responsible for loss prevention programs on the corporate level.

Every security system or service that is presented to a retail organization should be planned for the needs of the particular company buying that system or service. No stock item should be forced on a company unless it precisely meets the needs of the firm. In terms of basic functions, at least one of the following should be met by any security device or procedure: 1) The service or hardware should assist the company and its security personnel in deterring or detecting thefts of the company's money or merchandise or 2) The service or hardware should assist the company and its security personnel in apprehending individuals committing crimes against the company.

ALARM SYSTEMS—THE BASICS

The essential purpose of an alarm system is not primarily to catch a thief. The principal role is to minimize a loss, or better still, deter a criminal attempt. Burglar alarm systems should cover the possible entry points of a facility—doors, windows, roof entrances, skylights, ceilings, walls that may be shared in common with other operations, and other such entry points. Holdup alarms are basically notification devices manually triggered during the course of a robbery. Safe alarms provide localized, specialized burglary protection for a safe or vault.

Here, in outline form, are the basic alarm system formats:

1. Bell, Gong or Siren System

A local noise alarm powered by a transformer or battery that can be set up to cover as many "openings" as desired at a store or warehouse location. The wires themselves are encased in thin silver or tinfoil stripping and wired to the alarm sounding device, which is encased in a tamper-proof box. When the circuit is broken the alarm goes off. Skylights may be wired to the system by use of special screens consisting of fine wire. Walls and ceilings may be included with the addition of special sensors that, set for a predetermined tolerance, will open the circuit and trigger the alarm.

2. McCulloh or Circuit Alarm

This system starts with an outside noise alarm, but more importantly includes a line that terminates in a central alarm maintenance company. It utilizes leased telephone lines that may be shared with a number of customers. Thus, if there is a line failure, the source of the problem may not be isolated immediately; the alarm company will only receive a signal that the line is in trouble. The line cannot be repaired until telephone company personnel locate the problem. When the signal terminates at a central station it activates ticker tapes that punch out a coded message. An armed guard may respond if a signal is received.

3. Direct Line Systems

a) To police stations. This direct line system terminates at a police station or police answering service, and utilizes leased lines that are not shared with other customers. The system can be a silent alarm only or one wired to sound a local noise alarm as well. These lines are supervised. In large cities, police often may not handle direct lines, but in smaller cities or rural areas, police or sheriff departments may permit alarm lines or signals to terminate at their headquarters. When an entry is made, the broken contact triggers a signal at the alarm-monitoring station. This system can also be supplemented with a telephone dialer that can call an unlisted seven-digit number instead of, or in addition to, triggering an alarm at police headquarters or at maintenance companies.

b) To central stations. In this system power is supplied entirely by the central alarm system and monitored on a sensitive milliammeter at a central station. This system can detect any interference or tampering with telephone lines. Normally it is wired as a silent alarm only. Such a system has the maximum line integrity, and commands a larger discount on crime insurance policies than other alarm system installations. As with other alarm systems, an armed guard may respond when a signal is received.

4. Holdup Alarm or Police Call

This may be a separate system in a retail or office location, or it may be integrated with a burglar alarm system that can be adapted for "daytime" use by removing regular customer entry points from the circuit. As noted in the chapter on robbery and burglary, this type of alarm system cannot deter or stop an attempt; it can only summon help. Like burglar alarms, it can be a direct line to police or to alarm maintenance companies. In most cases, the alarm is triggered manually and sends a silent signal. The manual triggering devices range from simple concealed push-buttons to pressure sensitive tapes, cash register money clips or even remote control units similar to remote units for TV sets.

The money clip system has proven very popular. When the cash is removed from the clip, the prongs contact and the alarm is sent.

Cashiers function with the system deactivated since they are constantly putting in and removing cash from the register. In robberies involving this type of system, it is often the thief himself, grabbing money from the register, who ironically initiates the alarm.

It is at the "input" end of alarm systems that most technological change has occurred. The sensitivity to a break-in attempt or holdup is heightened; but response or follow-through by police or central station monitoring services cannot be increased. The added cushion of time or sensitivity of the new alarm system adaptations can, looking at the bottom line, speed response. They are also less easily "defeated" than simple "broken circuit" types of systems.

The new "space alarms" include:

- **Ultrasonic and Sonic Detectors**—Sound wave patterns transmitted throughout a location or channelled to a specific area; they cannot penetrate solid walls, and are most useful in defending individual areas with a combination of a master unit and remote sensors. The sound waves trigger an alarm when they are interrupted by either a preset amount of air turbulence or actual noises that bounce off the pulsing waves.
- **Microwave Units**—Radio waves that can fill an interior area. They can penetrate some materials, such as glass, and thus are not advisable for use near windows. The system sends an alarm when the wave pattern is interrupted by any motion.
- **Infrared Units**—Electric eye devices that can trigger an alarm when the invisible infrared beam is broken. Infrared units can measure both heat and motion in an area. Add-ons include photoelectric cells that can snap photographs as the beam is broken. Newer units can protect safes and vaults.
- **Stress Alarms, Heat Sensors, Radar Units**—Highly sophisticated systems that trigger alarms based on shifting weights on floors and surfaces, air temperature levels, or any motion within the protected area. In this group fall capacitor alarms earmarked for protection of safes and vaults, also discussed in the robbery and burglary chapter. Many of these newest systems are unstable and a broad tolerance for chance occurrence must be built-in to avoid a host of false alarms. Buildings do settle, sway, groan and creak; air temperature does rise and fall; an object can fall off a shelf if a stray breeze circulates; outside noises can be loud and intrusive—none of these should be able to trigger an alarm. Fine tuning any store's system for proper tolerance is vital.

Another alarm system add-on is a strobe light that can emit intense flashes of million-candlepower light when the alarm is given, to physiologically "jam" an intruder's vision. Obviously there is also a strong psychological reaction to such an on-site alarm mechanism.

Current State-of-the-Art

Large alarm systems suppliers prefer to sell complete packages to the retailer. One firm, for example, offers a "Lifeline" system that can be used in food retailing or fast food restaurants. It includes window and door protection involving simple electrical circuits as well as interior motion detectors; holdup protection via buttons, footrails, clips and wireless devices; fire protection from heat and smoke detectors; safe protectors; and access control systems to restrict customer and employee traffic in high risk areas. Underscoring the realities we have become accustomed to, other services offered are "hostage protection" via unlocking and alarm buttons located in large coolers and freezers to prevent possible lock-in after robbery, plus closed circuit TV surveillance systems with recording capabilities.

This firm offers 38 central security stations across the country, and a staff of 1,500 professionals providing service to approximately 45,000 subscribers. The equipment is installed by full-time locally trained representatives, and can be purchased outright with a monthly service contract, or leased.

Another major supplier offers a supermarket package including a burglar alarm, with optional ultrasonic or photoelectric intrusion detection, a fire alarm system, freezer supervison, paging and music inclusion plus a "rail TV" system (detailed in the closed circuit TV section in this chapter), safe alarm, holdup alarm, and an optional rear loading door closed circuit TV system. During daytime hours, an "annunciator" control panel indicates by sound and light an unauthorized opening anywhere in the store. This supplier's central station facilities include about 2,000 separate operations in major cities across the United States. Armed guard services are part of the central station package.

One firm offers a single monitoring station, centrally located in Columbus, Ohio, that operates via WATS (Wide Area Telephone Service) lines. It can monitor an alarm anywhere in the 50 states and Puerto Rico without utilizing leased lines or recurring telephone company charges to subscribers. Depending on the input—break-in, robbery, smoke or heat problems, holdup alarms—the service's operators

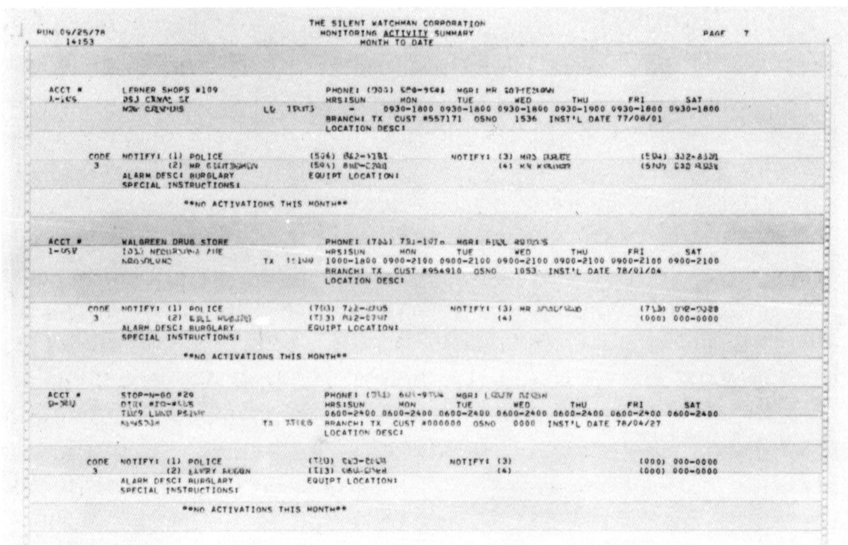

```
RUN 09/25/78                       THE SILENT WATCHMAN CORPORATION                             PAGE   7
   14:53                           MONITORING ACTIVITY SUMMARY
                                          MONTH TO DATE

ACCT #     LERNER SHOPS #109                   PHONE: [illegible]  MGR: MR [illegible]
[illegible] [illegible]                        HRS:SUN    MON       TUE       WED       THU       FRI       SAT
           [illegible]            [illegible]     -    0930-1800 0930-1800 0930-1800 0930-1900 0930-1800 0930-1800
                                               BRANCH: TX  CUST #557171  OSNO   1536  INST'L DATE 77/08/01
                                               LOCATION DESC:

     CODE  NOTIFY: (1) POLICE           [illegible]          NOTIFY: (3) [illegible]        [illegible]
      3            (2) [illegible]      [illegible]                  (4) [illegible]        [illegible]
           ALARM DESC: BURGLARY         EQUIPT LOCATION:
           SPECIAL INSTRUCTIONS:

                 **NO ACTIVATIONS THIS MONTH**

ACCT #     WALGREEN DRUG STORE                 PHONE: [illegible]  MGR: [illegible]
1-[illegible] [illegible]                      HRS:SUN    MON       TUE       WED       THU       FRI       SAT
           [illegible]            TX [illegible] 1000-1800 0900-2100 0900-2100 0900-2100 0900-2100 0900-2100 0900-2100
                                               BRANCH: TX  CUST #954910  OSNO   1053  INST'L DATE 78/01/04
                                               LOCATION DESC:

     CODE  NOTIFY: (1) POLICE           [illegible]          NOTIFY: (3) MR [illegible]     [illegible]
      3            (2) [illegible]      [illegible]                  (4)                    (000) 000-0000
           ALARM DESC: BURGLARY         EQUIPT LOCATION:
           SPECIAL INSTRUCTIONS:

                 **NO ACTIVATIONS THIS MONTH**

ACCT #     STOP-N-GO #29                       PHONE: [illegible]  MGR: [illegible]
[illegible] [illegible]                        HRS:SUN    MON       TUE       WED       THU       FRI       SAT
           [illegible]                         0600-2400 0600-2400 0600-2400 0600-2400 0600-2400 0600-2400 0600-2400
           [illegible]            TX [illegible] BRANCH: TX  CUST #000000  OSNO   0000  INST'L DATE 78/04/27
                                               LOCATION DESC:

     CODE  NOTIFY: (1) POLICE           [illegible]          NOTIFY: (3)                    (000) 000-0000
      3            (2) [illegible]      [illegible]                  (4)                    (000) 000-0000
           ALARM DESC: BURGLARY         EQUIPT LOCATION:
           SPECIAL INSTRUCTIONS:

                 **NO ACTIVATIONS THIS MONTH**
```

Photo courtesy of The Silent Watchman Corp.

Centralized security monitoring via a WATS line offers extensive electronic services on an economic basis. A typical report printout confirms the extent of each store's alarm systems, the dialing and instruction codes, and any WATS line activity during the month.

will call police or fire officials in the local community as the subscriber name is displayed, along with telephone numbers and names to contact, on a CRT terminal screen.

Another company offers a computer-based "Security Management System" that can interface all on-premise loss prevention equipment, from recording door locks to passive infrared intrusion sensors with host computer hardware and software at a central station. The result is a system that stores, collates, evaluates and reports on a continuous stream of incoming data. Loss prevention directors or corporate management receive complete location-by-location summaries of all equipment signals transmitted to the central station, including those caused by operator error or false alarms.

Today's automatic telephone dialers can permit two operating channels for separate burglar and fire alarms. They also have a "positive priority override" feature that assures complete play of a priority message (such as a fire alarm) overriding any other message that might interfere. Ultrasonic alarms (in "transceiver" units) can be hooked to "range expanders" to increase their coverage by 50-90%, but without so-called "receiver gain" increases that can produce more false alarms.

In this era of power failures and brownouts, special rechargeable battery packs can operate protective circuits, including digital dialers, for up to ten days on a standby basis. Modern day/night alarm control panels feature built-in transformers for low-voltage AC input, Light-Emitting Diode (LED) indicators to indicate arm/disarm status, with a light optionally pulsating during alarm, entry/exit alarm delay features, and so-called open loop interlocks to prevent arming the alarm system when any protective circuits are not "secure." Going beyond this, a number of firms offer programmable alarm systems, termed "digital communicators." Without any additional wiring or screws, but utilizing entry keyboards, the units can select optional telephone and account numbers to dial, permit entry and exit delays prior to sending the alarm, phase-out a noise alarm, display opening and closing reports, arm either an entire system or only designated zones, and self-troubleshoot for any loop faults or other problems.

New alarm systems using infrared detectors only to sense the movement of body heat (which are theoretically less susceptible to false alarms caused by air turbulence) have been developed on a self-contained basis, making such units easy to install and portable. The alarm is a local noise alarm producing a 122-decibel warbling siren, plus a control panel which sends a silent alarm to a central station.

Annunciator Systems

Mentioned briefly earlier in this chapter, the most sophisticated of today's alarm systems offer daytime "annunciator" systems, a control panel that monitors all of the openings in a store or warehouse that are wired to the alarm system. Full perimeter coverage can include front doors, fire exits, receiving dock, and all side and rear doors. Internal protection can include offices or areas with cash-on-hand, food freezers or refrigeration equipment, jewelry showcases, etc.

Essentially, an annunciator immediately displays which unauthorized doors have been opened. If such doors are used for deliveries, the appropriate door's control can be placed in an "access" mode, all indicated by an LED (Light-Emitting Diode) readout. No alarm will be sounded at either the panel or the particular door until the delivery is made and the door's security restored by the touch of a button. After closing, the night setting puts all the protected openings into one alarm loop.

CLOSED CIRCUIT TELEVISION SYSTEMS (CCTV)

The proper use of closed circuit TV systems today affords one of the best ways to deter or apprehend dishonest employees or shoppers. Such equipment should be installed in response to a real need, since the costs can be high. An objective survey should be conducted by management or a loss prevention department to measure the extent of theft and pilferage by customers and employees vs. the cost of the equipment. Vendors, naturally, are often more interested in selling the hardware regardless of the true needs of the customer.

Once a company has decided to proceed with CCTV installations at retail stores and/or distribution centers, the commitment must be total to derive real benefits from all of this electronic wizardry. Merely *having* the equipment mounted in stores or warehouses, and seeing that it is maintained, is not the answer. The system must be properly designed, properly used and monitored by designated personnel. Installations should be carried out by vendors and service companies thoroughly familiar with the store or company's operation, resulting in systems tailor-made for each of the premises to be protected.

Loss prevention experts generally espouse a rule of thumb stating that cameras should be installed so that store personnel are observed 75% of the time, and customers, vendors or salespeople working the store are observed 25% of the time.

Pan, tilt and zoom-lens cameras are important extras in closed circuit systems. A camera can zoom in on a register to read the exact amount of a ringup. Then it can pan around to spot a customer walking out with unpaid merchandise on the bottom of a shopping cart. A customer suspected of shoplifting can be followed up an aisle and the camera can then zoom in to observe exactly where the customer is secreting the stolen merchandise. Receiving doors, employee parking lots, courtesy booths . . . all can be monitored in like fashion.

Newest Developments in CCTV

The newest development in CCTV utilization in loss prevention is the overhead rail system. This involves mobile cameras enclosed in a one-way viewing acrylic tunnel, so that the camera can see out of the tunnel, without customers or employees being able to see into the tunnel to note the momentary location of the camera. The camera itself glides along noiselessly in its carrier, aimed by remote control at almost any area of concentration. Two cameras—a telephoto and wide-angle unit—can operate simultaneously on a rail system, feeding into one monitor.

Primary usage for rail systems is at the front end of the store to minimize cashier theft and collusion with customers. They can also be used in freight terminals and warehouses, and employee entrances. The systems are expandable to include videotape recording for documentation, and can be integrated into existing protection systems.

For small stores, basic TV network systems, which include a single camera and monitor plus accessory equipment such as intercom systems and ceiling and wall mount brackets, may be sufficient.

Basic systems expand into multi-monitor systems via a multi-camera interface, which permits the viewing of more than one location at the same time. With this equipment, one operator seated at a console controls access to all cameras throughout an installation. This permits watching every door, surveying an entire area while keeping monitoring personnel down to a minimum. With more sophisticated equipment, viewing cameras can act as intrusion sensors, automatically tripping an alarm upon any motion in the camera's field of vision. The TV network can also coordinate with heat and smoke detectors and door access controls.

Time lapse video recorders or mounted 35mm cameras afford nighttime surveillance recorded on a stop-action, time-lapse basis on erasable, reusable magnetic tape or on permanent film. Retail appli-

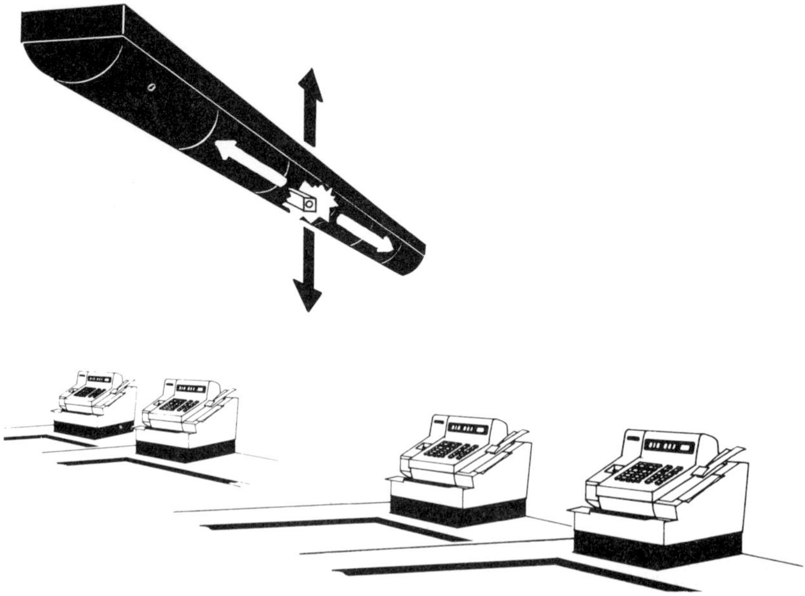

Photos courtesy of ADT Security Systems and Checkpoint Systems

Operation of a rail TV system designed to monitor the entire front end of a store is depicted in the diagram above. The photo illustrates an "article surveillance" tag (embedded in the "nice place to shop" design) containing a miniature relay circuit that can trigger an alarm if the item is stolen and the tag is not "desensitized" by special equipment at store checkouts.

cations can include recording cash register, stockroom and loading dock activity.

SHOPLIFTING ALARM SYSTEMS

Great strides in miniaturized circuitry, and trial-and-error testing that has continued for more than a decade, have brought about the development of electronic shoplifting controls—euphemistically called "article surveillance"—to the threshold of widespread use.

A number of systems are now in use—in department stores, clothing stores, drugstores, and in trend-setting supermarket units in some areas. All of the systems involve a special low-frequency circuit or microwave relay on a price tag, wafer, strip or element attached to merchandise. Or, the tag can incorporate a magnetic sensor for greater reliability. Each tag, with a printed circuit embedded within, must be desensitized or "detuned" by special equipment at the checkout; otherwise, the "live" security tag will trigger a visible or audible alarm as the shoplifter passes detection monitors at store exits. The monitors will trigger the alarm no matter where the item has been placed or secreted—even in metal boxes.

In its earliest incarnations, these systems involved large bulky tags and were tricky to use when any metal was involved. In addition, the detection systems were easily "spooked," and could be accidentally triggered by transistor radios, even customers with pacemakers. Magnetic sensors are less easily "fooled" and function at 98% reliability.

One system, using a reusable plastic tag or wafer for clothing or other soft goods, is virtually impossible to remove (requiring 200 pounds of pressure) without a special removal tool which the store maintains at the checkouts. For fast moving grocery merchandise, the circuit can be embedded on flexible non-reusable paper-thin strips.

Another firm offers non-magnetic, Underwriters' Laboratories-approved tags that double as merchandise price tags. This program utilizes a pair of slender sensing screens built into each checkstand, and yields a "Teeny Beeper" alarm when not properly desensitized or detuned. The system is designed to protect meats, fish, poultry, deli, dairy, cosmetics, drugs, wines, liquors and most other foods and non-foods.

In addition to gaining greater accuracy in use, these systems are quite costly when the merchandise needs of a convenience store with 2,000 items, a supermarket, carrying 15,000 items, a drugstore with 7,000 or more items, and department stores, with even greater total item counts, are taken into consideration. Estimates suggest that such sensing systems may cost a company from .7% to 1.8% of gross sales. With system costs this high, a decision to adopt this protection which, in effect, watches the merchandise—not the thief—is not impulsive by any means. The company, which first marketed article surveillance equipment in 1968, didn't make one cent of profit until 1973, and even today considers that, according to a *Fortune* magazine profile, "95% of its potential market has yet to be penetrated."[1] At the same time, in a test supermarket (one of the top chains in the country) using an article surveillance system, savings on merchandise not stolen have already gone into six figures.

These sophisticated systems can play a role in the reduction of employee pilferage as well as customer shoplifting, and also make a definite statement about a retail organization's seriousness in minimizing pilferage of all types. While the extensive costs of a merchandise protection system may approach or in some cases exceed that of the cost of shoplifting itself, the system may build a deterrent that spills over into other potential areas of crime, telling the world at large that this retailer's loss prevention program means business.

CHECK CASHING SYSTEMS

Dual lens cameras, taking photographs simultaneously of check and identification and the check passer, have long been the primary item of hardware to minimize bad check losses. Professional thieves tend to avoid retail operations where these camera systems, which can record up to 2,000 transactions on a 100-ft. roll of film, are in use. Each unit operates automatically by a touch; lenses are pre-set and pre-focused; cameras are operated with 16mm film.

A newer, less expensive system involves inkless fingerprinting of customers. The units involve no special machinery, the evidence provided is admissable in court trials, and the system utilizes rolls of 500 chemically-treated, pressure sensitive stickers that pop up one at a time to take thumb prints, placing the printed stickers on the back of the check.

Users put the fingerprinting system into play after checking conventional identification. A sticker is removed from the dispenser and placed on the back of the check or document. The customer's right thumb is gently pressed to the activating thumb pad and then to the sticker, producing a permanent print. The thumb pad contains a colorless non-toxic activator that cannot smudge or stain. Store kits for use along with the system include signs and decals for installation at courtesy booths and checkouts, explaining the protective device to customers. Since fingerprinting is so clearly associated with police stations, use of an in-store fingerprinting system may pose a customer-relations headache of some magnitude, despite the marketing organization's claim that the system "causes no embarassment to legitimate customers, but stops the phonies immediately." The main attraction of fingerprinting systems like this is the exceedingly low cost. Bad checks in one chain's stores where a fingerprinting unit was installed were reduced from 30-35 bad checks per week to 3-4 returns.

Currency validators are now on the market, promising help in minimizing acceptance of counterfeit currency. These systems are solid state electronic devices that can authenticate all denominations of U.S. currency when the portrait side of the bill is placed face down.

Computer systems to reduce bad check loss include one recently established service that is essentially a name memory bank of bad check passers. It is based on the assumption that most bad checks (other than casual insufficient funds checks) are written by a small group of repeat offenders (said to total around 300,000 individuals). With terminals connected to the main data processor by WATS lines, this service handles more than 2,500,000 check acceptances in the 24 states in which it operates, while rejecting some 25,000 checks from those areas. The system operates through franchised firms with local data banks that are constantly reviewed and updated. Access to the entire data bank in all areas of operation makes it possible to handle check cashing from out-of-state locations.

MONEY SAFES

Money safes have not grown technologically with the lightning speed seen in alarm systems and article surveillance equipment. As noted earlier in this text, a majority of older safes in the country are not truly effective in burglary protection since they were built mainly for protection from fires. As with alarm systems, Underwriters' Laboratories has a rating system for safes indicating that for retail locations, safes rated "E" are required as a minimum. This means that the safe has a degree of fire resistance and burglary resistance. Most safes presently on the market are classified according to UL ratings, so that comparability from brand to brand can be tracked in addition to costs.

For high-volume retail locations, a "dual safe" is important. This is a unit weighing a ton or more, with a separate locker for storage of cash trays and small change, plus a bulk cash armored steel money safe. Its essentials were described in the chapter on robbery and burglary.

Adaptations to the dual safe are drop safes, which function as one-way systems. A slit atop the safe allows bagged cash to be dropped into an armored compartment, but not extracted back through the slit. This is for temporary cash storage. Below the drop-box is the more heavily armored bulk cash vault.

Burglar safes today can be designed in numerous shapes and sizes by the major manufacturers to meet such requests as concealed installation, under-the-counter installation, and so on. Special locks are available, including silent signal locks, which will activate an alarm unless the combination is turned in a certain manner. Time delay locks, which activate a special timing mechanism when the combination dial is not turned in a certain manner, make it impossible to fully dial the combination for as long as 15 minutes. Small drop-boxes with large hoppers to accept rolls of coins, bags and loose change and a dual key format to extract the money, have become popular in high-volume stores for use directly at checkouts, to minimize a store's exposure in the event of a robbery.

As noted earlier in the text, the choice of safe for a retail location is important in helping insurance companies base premium rates for robbery and burglary coverage. The safe type is often the single most important determinant of that premium charge.

LOCKING SYSTEMS

Electronics and chip technologies have created a new generation of locking systems, but the old adage that no door lock is pick-proof or absolutely un-openable must still be regarded as true. A number of basic locking systems, covering long deadbolt latches, three-point locking systems and latches containing roll-pins to prevent saw-throughs, were described in the chapter on robbery and burglary.

Time-recording locks have been on the security scene for many years, since 1893 to be exact, and very few systems have been devised to effect a more methodical and orderly store or warehouse location opening and closing procedure. In fact, in some areas of the country, up to 90% of the supermarkets utilize the time recording lock system.

The system works by a simple concept: the final exit door is fitted with a master recording lock, housing a precision mechanism that records the time of every opening, closing, and re-entry made by key, 24 hours a day, seven days a week. All other doors are equipped with two-key interlocks. These must be locked in sequence starting with Interlock No. 1, progressing through all interlocks in a predetermined order, and ending with the master lock. The system works without wires; with the overlapping arrangement, missing a door in the locking or unlocking sequence is impossible. When the master lock is locked, the time is recorded and all doors are secured. For each location equipped with the system, a weekly report is provided, showing all opening, closing and re-entry times. When "key" employees leave the company, lock manufacturer supervisors can install a new cylinder in seconds with a special key. All cores are completely interchangeable.

Updated versions of time recording locks can also involve electrical hookups, so that alarm systems can be automatically armed as the last lock in the system is secured. This prevents a store manager or employee from forgetting to arm the system at closings. The lock, as with basic time recording systems, provides a hard-copy printout of the time, day and specially coded key used to open or close the lock, ensuring that only authorized personnel with keys properly coded have closed the lock and armed the system.

Magnetic and Electrical Locks

Magnetic locks, using low voltage to provide up to 3,000 lbs. of holding force are available, with flexibility to accommodate identification card activators, toggle or key switches or push-buttons. Such locks offer battery powered backups ranging from several days to a few weeks, according to specific requirements. Desk command modules can operate or actuate any or all doors tied into the system, with built-in "man-trap" provisions to prevent accidental locking-in of employees in refrigerated rooms or special security areas. The systems can also be tied into sensing systems, such as smoke and fire alarms, that can override the magnetic locks.

Electrical locking systems include digital access control systems with miniature stored memories to instantly change unlocking combinations (up to 10,000 combinations in a single system) so that each new code entered erases the previous one. These systems also have adaptations for card-key readers. Remote control exit locks, wired to alarm systems, alarmed emergency exits, electric deadbolts for inswinging or double-acting doors that lock the door only with the power switched on, and electrified knob locks, are all currently available. All locks of this type can be wired to a monitoring console with visible and audible signals to indicate authorized or unauthorized openings. The monitors can also handle fire and smoke alarms, magnetic doors and other security network functions.

ELECTRONIC INTERVIEWING EQUIPMENT

Electronic interviewing equipment is rarely, if ever, handled by regular retail employees. However, with increased use of polygraphs and voice stress analyzers (VSA) in business situations of all types, employees may find themselves on the receiving end of such examinations, either as a pre-employment requirement, or as a periodic checkup mandated by the company. As employees are promoted to managerial levels, they may find themselves directing the use of such equipment or responsible for actions based on the results. The lower costs of this equipment compared with the costs of background checks (about 50% of the cost, in fact), makes polygraph or VSA testing very appealing to businesses. This is so in spite of questions of legality that arise in many states, and an industry-wide debate on the accuracy rate of the testing.

In a recent *Time Magazine* article[2], a college psychiatry professor stated that the most prevalent type of polygraph test is correct only two-thirds of the time, and more critically, is far more likely to err when the person tested is truthful. The implication is that the caliber, ethics and expertise of the examiners plays a large role in the quality and accuracy of the results.

Basic lie detectors and pre-employment honesty testing was described in the chapter on internal theft. The state-of-the-art in electronic lie-detection equipment today is the voice stress analyzer system. This equipment measures stress in a speaker's voice and can display the results in simple numerics, providing the user with a continuous reading of deception that claims to be more precise than anything used before. A major advantage of VSA is that it needs no attachment to the subject, eliminating the sensors and confining wires that have in the past contributed somewhat to inaccurate results. The equipment can even be used without the knowledge of the person being interviewed; or a tape recording of the interview can be run through the voice stress analyzer following a non-monitored interview.

The newest systems provide housing in a regular attache case, operation on wall current or battery, hookup to a 6-hour capacity cassette recorder, etc. As a suspect talks, or a tape is played, modulations in the subject's voice appear as a numeric readout on a screen. By querying the subject initially with questions that can be easily answered truthfully, the normal range of the subject's voice modulations are established. When answers to critical questions prompt higher-than-normal numbers on the screen, the subject's stress is immediately apparent. The analyzer can detect changes in the subject's voice that are below the audible range of the human ear, helping to eliminate the kind of guesswork frequently needed in conventional lie detector testing, which can measure breathing, pulse rate, skin conductivity and changes in blood pressure.

VISUAL DETERRENTS AND AIDS

Other than festooning a store with signs and decals warning customers and employees about prison sentences that can be meted out for retail crimes, two visual deterrents can be used which have a silent impact on the reduction of store pilferage and theft. One is the use of mirrors, with the latest advance the panoramic view "moon mirror" that permits a full 360-degree view, allows coverage of an extensive area with one mirror, and is lightweight and relatively inexpensive for pilferage prevention equipment. Manufacturers now make panoramic mirrors for use in drop ceiling grids, which are very popular with many of today's retail installations, as well as flush mounted into a standard ceiling. A large supermarket might require two dozen such mirrors to provide 100% coverage of the selling floor, due to interaisle obstructions.

While the use of mirrors is essentially a passive deterrent to pilferage, employees trained to routinely scan any mirrors in their areas can turn this tool into an extension of a concerned employee's constant "eyeballing" of the store and its customers.

The use of dummy cameras is a second visual deterrent to crime, with newer units growing ever more realistic, with simulated F-stops on camera lenses, convex lens optics, or realistic looking coaxial cables and wall-plates. Some dummy models are motorized to oscillate back and forth. "ON" lights or blinking red lights mounted atop the cameras are additional realistic extras. Warning decals for store doors and windows relating to the cameras are final touches of authenticity.

While these cameras are relatively inexpensive props and can be effective as deterrents, they also have a "straw man" disadvantage

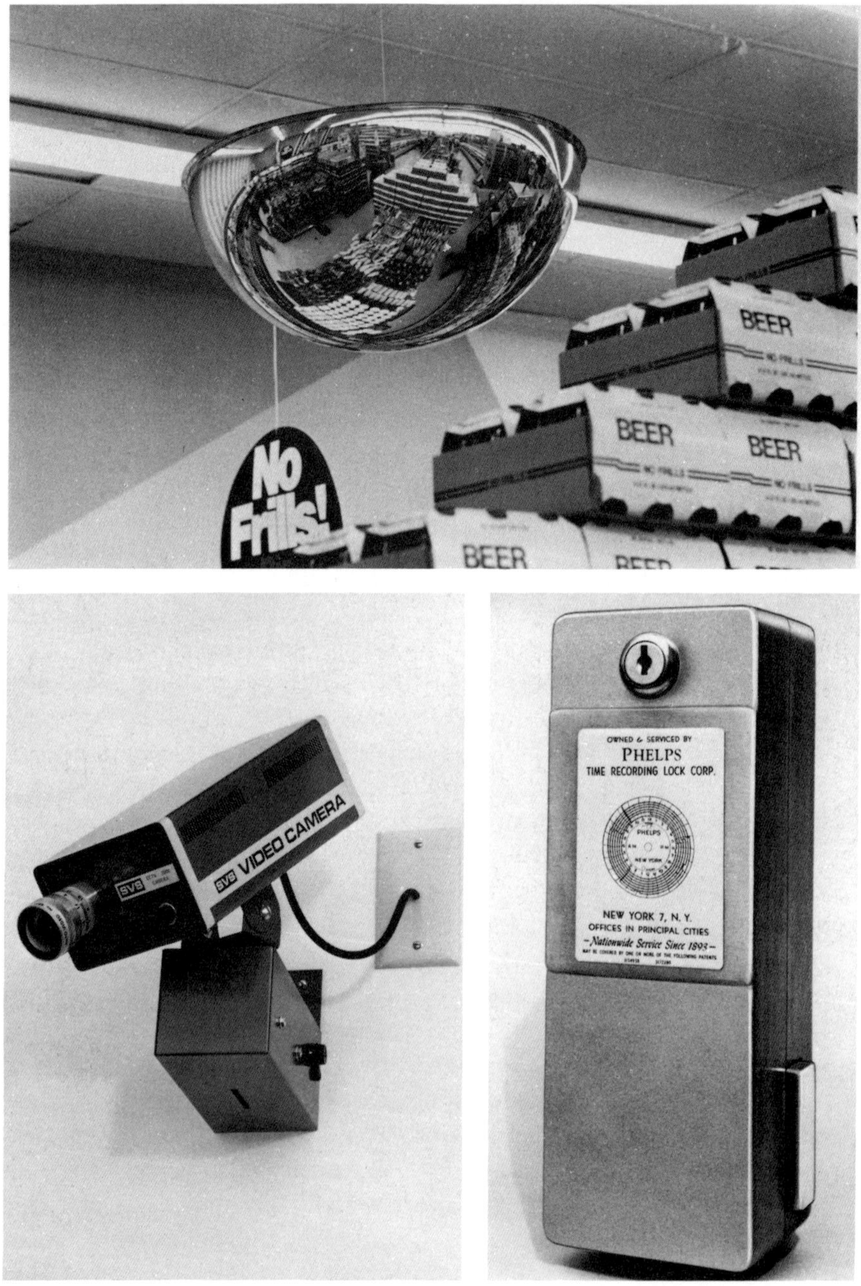

Photos courtesy of Global Marketing Corp., Surveillance Video Systems and Phelps Time Lock Recording Corp.

Basic security equipment for retail locations may include hemispheric/panoramic viewing mirrors, realistic dummy videotape recorders, and one of the oldest and most reliable locking systems—the time recording lock.

because their value is reduced to near zero if customers and potential thieves discover that they are not genuine. Installation of such camouflage equipment should be conducted on a discreet basis with a minimum of people in the company aware of the sham.

SHOPPING CART SYSTEMS

All mass merchandiser types of retail locations utilize shopping carts. Supermarkets wouldn't be supermarkets without them. One critical problem relating to the carts is loss due to bottom-of-the-cart shrinkage, either via deliberate theft, checker-customer collusion, or innocent error. The bottom rack of the cart is often used for large bulky items, such as bags of dog food, garden supplies, and charcoal.

A number of new carts have been designed with a series of claws on the bottom rack that makes it impossible for any merchandise to be placed below the main shopping basket, while the carts can still "nest" for easy storage. Such carts can require a shift in merchandising policies, such as up-front location of all bulky items, added carryout services, etc.

A second shopping cart problem is loss of the cart itself, via damage, vandalism or outright theft. Retail locations less dependent on the carts, such as drug chains or mass merchandiser stores, frequently use high antenna-like welded pieces of metal on the carts to prevent their easy removal through store doors. Other stores have installed heavy stanchions at the exits to prevent the carts from being wheeled away from a cart unloading area.

A new system offers an incentive for customers to return their own carts from a parking lot after they have unloaded the contents into their cars. As the cart is pushed by the customer through a special turnstile, a special stamp with a value anywhere from 25¢ to $1 is dispensed. Customers can then save the coupons or stamps and redeem them for store merchandise. Regular store trading stamps could also be incorporated into the system. The units are battery operated, and the stamps or coupons that are dispensed are supplied by the retailer.

SUMMARY

Retail employees may come in contact with security equipment during the normal course of their duties. As employees move into managerial ranks, they may have jurisdiction over, or additional

Photo courtesy of Franklin Electric Corp.

The Return-A-Cart system, which dispenses trading stamps or special savings coupons when customers return shopping carts from the parking lot, is one way to reduce costly shopping cart damage or outright theft.

responsibilities regarding handling a firm's security hardware, interactions with loss prevention personnel proficient in the security systems, or involvement in the purchase or lease of security systems. A basic grounding in the primary types of retail security equipment and knowledge of some new "state-of-the-art" advances is important to complete the security orientation of retail employees.

In addition to the four basic types of alarm systems, new adaptations, such as weight stress sensing equipment and strobe-light flashers, along with solid state central monitoring consoles and "annunciator" systems, are becoming commonplace in retail use. Included in some of the new package systems are "hostage protection" manual alarms or unlocking controls.

Closed circuit TV or videotaping systems now include rail cameras mounted in one-way acrylic tunnels over checkouts to zoom in on checkouts and customers on a hidden basis. Shoplifting "article surveillance" systems—miniature alarm systems on a clothing tag or merchandise pressure-sensitive tape that must be desensitized or "detuned" at checkouts or else alarms will sound—have made great strides in the past ten years, and now are on the threshold of major retail utilization.

Check cashing equipment and systems, however, have changed little in the past decade. Commonly used systems include dual cameras to simultaneously photograph the check passer and the check, identification or store card. An inkless customer fingerprinting system is now available. Electronic credit reporting terminals or professional bad check passer information banks are good ways to minimize bad check loss from professional "paperhangers."

Money safes with time delay locks or silent alarm-wired combinations are new features of what is essentially a static and little-changing piece of security hardware. New electronic controls on locks, magnetic force locks, and updated versions of the time recording locks that have been in use for nearly 100 years are bringing new sophistication to the most primitive of all security elements.

While most employees will rarely if ever be involved with electronic interviewing equipment, other than on the receiving end, it is probably a good policy under the banner of "full disclosure" to orient employees to the concept and use of polygraphs and voice stress analyzers to the degree they are used in a given company.

Along with "working" security hardware, purely visual deterrents, such as panoramic mirrors or dummy TV cameras, have their place in the loss prevention picture and should be appreciated for what they can produce in terms of forestalling customer and employee pilferage attempts.

New types of shopping cart protective systems include positive loss prevention controls in the form of automatic equipment which dispenses free coupons or stamps to customers as a bonus for returning their carts through a special turnstile.

NOTES

[1] "Sensormatic Collars the Shoplifter," **Fortune Magazine,** February 25, 1980, p. 115.

[2] "Blood, Sweat and Fears," **Time Magazine,** September 8, 1980.

APPENDIX A

A STATISTICAL REPORT ON SHOPLIFTING

(Seventeenth Annual Survey of Shoplifting, 1979,
Commercial Services Systems, Inc., Van Nuys, CA, Reprinted with permission).

	TOTAL CASES			TOTAL MALES			TOTAL FEMALES			TOTAL ADULTS			TOTAL JUVENILES			TOTAL MALE JUVENILES			TOTAL FEMALE JUVENILES		
	Sup Mkt	Drug	Disc	Sup Mkt	Drug	Disc	Sup Mkt	Drug	Disc	Sup Mkt	Drug	Disc	Sup Mkt	Drug	Disc	Sup Mkt	Drug	Disc	Sup Mkt	Drug	Disc
Total Cases	14,656	4015	1440	8137	2120	736	6424	1849	695	9126	1926	889	4605	1917	511	2903	1135	306	1682	778	202
Shoplifters Booked (%)	30.8	28.0	54.9	30.6	24.4	49.7	31.0	32.1	60.3	34.1	36.7	63.4	24.7	18.4	39.7	22.5	16.1	35.6	28.4	21.7	46.5
Shoplifters Released (%)	69.2	72.0	45.1	69.4	75.6	50.3	69.0	67.9	39.7	65.9	63.3	36.6	75.3	81.6	60.3	77.5	83.9	64.4	71.6	78.3	53.5
Average Number of Articles Recovered	3.1	2.6	4.5	2.5	2.1	3.6	3.8	3.2	5.6	3.3	2.4	5.1	2.6	2.7	3.4	2.2	2.3	2.7	3.4	3.3	4.5
Average Value Recovered	$7.37	9.07	25.44	6.49	7.57	22.34	8.47	10.76	28.29	8.61	10.85	28.65	4.73	6.97	19.42	3.68	5.97	19.53	6.46	8.45	19.24
Sex (%)																					
Male	55.3	52.8	51.1	—	—	—	—	—	—	50.8	46.8	45.8	63.0	59.2	59.9	—	—	—	—	—	—
Female	43.6	46.1	48.3	—	—	—	—	—	—	48.0	51.6	53.7	36.5	40.6	39.5	—	—	—	—	—	—

	TOTAL CASES			TOTAL MALES			TOTAL FEMALES			TOTAL ADULTS			TOTAL JUVENILES			TOTAL MALE JUVENILES			TOTAL FEMALE JUVENILES		
	Sup Mkt	Drug	Disc	Sup Mkt	Drug	Disc	Sup Mkt	Drug	Disc	Sup Mkt	Drug	Disc	Sup Mkt	Drug	Disc	Sup Mkt	Drug	Disc	Sup Mkt	Drug	Disc
METHODS OF CONCEALMENT (%)																					
In Purse	30.6	24.0	29.6	2.5	.6	1.2	66.3	50.9	59.7	39.3	32.9	36.1	15.5	15.9	19.2	1.1	.3	.3	40.4	38.7	48.0
Shopping Bag	2.8	4.3	15.9	2.8	3.5	19.0	2.9	5.4	12.8	2.4	2.9	15.2	3.6	5.6	16.8	2.9	4.1	19.0	4.9	7.8	13.9
Other Bag	3.3	4.5	2.7	3.2	4.3	2.7	3.4	4.8	2.7	2.6	3.5	2.4	4.6	5.6	3.5	3.7	4.9	3.6	6.4	6.4	3.5
Professional	.5	.3	1.4	.7	.5	1.6	.2	.1	1.2	.7	.5	1.8	.1	.1	.4	.0	.2	—	.1	—	1.0
In Pocket	21.8	29.5	15.6	34.0	46.2	27.4	6.4	10.5	2.7	19.7	24.8	15.1	26.4	34.4	16.6	34.2	46.9	23.5	13.1	16.2	5.9
Label Switcher	1.9	2.5	5.6	1.5	1.9	8.2	2.4	3.2	2.9	2.5	3.7	5.4	1.0	1.5	6.1	.8	1.5	9.5	1.2	1.5	1.0
Accomplice	2.7	3.4	4.9	2.9	3.8	5.7	2.5	3.0	4.2	2.2	1.9	3.1	3.9	5.1	7.4	3.4	5.1	6.9	4.6	5.1	8.4
Under Clothing	25.6	13.7	9.8	39.4	20.2	15.6	8.1	6.1	3.6	22.6	11.7	7.4	30.5	16.1	13.9	38.6	20.4	18.6	16.4	9.9	6.4
Other Method	7.9	12.7	11.9	9.6	13.8	15.4	5.7	11.2	8.3	6.0	13.8	11.6	11.1	11.7	12.3	11.4	12.7	14.7	10.6	10.3	8.9
Not Indicated	3.0	5.0	2.6	3.4	5.1	3.1	2.2	4.8	1.9	2.0	4.3	1.9	3.2	4.0	3.7	3.7	4.0	3.9	2.3	4.0	3.0
MERCHANDISE STOLEN (%)																					
Fresh Meat	11.8	.1	1.7	12.4	.0	1.7	11.1	—	1.7	15.8	.1	2.5	2.4	—	—	2.4	—	—	2.4	—	—
Deli	8.7	.2	1.0	8.6	.1	.8	8.7	.2	1.3	10.8	.3	1.4	4.1	.1	.2	4.0	—	—	4.3	.1	.5
Other Food	21.4	6.0	4.3	21.9	7.1	3.1	21.0	4.8	5.3	17.7	3.4	4.1	30.3	8.8	4.3	32.4	10.6	2.9	27.0	6.4	6.4
Liquor	6.9	3.5	.8	10.0	5.6	.5	3.6	1.2	1.0	7.9	6.0	1.0	4.2	.5	.2	5.9	.7	—	1.6	.3	.5
Cigarettes	5.2	1.8	1.2	6.3	2.7	1.4	3.9	.9	.9	5.2	1.9	1.3	5.2	1.8	.8	5.5	2.3	.3	4.6	1.2	1.5
Vitamins	.9	1.2	.8	.8	1.2	.8	1.1	1.2	.8	1.1	2.1	1.1	.4	.3	.2	.4	.3	.3	.3	.4	—
Sundries	7.5	9.3	1.0	6.0	9.4	.5	9.0	8.7	1.5	8.3	15.6	1.3	5.2	2.4	.6	4.2	2.6	.3	6.9	2.1	1.0
Clothing	7.7	9.5	17.4	5.3	6.3	8.1	10.2	12.9	26.8	6.9	11.2	17.9	9.0	7.3	16.2	5.9	4.5	9.4	13.7	10.9	26.6
Other Non-Food	30.0	68.5	71.9	28.8	67.5	83.1	31.4	70.0	60.6	26.3	59.6	69.3	39.2	78.9	77.6	39.3	79.0	86.6	39.1	78.7	63.5

	TOTAL CASES			TOTAL MALES			TOTAL FEMALES			TOTAL ADULTS			TOTAL JUVENILES			TOTAL MALE JUVENILES			TOTAL FEMALE JUVENILES		
	Sup Mkt	Drug	Disc	Sup Mkt	Drug	Disc	Sup Mkt	Drug	Disc	Sup Mkt	Drug	Disc	Sup Mkt	Drug	Disc	Sup Mkt	Drug	Disc	Sup Mkt	Drug	Disc
MONTH (%)																					
JANUARY	10.0	7.7	7.0	11.0	7.6	6.3	8.8	7.7	7.9	9.3	8.8	7.2	10.8	6.5	6.8	11.4	6.3	6.5	9.9	6.8	7.4
FEBRUARY	10.3	5.7	7.9	10.7	5.7	7.3	9.7	5.7	8.6	9.4	4.8	8.8	11.0	6.4	5.5	11.2	5.3	5.2	10.7	7.8	5.9
MARCH	11.6	7.3	9.9	12.2	8.4	10.5	10.7	5.9	9.4	11.1	6.6	9.4	11.5	7.7	10.4	12.4	9.1	10.5	9.7	5.4	10.4
APRIL	9.0	6.2	7.8	9.2	6.2	6.7	8.6	6.1	8.9	8.5	6.1	8.9	8.7	5.9	5.7	8.7	6.0	5.6	8.5	5.8	5.9
MAY	8.5	7.0	8.1	8.3	6.1	8.2	8.8	8.1	7.9	8.2	6.4	7.9	8.9	7.7	8.2	8.2	6.5	8.5	10.1	9.5	7.9
JUNE	8.0	7.4	6.4	7.3	7.5	7.1	8.8	7.2	5.6	7.5	5.1	6.5	8.2	9.4	6.1	7.4	10.0	6.2	9.6	8.7	5.9
JULY	7.2	7.9	9.0	6.7	8.0	8.8	8.0	7.6	9.2	7.6	8.7	8.0	6.9	6.9	10.2	6.5	7.0	8.5	7.6	6.7	12.4
AUGUST	7.4	8.5	7.8	7.0	7.9	8.3	7.9	9.2	7.3	7.7	9.6	6.6	7.7	7.9	10.2	7.5	8.4	10.5	7.7	7.1	9.9
SEPTEMBER	5.8	8.8	8.1	5.6	7.2	9.0	5.9	10.7	6.9	6.6	9.2	8.3	5.0	8.8	8.2	5.2	7.4	9.2	4.5	10.9	5.9
OCTOBER	7.9	9.3	7.6	7.1	9.8	6.9	8.9	9.0	8.3	8.6	10.0	7.6	7.8	9.2	8.0	7.3	9.5	8.2	8.6	8.7	7.9
NOVEMBER	6.5	10.8	9.9	6.4	10.8	8.8	6.7	11.0	11.1	7.1	11.4	11.1	6.4	10.7	8.4	6.3	10.8	7.5	6.7	10.5	9.9
DECEMBER	7.1	12.2	9.9	7.6	13.5	11.5	6.7	10.9	8.3	7.9	12.4	9.2	6.2	11.7	11.5	6.7	12.6	12.7	5.5	10.4	9.9
NOT INDICATED	.8	1.2	.6	.9	1.2	.7	.6	1.0	.4	.6	.9	.3	1.0	1.3	.8	1.1	1.1	1.0	.9	1.5	.5
DAY OF WEEK (%)																					
MONDAY	14.7	13.6	1.9	14.5	13.3	2.3	14.8	13.6	1.6	14.5	13.7	2.2	15.4	13.4	1.2	15.2	14.2	.7	15.8	12.2	2.0
TUESDAY	14.7	11.6	16.5	14.5	11.9	16.0	14.8	11.2	17.0	14.4	11.8	16.5	14.8	11.0	16.2	14.8	11.9	19.3	14.8	9.8	11.4
WEDNESDAY	14.0	10.4	15.8	13.8	9.9	15.8	14.5	11.1	15.8	13.6	11.0	16.8	15.4	10.0	14.5	15.4	8.5	15.4	15.2	12.1	12.9
THURSDAY	14.0	12.9	17.4	13.5	12.3	16.8	14.8	13.5	18.1	13.4	12.3	17.8	15.2	13.6	16.2	15.0	13.1	17.0	15.8	14.1	15.3
FRIDAY	13.4	16.4	15.2	13.9	16.4	13.6	12.8	16.5	16.8	14.0	18.1	14.7	12.7	15.4	15.9	13.3	15.5	13.7	11.7	15.4	19.3
SATURDAY	12.7	18.2	15.4	12.6	18.0	16.7	12.8	18.4	14.1	13.4	17.5	15.5	11.1	18.8	15.5	10.7	17.7	15.7	11.6	20.2	15.3
SUNDAY	12.7	13.0	15.7	13.1	13.4	16.6	12.1	12.7	14.8	13.2	12.1	14.8	11.8	14.1	17.8	11.8	14.6	15.7	11.7	13.4	20.8
NOT INDICATED	3.8	4.0	2.1	4.2	4.8	2.2	3.3	3.0	1.7	3.6	3.5	1.6	3.7	3.8	2.7	3.8	4.4	2.6	3.6	2.8	3.0

SUPERMARKET SHOPLIFTING DATA 1968–1979

Year and Number of Cases	Percent of Adults Prosecuted	Percent of Juveniles to Police	Day When Most Shoplifters Were Caught	Month When Most Shoplifters Were Caught	Time Period When Most Shoplifters Were Caught	Age Group Most Often Apprehended	Percent of Shoplifters Under Thirty Years Old	Ratio of Male–Female Apprehensions	Percent Concealed in Pocket-Purse or Under Clothing	Average Number of Articles Recovered	Average Value of Merchandise Recovered
1979 14,656	34.1%	24.7%	Monday Tuesday	March	3–6 PM	18–29	66.6%	53.3% M 43.6% F	78.0%	3.1	$7.37
1978 17,326	33.0%	21.7%	Wednesday	April	3–6 PM	18–29	70.6%	54.9% M 44.3% F	78.4%	3.2	$6.39
1977 16,255	35.3%	24.7%	Friday Monday	May	3–6 PM	18–29	70.2%	52.6% M 47.3% F	80.6%	3.2	$5.99
1976 16,100	35.7%	24.9%	Thursday	March	3–6 PM	18–29	71.6%	51.4% M 48.6% F	81.3%	3.2	$5.90
1975 18,303	37.3%	24.1%	Wednesday	January	3–6 PM	18–29	71.2%	54.2% M 45.7% F	81.1%	3.0	$4.91
1974 18,165	42.3%	25.8%	Friday	March April	3–6 PM	12–17	71.3%	56.5% M 43.5% F	79.2%	3.1	$4.97
1973 14,790	42.6%	25.0%	Thursday	October November	3–6 PM	12–17	69.5%	51.2% M 48.8% F	79.4%	3.0	$4.32
1972 15,542	39.4%	23.6%	Friday	March	3–6 PM	12–17	66.5%	50.3% M 49.7% F	79.9%	3.0	$3.85
1971 13,599	37.1%	22.9%	Wednesday	December	3–6 PM	12–17	68.2%	57.0% M 42.9% F	78.0%	3.1	$4.35
1970 13,439	36.3%	20.9%	Thursday	February April	3–6 PM	12–17	68.3%	56.1% M 43.9% F	77.3%	3.1	$3.81
1969 12,460	30.6%	22.9%	Thursday	March	3–6 PM	12–17	67.3%	56.2% M 43.8% F	77.0%	3.2	$3.80
1968 10,212	30.8%	20.4%	Friday	October	3–6 PM	12–17	66.3%	50.7% M 49.3% F	78.7%	3.1	$3.40

	TOTAL CASES			TOTAL MALES			TOTAL FEMALES			TOTAL ADULTS			TOTAL JUVENILES			TOTAL MALE JUVENILES			TOTAL FEMALE JUVENILES		
	Sup Mkt	Drug	Disc	Sup Mkt	Drug	Disc	Sup Mkt	Drug	Disc	Sup Mkt	Drug	Disc	Sup Mkt	Drug	Disc	Sup Mkt	Drug	Disc	Sup Mkt	Drug	Disc
TIME OF DAY (%)																					
Opening																					
Till Noon	8.4	8.1	9.2	8.5	8.7	10.7	8.3	7.4	7.8	9.1	8.2	10.3	7.7	8.0	7.2	7.9	9.0	8.8	7.4	6.7	5.0
Noon - 3 PM	22.5	26.5	34.7	20.3	25.7	29.1	25.3	27.7	40.7	23.2	26.1	37.5	22.0	27.5	31.5	21.8	25.7	27.8	22.4	29.9	37.6
3 PM - 6 PM	37.6	35.4	34.7	35.9	35.0	36.4	39.8	35.9	32.7	35.5	33.6	29.4	42.8	37.0	44.0	41.0	37.0	46.4	45.8	37.0	39.6
6 PM - 9 PM	20.8	22.5	18.0	23.4	22.9	20.1	17.6	22.1	15.8	21.6	25.2	20.5	18.9	20.3	12.5	20.3	20.6	13.7	16.7	19.9	10.9
9 PM - 12M	5.7	2.6	1.0	6.9	2.7	.8	4.2	2.5	1.2	6.2	3.4	.4	4.1	1.8	1.8	4.7	2.2	.7	3.2	1.2	3.5
After Midnight	.5	.2	.1	.6	.2	.1	.3	.2	—	.5	.3	.1	.3	.1	—	.3	.1	—	.2	—	—
Not Indicated	4.5	4.6	2.4	4.4	4.8	2.7	4.5	4.2	1.9	3.8	3.3	1.8	4.2	5.4	2.9	4.1	5.4	2.6	4.4	5.3	3.5
AGE GROUPINGS (%)																					
Under 12	6.2	13.1	6.3	8.0	18.6	9.4	4.1	7.1	2.7	—	—	—	19.9	27.5	17.8	22.4	34.7	22.5	15.7	16.8	9.4
12 to 17	26.7	34.6	29.2	27.0	35.0	32.2	22.1	35.0	26.3	—	—	—	80.1	72.5	82.2	77.6	65.3	77.5	84.3	83.2	90.6
18 to 29	33.7	26.2	29.0	30.4	23.0	24.0	33.1	29.5	34.7	51.0	54.5	47.0	—	—	—	—	—	—	—	—	—
30 to 39	12.8	9.1	15.5	10.8	8.1	14.7	13.7	10.2	16.3	19.4	19.0	25.1	—	—	—	—	—	—	—	—	—
40 to 49	7.0	4.7	7.8	5.6	3.9	8.2	7.7	5.5	7.6	10.5	9.8	12.7	—	—	—	—	—	—	—	—	—
50 to 59	5.4	4.1	5.8	4.0	3.9	5.0	6.4	4.3	6.3	8.2	8.6	9.3	—	—	—	—	—	—	—	—	—
60 and over	7.1	3.9	3.6	6.2	3.7	3.4	7.3	4.2	3.7	10.8	8.2	5.8	—	—	—	—	—	—	—	—	—
Not Indicated	1.1	4.3	2.8	7.4	3.9	3.1	5.7	4.2	2.3	—	—	—	—	—	—	—	—	—	—	—	—

APPENDIX B
A SUMMARY OF SHOPLIFTING LAWS IN 8 STATES

Throughout this text, reference has been made to the diversity and relative toughness of the myriad laws that apply to the retail crimes discussed here. Criminal jurisdiction, other than for interstate offenses, resides within the states, and every state has evolved its own laws. Some seem highly favorable or protective of the rights of the merchant; others seem to provide little guidance as to what to do when an offense is committed.

Obviously, the more serious or violent crimes of robbery and burglary will be more often uniformly treated as major crimes by the states. But it is in the shoplifting laws particularly that vast differences have arisen. Some states explicitly provide false arrest protection for the merchant; others do not. . . . Some states allow merchants to bring suit against parents of apprehended minors; others do not. . . . Some states restrict detentions to no more than 30 minutes; others have only vague guidelines as to what constitutes "reasonable" detention.

To provide some appreciation of the many nuances of these laws, the shoplifting statutes of 8 states are presented here in summary form. Some of them are completely new, or have recently been amended, mostly in the direction of better protection for the merchant.

Scanning the specifics of these various laws should indicate clearly why the security program of every retail organization must be grounded in a clear understanding of the laws operative in the states where the company maintains stores and other facilities.

ARIZONA Revised Statutes 13–1805

1. Definition of crime

a. Removal from display without paying.
b. Charging price to fictitious person or unwitting person.
c. Price tag switching, cap switching, container switching.
d. Concealment within the mercantile establishment.

2. Who can detain? Where? How long?
Merchant, his agent or employees may detain on the premises in a reasonable manner and for a reasonable time.

3. Reasons for detention
Reasonable cause.

4. False arrest provision?
Yes. Reasonable cause is a defense to a civil or criminal action against merchant, agent, employee or peace officer.

5. Handling of juveniles
Merchant can sue parent or legal guardian of minors apprehended while shoplifting.

6. Type of offense and penalties
Property valued more than $1,000 is a Class 5 Felony.
Property valued $100-$999 is a Class 6 Felony.
Property valued under $100 is a Class 1 Misdemeanor.
All firearm shoplifting is a Class 6 Felony.
Penalties may include public services in lieu of sentence and/or fines.

FLORIDA H.B. 1068 (1978)

1. Definition of crime

a. Person knowingly obtains or uses, or attempts to obtain or use, property of another with intent to appropriate property to his own use . . .
b. . . . To deprive the other person of the right to the property or benefit.
c. Retail theft includes price tag switching, container transferring, theft of shopping carts.

2. Who can detain? Where? How long?
Peace officer, merchant, his agent or employees may detain person by taking into custody in a reasonable manner for a reasonable length of time.

3. Reasons for detention
Probable cause to believe that merchandise has been unlawfully taken.

4. False arrest provision?
Yes. No liability for peace officer, merchant, agent or employee if custody and detention is done in compliance with law as above. However, if merchant, agent or employee takes the suspect into custody, peace officer must be immediately called to the scene.

5. Handling of juveniles
No provision.

6. Type of offense and penalties
When reasonable efforts to recover merchandise are resisted and individual is found to be guilty of theft, individual is guilty of a misdemeanor of the first degree.
Punishment includes fingerprinting of convicted thief in open court on face of written judgment, becoming admissable evidence.
Second or subsequent convictions may be punishable by a fine of \$50–\$1,000, or public services in lieu of the fine, but no less than number of hours required to satisfy the fine at minimum wages prevailing in the state.

IDAHO Section 18–4601 Idaho Code and Willful Concealment Act, Section 18–4626 (amended 1973)

1. Definition of crime

a. As larceny, defined as felonious stealing, taking, carrying, leading or driving away of the personal property of another. Tag, cap switching, etc., is now included.
b. Under willful concealment: concealment of goods, wares of merchandise while still upon the premises of the store or merchant.

2. Who can detain? Where? How long?
Any owner, agent or employee may apprehend or detain in the immediate vicinity of the premises to investigate or question as to ownership of goods. Photographs of stolen property, when signed and identified may be used as evidence instead of actual merchandise.

3. Reasons for detention
Probable cause; willful concealment.

4. False arrest provision?

Yes. Probable cause is a defense to a civil or criminal action against merchant. Merchant also obtains immunity from liability by posting the Anti-Shoplifting Act as a notice 13″ wide by 21″ long in a prominent place on premises.

5. Handling of juveniles

Merchant may bring civil action against parent or guardian of minor, or an adult, for retail value of merchandise plus damages of $100–$250 plus costs of suit and attorney's fees.

6. Type of offense and penalties

a. As larceny: Grand larceny involves property over $150 in value; punishable by imprisonment for 1–14 years. Petit larceny is punishable by fine up to $300, or up to 6 months in jail, or both.
b. Under willful concealment: Misdemeanor punishable as petit larceny above. Note civil liability under "handling of juveniles" above.

MAINE Criminal Code, Chapter 113–114, effective May 1, 1976

1. Definition of crime

Unlawful concealment of merchandise while still on the premises of a store.

2. Who can detain? Where? How long?

Store owner, manager or supervisor may detain on the premises in a reasonable manner for a period of time not to exceed 30 minutes.

3. Reasons for detention

Probable cause to believe individual is concealing merchandise.

4. False arrest provision?

None specifically stated.

5. Handling of juveniles

No provision.

6. Type of offense and penalties

Misdemeanor punishable by fine up to $100 and/or imprisonment up to 6 months.

MARYLAND, Article 27, Annotated Code of Maryland, July 1, 1979

1. Definition of crime

Under general theft statutes, including larceny, larceny by trick, larceny after trust, embezzlement, false pretenses, shoplifting and receiving stolen property. Most applicable in shoplifting: Willful or knowing use, concealment or abandoning of property in such manner as to deprive the owner of the property.

2. Who can detain? Where? How long?

Merchant, agent or employee.

3. Reasons for detention

Probable cause to believe the individual had committed the crime of theft.

4. False arrest provision?

Yes. No civil liability if probable cause has been established.

5. Handling of juveniles

No provision specifically stated.

6. Type of offense and penalties

Under $300: Misdemeanor punishable by fine up to $100 and/or up to 18 months imprisonment. Over $300: Felony punishable by fine up to $1,000 and/or up to 15 years imprisonment.

MONTANA, 46-6-501, 502, 503, 504 Criminal Procedures Code, 1974

1. Definition of crime

Concealment—any act of deception done purposely or knowingly upon or outside the premises of a retail store with intent to deprive the merchant of all or part of the value of the merchandise. Includes price switching, transferring containers, etc.

2. Who can detain? Where? How long?
Merchant, in a reasonable manner or time. After 30 minutes, merchant must allow suspect to go or turn suspect over to custody of peace officer.

3. Reasons for detention
Reasonable grounds to believe an offense has been committed; probable cause to believe an act of shoplifting is occurring in his presence.

4. False arrest provision?
Yes, unless merchant does not comply with time restrictions; must inform suspect of reason for detention; may take into possession any merchandise which has been concealed from full view (meaning only search of coat and outer garments and any package, briefcase or other container).

5. Handling of juveniles
None specifically stated.

6. Type of offense and penalties
N/A

NORTH CAROLINA G.S. 14–72.1

1. Definition of crime
Willful concealment of the goods or merchandise of any store not purchased by the individual.

2. Who can detain? Where? How long?
Explicit reference only to observation of willful concealment on store premises.

3. Reasons for detention
Probable cause; goods or merchandise found concealed on or about the suspect.

4. False arrest provision?
Not specifically stated.

5. Handling of juveniles
No provision specifically stated.

6. Type of offense and penalties
Misdemeanor; fine up to $100 and/or imprisonment up to 6 months.

OHIO, Sections 2913.02, 2935.041 and 3109.09, last amended July 4, 1978

1. Definition of crime
Under general theft statute: Theft occurs when owner of property or services is deprived without consent of owner, by deception, by threat.

2. Who can detain? Where? How long?
Merchant, employee, agent or police officer can detain inside or outside a store in a reasonable manner for a reasonable length of time to recover merchandise believed taken, or to arrest individual. No search permitted.

3. Reasons for detention
Probable cause for believing that items offered for sale have been unlawfully taken.

4. False arrest provision?
Not specifically stated.

5. Handling of juveniles
Civil action may be brought against parents of minors to recover damages not to exceed $3,000 plus legal costs in convictions for willfully damaging property or any act recognizable as "theft offense."

6. Type of offense and penalties
Under $150: Misdemeanor subject to fine up to $1,000 and/or imprisonment up to 6 months. Second convictions regardless of value: 4th degree felony with fine up to $2,500 and/or imprisonment from 2–5 years. Felony penalty also applies on first offense if value of property stolen is over $150.

WHERE TO GET MORE INFORMATION

GENERAL

Crime in Retailing, U.S. Department of Commerce (Annual Statistical Report), U.S. Government Printing Office, Washington, D.C. 20402.

INTERNAL OR EMPLOYEE THEFT

London House Managment Journal (ongoing newsletter), London House Management Consultants, Inc., 1500 North Northwest Highway, Park Ridge, IL 60068.

Preventing Embezzlement, Small Business Administration Small Marketer Aids No. 151. Small Business Administration, Washington, D.C. 20416.

Preventing Employee Pilferage, Small Business Administration Management Aids No. 209. Small Business Administration, Washington, D.C. 20416.

Preventing Retail Theft, Small Business Administration Small Marketer Aids No. 119. Small Business Administration, Washington, D.C. 20416.

The Reid Report: The search for an Honest Employee, John E. Reid and Associates, 215 North Dearborn Street, Chicago, IL 60601.

SHOPLIFTING

"The High Cost of Shoplifting," **Nation's Business,** November 1978, p. 44.

"How Shoplifting is Draining the Economy," **Business Week,** October 15, 1970, pp. 119–123.

Basic Shoplifting Procedures, A Policy Outline, Commercial Service Systems, Inc., P.O. Box 3307, Van Nuys, CA 91407.

The Booster and the Snitch; Department Store Shoplifting, Mary Owen Cameron, The Free Press of Glencoe, Crowell-Collier Publishing Co., New York, 1964.

CHECK CASHING

Driver's License Guide, 1492 Oddstad Drive, Redwood City, CA 94063.

Outwitting Bad Check Passers, Small Business Administration Small Marketer Aids No. 137. Small Business Administration, Washington, D.C. 20416.

ROBBERY & BURGLARY

Armed Robbery—An In-Depth Study Prepared By Philip Morris USA and the National Association of Convenience Stores, Copyright Philip Morris, Inc., 1979. (Write Account Management Department, Philip Morris USA, 100 Park Avenue, New York, NY 10017.)

Preventing Burglary and Robbery Loss, Small Business Administration Small Marketer Aids No. 134. Small Business Administration, Washington, D.C. 20416.

INDEX